KB270944

ALL ABOUT JUNIOR TOEFL
[LISTENING]

Intermediate Course

Bansok Junior

ALL ABOUT JUNIOR TOEFL LISTENING (Intermediate Course)

1st edition : Printed in Aug. 1, 2008(1st impression)

Authors : Naomi Kim, Alan Hahn
Publisher : Mi-soon Ko
Editor in chief : Seung-ju Kang
Editors : Min-jung Kwon, Dam-hee Cho
Marketing Department : Keum-hee Kim
Design : Eun-ryoung Kim
Publisher : Bansok Publishing Company
Address : 87-5 Anam-dong, Seongbuk-gu, Seoul
Registration No. : 9-33
Web site : www.bansok.co.kr
E-mail : bansok@bansok.co.kr
Phone : 02-928-0027
Fax : 02-928-3415

ISBN 978-89-7172-485-9   13740
Printed in Korea

ALL ABOUT JUNIOR TOEFL
[LISTENING]

Intermediate Course

Bansok Junior

PREFACE

iBT 토플이 국내에서 시행된 지 벌써 1년이 넘었습니다. 언어의 4가지 구성 영역인 Reading, Listening, Speaking, Writing 능력을 골고루 측정하는 iBT 토플은 언어 이해력과 논리력, 분석력, 표현력, 응용력 등을 종합적이고 총체적으로 평가하는 시험입니다. 영어를 학습함에 있어 어느 한쪽으로 치우침 없이 각 영역이 서로 균형 있게 조화를 이루는 학습의 중요성을 확산시킨 데에 iBT 토플의 역할이 크다고 할 수 있습니다.

4 영역의 통합형 문제의 등장으로, 토플 시험에서 리스닝 섹션이 차지하는 비중이 여느 때보다 크게 증가했습니다. 문제는 청취력은 짧은 시간 집중적으로 공부한다고 해서 실력이 부쩍 늘어나지는 않는다는 것입니다. 글로 써있을 때는 무슨 의미인지 쉽게 알 수 있는 내용도 원어민의 발음으로 들려주면 무슨 내용인지 도무지 모를 때가 많습니다. 청취력을 향상시키기 위해서는 무엇보다도 매일매일 영어 듣기 환경에 귀를 노출시키고 청취 절대시간을 늘리는 것이 중요합니다. 배경 음악처럼 영어 테이프나 라디오를 틀어 놓고 무의식 중에 귀를 영어에 노출시키는 것도 좋지만, 하루에 일정 시간 이상은 오로지 듣기에만 집중하여 청취 학습을 하는 습관을 들여야 합니다. 듣기 학습은 받아 쓰기와 따라 읽기를 병행하는 것이 최상의 방법입니다. 짧은 문장이라도 원어민이 말하는 것을 반복해서 들으며 받아 적는 연습을 하면 원어민의 발음과 문장의 리듬에 익숙해질 뿐만 아니라 놓치기 쉬운 세세한 발음까지 잡아 내어 문장이 어떻게 구성되는지를 자연스럽게 터득하게 되는 효과도 있습니다. 여러 번 들어도 잘 안 들리는 부분은 스크립트를 보고 원어민처럼 말할 수 있을 때까지 계속 따라 읽으며 외우는 것이 효과적입니다. 다음 단어가 저절로 나올 정도로 따라 읽어 표현이 입에 붙은 문장은 잘 잊혀지지 않습니다. 하지만 아무리 효과적이고 뛰어난 듣기 학습법을 알고 있어도 직접 이러한 방법을 활용하여 공부하지 않으면 아무런 소용이 없습니다. 듣기 공부는 하루도 빼놓지 않고 해야 한다는 것을 기억하고 실천하는 것이 토플 리스닝 시험에서 높은 점수를 받을 수 있는 가장 확실하고 빠른 길입니다.

iBT Listening 섹션 준비의 지침서가 될 본 교재는 기본적인 청취력 향상과 토플 리스닝 정복이라는 두 가지 기본 목표를 가지고 집필 되었습니다. 리스닝 섹션의 출제경향을 철저히 분석하여 각 문제 유형별로 최적의 전략과 학습방법을 제시하고 있습니다. 또한 실제 시험에 자주 출제되는 대화 상황과 강의 주제를 중심으로 지문을 제작하여 실전 시험과의 유사성을 높였으며, 학습 효과를 극대화 하기 위해 난이도가 높은 문제들을 뒤쪽에 배치하여 자연스럽게 난이도를 조금씩 높여가며 공부할 수 있도록 하였습니다. 4주 학습 완성을 목표로 구성된 학습 계획표에 맞추어 본 교재를 차근차근 공부해나가면 부쩍 향상된 청취 실력과 더불어 iBT 토플 시험에 완벽하게 준비된 자신감에 넘치는 자신의 모습을 발견할 수 있을 것입니다.

Naomi Kim, Alan Hahn

CONTENTS

이 책의 구성과 특징

Overview

각 문제 유형에 대한 소개와 분석이 들어 있으며
문제에 효과적으로 접근할 수 있는 핵심 전략이
제시되어 있다.

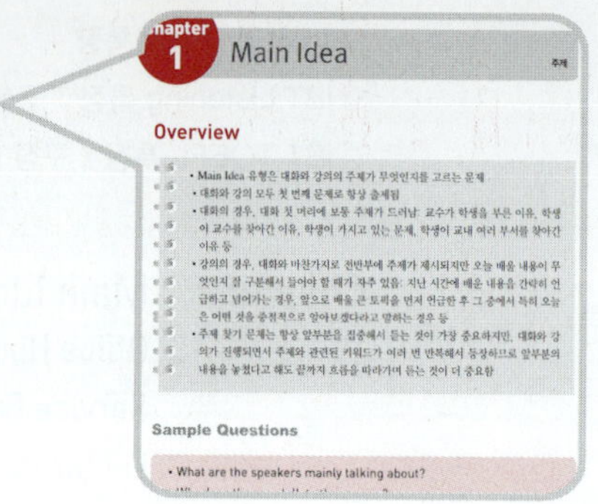

Preview

실제 문제를 풀어보며 앞서 제시된 전략을 적용
해보는 코너이다. 문제 접근법과 해결법이 문제
풀이 과정과 자세한 해설을 통해 구체적으로 설
명되어 있다.

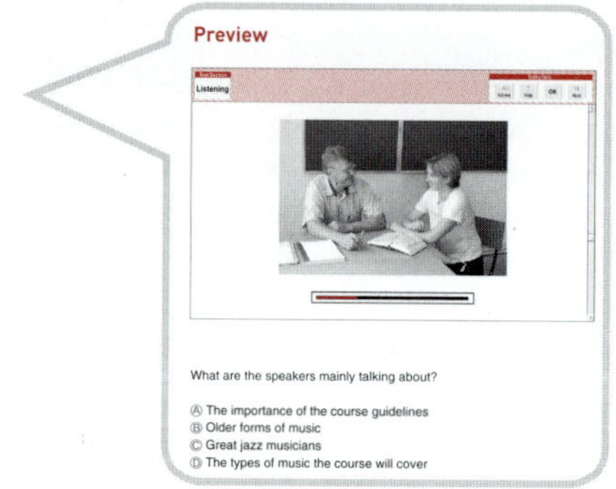

Office Hours/Service Encounters/Lectures

실전보다 짧은 길이의 다양한 스크립트를 듣고
문제를 풀어본다. 각 문제 유형을 단계적으로 공
략할 수 있도록 난이도가 조정되어 있다. 대화는
문항당 1 문제, 렉쳐는 문항당 2문제 이상이 출제
되어 있다.

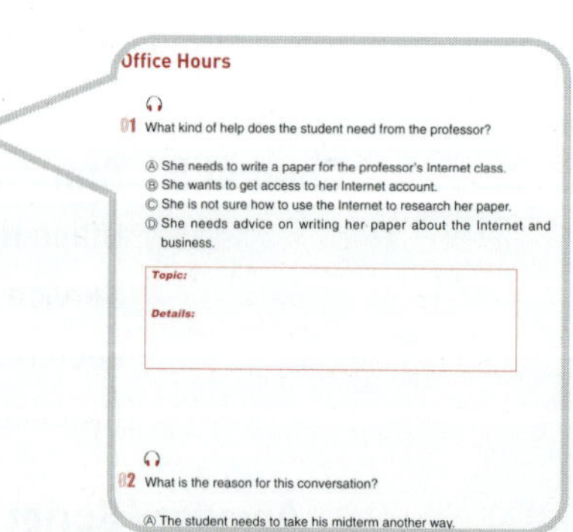

Dictation

Office Hours, Service Encounters, Lectures 의 모든 문제를 풀어본 후, 스크립트를 다시 들어 보면서 빈 칸에 받아 쓰기를 한다. 내용의 흐름을 다시 한 번 확인하고, 단어의 정확한 발음과 강세, 끊어 읽기, 스펠링 등 청취의 기본 요소들을 점검한다.

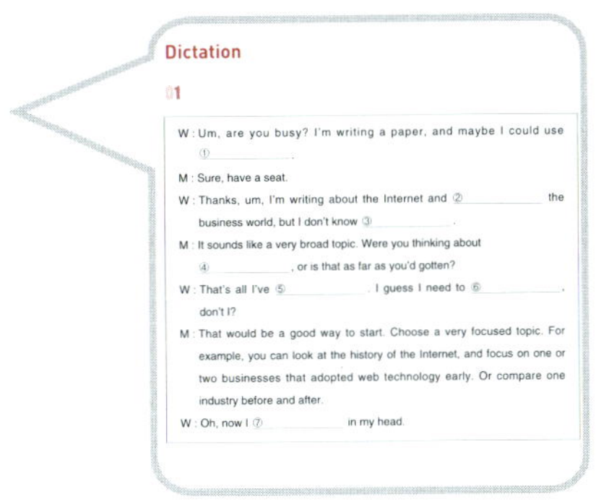

Practice

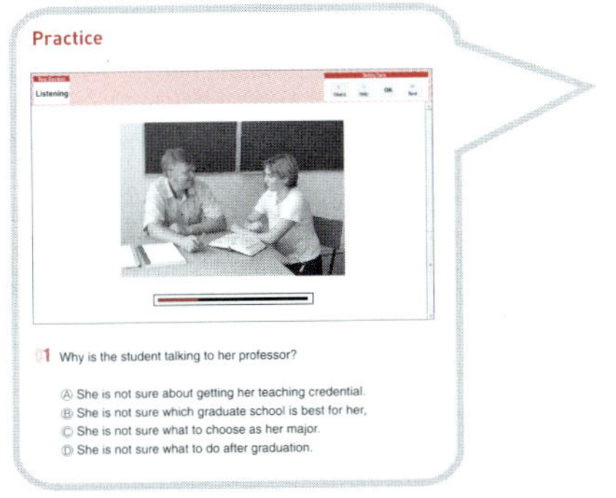

앞 코너에서 각 문제 유형을 집중적으로 학습한 후 Practice에서는 실전과 동일하게 제작된 문제들을 풀어본다. 실전과 마찬가지로 하나의 스크립트에 모든 문제 유형이 출제되어 있다.

Review

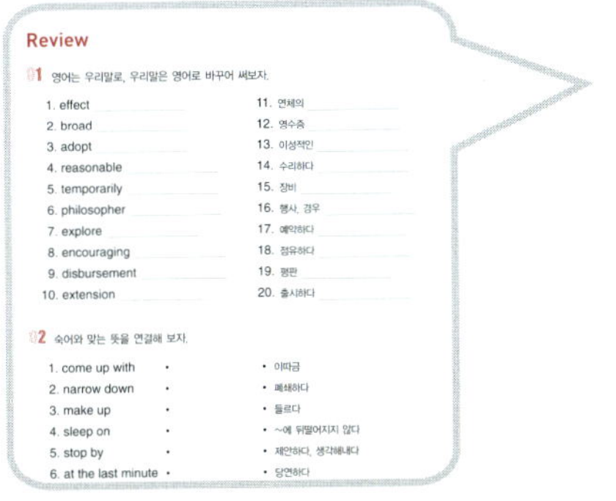

중요한 어휘의 의미와 쓰임새를 최종적으로 확인하며 학습 효과를 극대화시킨다.

iBT Listening 특징!

iBT Listening 섹션은 기존 CBT의 짧은 대화 지문이 없어지고 긴 대화 지문과 강의로만 이루어져 있다. 대화와 강의 모두 CBT에 비해 지문이 상당히 길어졌으며 실제 대화와 수업과 같이 말을 하다가 잠시 쉬는 부분이나, 머뭇거리는 부분 등 보다 현실감 있게 구성되어 있다. Listening 섹션의 주요 특징은 다음과 같다.

1. 2~3개의 파트로 구성된다.

한 개의 파트는 대화(conversation) 1개, 강의(lecture) 2개로 이루어져 있다. 따라서 시험이 2개 파트로 구성되어 있으면 총 2개의 대화와 4개의 강의가 출제되며, 시험이 3개 파트로 구성되어 있으면 총 3개의 대화와 6개의 강의가 출제된다.

2. 대화는 지문당 5개, 강의는 지문당 6개의 문제가 출제된다.

대화는 약 3분간 들려주고, 지문은 약 400~500자로 이루어져 있으며 각 지문당 5개의 관련 문제가 출제된다. 강의는 약 3~5분간 들려주고, 지문은 약 500~800자로 이루어져 있으며 각 지문당 6개의 관련 문제가 출제된다.

3. 대화는 Office Hours와 Service Encounters로 나뉘어져 있다.

Office Hours 대화에서는 학생과 교수가 대화를 나누고, Service Encounters 대화에서는 학생과 사서, 기숙사 직원과 같은 학교 직원이 대화를 나눈다.

4. 강의는 Monologue와 Discussion으로 나뉘어져 있다.

Monologue 강의에서는 교수가 혼자 강의 주제를 설명해나가고, Discussion에서는 학생과 교수의 질의 응답으로 강의가 진행된다.

5. Note-taking이 허용된다.

지문의 길이가 상당히 긴 편이므로 note-taking을 적극 활용하는 것이 좋다.

6. 대화와 강의 환경이 실제 상황과 유사하다.

CBT에서는 화자의 말이 딱딱 끊어지는 느낌이 나고 정형화되어 있었으나, iBT Listening에서는 화자가 말을 하며 머뭇거린다거나 말을 더듬는 등 대화와 강의 상황이 실제와 같이 보다 자연스럽게 이루어져 있다.

7. 다양한 영어권 국가의 발음과 억양을 들려준다.

미국식 화자의 음성 외에도 영국이나 호주식 화자의 음성을 들려준다.

8. 지문의 일부를 다시 듣고 푸는 문제가 출제된다.

화자의 태도나 말한 의도 및 목적을 묻는 문제(stance/function question)에는 헤드셋 표시가 나오고 지문의 해당 부분을 다시 한 번 들려준다.

9. 2점의 배점이 주어지는 문제도 출제된다.

대부분의 문제는 1점짜리 이지만 2점짜리 문제도 간혹 출제되며 배점이 따로 표시된다.

iBT Listening 구성

문제 유형		특 징
Basic Comprehension	Main Idea	지문의 주제 찾기
	Details	지문에 직접적으로 언급되어 있는 세부 정보를 찾기
Connecting Information	Inference	지문에 직접적으로 언급되어 있지는 않지만 지문에 흩어져 있는 정보를 바탕으로 논리적으로 추론할 수 있는 것을 고르거나 결론을 도출하기
	Connecting Information	지문에 정보가 어떻게 조직되어 있는지 내용상, 구조상의 전개방식을 이해하고 내용들 사이의 관계를 바탕으로 정보를 연결하기
Pragmatic Understanding	Stance/Function	지문에 제시되는 정보에 대한 화자의 입장과 태도를 파악하고 발화 목적과 의도를 알아내기

		화자	토픽
Conversation	Office Hours	학생과 교수	시험, 성적, 수업 참여도, 과제물, 수업 내용, 현장 학습, 전공 선택, 인턴, 진로 등
	Service Encounters	학생과 학교 직원	기숙사 생활, 도서 대출, 교재 구입, 수강 신청, 카페테리아 이용, 학비 납부 및 장학금 신청, 실습실 이용, 학교 행사, 동아리 활동 등
Lecture	Monologue	교수	history(역사학), literature(문학), economics(경제학), political science(정치학), psychology(심리학), film(영화), anthropology(인류학), archaeology(고고학), photography(사진), biology(생물학), astronomy(천문학), geology(지질학), paleontology(고생물학), urban planning(도시공학)
	Discussion	교수와 학생	

1. 어휘력을 기른다.

시험에 자주 등장하는 토플 수준의 다양한 어휘와 표현(이디엄)을 외워둔다. 글자만 외울 것이 아니라 소리 내어 읽으며 외워서 정확한 표현을 실제 대화 상황에서 써먹을 수 있을 정도로 외운다. 단어와 표현을 외울 때는 정확한 발음을 알아두도록 한다. 발음을 잘못 알고 있으면 의미를 아는 단어라도 제대로 알아 듣기가 힘들다.

2. 많이 듣고 따라 읽는다.

토플 리스닝 교재나 기타 듣기 자료 등을 활용하여 무조건 많이 듣는다. 일주일치 학습량을 하루에 몰아서 듣고 그 다음 주까지 아무 것도 듣지 않는 것보다 매일매일 조금씩 꾸준히 듣는 것이 훨씬 효과적이다. 내용의 이해가 최우선이지만 발음과 억양에도 신경을 집중하고 들으며 따라 읽는 연습을 한다.

3. 들으면서 note-taking을 한다.

듣기 연습을 할 때 note-taking을 하는 습관을 기르도록 한다. 키워드의 개념 정리를 시작으로 핵심 내용을 빠르고 체계적으로 적는다. Note-taking은 단순한 받아 적기가 아니라 듣는 사람이 자기만의 방식으로 내용을 간단하게 메모하는 것이다. 시험장에서 들려주는 내용을 놓치는 일 없이 note-taking을 제대로 활용하기 위해서는 많은 연습이 필요하다. Note-taking을 다 한 후에는 적어 놓은 내용이 스크립트의 흐름과 맥을 같이 하는지 확인해보고 본인이 적은 내용만 보고도 글의 내용을 이해할 수 있는지 확인해본다.

4. 글을 요약하는 연습을 한다.

들은 후 핵심 내용을 재대로 이해했는지 들은 내용을 요약해 보도록 한다. 요약 연습은 note-taking과 연계하여 해보는 것이 좋다. 메모에 스크립트의 중요 사항이 흐름대로 잘 적혀있다면, 이 메모가 요약의 틀을 짜는 바탕이 될 수 있기 때문이다. 요약할 때는 되도록 들려준 그대로의 어휘나 표현을 사용하지 말고 본인만의 표현으로 바꾸어 나타내본다.

5. 많이 읽는다.

토플 리스닝 강의에 등장하는 지문은 길이도 길뿐만 아니라 다양한 분야의 학구적인 내용을 다루기 때문에 내용 자체도 어려운 편이다. 낯선 분야의 강의 내용을 사전 지식 없이 바로 들으면 무슨 내용인지 이해하지 못할 때가 많다. 따라서 듣기와 더불어 평소에 많은 글을 접하여 읽어 본다.

6. 배경 지식을 늘린다.

토플 시험에 등장할만한 다양한 분야의 글을 읽고 들으며 배경지식을 쌓도록 한다. 특히 시험에 자주 등장하는 토픽은 내용을 간략히 정리해두는 것도 좋다. 대화 파트를 위해서는 영어 회화를 많이 해보고 대화 상황을 들으며 구어체 표현을 익히는 것이 효과적이다.

iBT Listening Note-taking

iBT Listening에서는 노트 테이킹이 허용된다. CBT에 비해 지문의 길이가 많이 길어졌지만, 내용이 많아지고 길어진 만큼 지문을 들으면서 내용을 적을 수 있기 때문에 노트 테이킹을 효과적으로 활용하면 더 높은 점수를 받을 수 있는 가능성도 높아졌다. 지문을 들으면서 노트 테이킹을 하면 내용의 전체적인 주제와 전반적인 흐름을 이해하고 세부 정보를 정리하여 기억해내는데 효과적이다. 노트 테이킹을 할 때는 먼저 도입부에 제시되는 글 전체의 주제를 파악하고 이 주제를 전개하기 위해 언급되는 중심 정보와 세부 정보를 간단명료하게 적는 것이 중요하다. 노트 테이킹의 목적은 지문에 언급되는 모든 정보를 얼마나 잘 정리하느냐에 달린 것이 아니라 듣고 적은 내용이 문제를 풀며 내용을 기억해내고 정보간의 관계를 파악하는데 얼마나 도움을 주느냐에 있다. 따라서 내용 이해에 방해가 되지 않는 선에서 노트 테이킹을 해야 하며, 지문을 한 번밖에 들을 수가 없고 들려주는 내용의 양이 상당히 많다는 Listening 섹션의 특성을 고려하여 내용을 효율적으로 받아 적을 요령이 필요하다.

Note-taking 핵심 요령

1. 주제 (main topic)를 먼저 명료하게 적는다.

도입부를 들으면서 핵심어(keyword)를 중심으로 앞으로 전개될 대화와 강의의 주제를 먼저 적는다.

2. 세부 정보를 하위 주제에 따라 구분하여 적는다.

도입부에 대화와 강의의 중심 정보가 나온 후, 그 뒤에는 이 중심 정보와 관련된 세부 정보가 언급된다. iBT Listening에서는 한 지문당 듣기 시간이 상당히 긴 편이므로, 이 세부 정보 역시 하위 주제별로 구분하여 정리해 두어야 한다. 특히 강의를 들을 때는 하위 주제가 전환될 때 이를 알려주는 전환어가 자주 등장하므로 이를 듣고 화제가 바뀌고 있음을 알 수 있다.

3. 가능한 간단히 적는다.

완전한 문장으로 적을 필요는 없다. 구(Phrase)를 사용하여 최대한 간단히 적는다.

4. 약어와 부호를 이용해 적는다.

자주 등장하는 어휘나 표현의 부호와 약어를 충분히 익혀두고 노트 테이킹을 할 때 적극 활용한다. 시간을 절약하는데 도움을 준다.

5. 잘 듣지 못한 부분은 넘어간다.

대화와 강의를 들으면서 알아듣지 못한 부분이나 놓친 부분은 넘어간다. 알아들었다고 해도 앞부분의 내용을 먼저 적다가 잊어버리는 수도 있다. 특히 이런 경우에는 지나간 내용에 집착하게 되는데, 잊어버린 내용을 기억해내려고 하는 동안에도 화자의 말은 계속 되고 있음을 잊지 말아야 한다. 한 번 지나간 부분은 다시 들을 수 없다. 따라서 놓친 부분에 연연해하지 말고 앞으로 들어야 할 내용에 더 신경을 쓴다.

iBT TOEFL 특징

토플은 비영어권 국가의 수험생들의 영어 능력 측정을 목표로 한다. 특히 영어권 국가의 대학 생활과 같은 학술적 환경에서의 영어 사용 능력을 측정하는 데 초점을 맞추고 있다. 학문적 지식이나 컴퓨터 활용 능력을 평가하려는 것이 아니므로 모든 문제는 시험에 제시되는 내용만을 근거로 정답을 골라야 한다. iBT (Internet-based test) 토플은 인터넷을 통해 시험이 치러지며 언어의 네 가지 영역인 읽기(Reading), 듣기 (Listening), 말하기(Speaking), 쓰기(Writing) 능력을 종합적으로 평가한다.

1. Speaking(말하기) 영역이 평가된다.

영어를 읽고 듣고 쓰는 능력에 비해 말하기 실력이 부족한 사람들이 많다는 것을 감안해 iBT 토플에서는 Speaking 영역이 평가된다. 글을 듣거나 읽으면서 이해하는 것으로만 그치지 않고 이해한 내용을 체계적으로 말할 수 있어야 한다.

2. 언어의 통합적(Integrated) 사용 능력이 중요하다.

Speaking과 Writing에서는 말하고 쓰는 독립적 능력 외에, 언어의 통합적 사용 능력이 함께 평가된다. Speaking 영역에서는 강의나 대화를 듣고 말하거나 지문을 읽고 강의나 대화를 들은 후 말하는 통합형 문제가 출제된다. Writing 영역에서는 지문을 읽고 강의를 들은 후 내용을 요약해야 하는 통합형 문제가 출제된다.

3. 문법 실력만을 측정하는 별도의 영역은 없다.

CBT에서는 문법(Grammar) 영역이 별도로 있었으나 iBT에서는 문법 실력만을 별도로 측정하는 영역은 없다. 이는 문법이 언어 구사에 있어 기본적인 요소인 만큼 읽고 듣고 말하고 쓰는 실용적 상황에서의 기본적인 문법 활용을 측정하기 위함이다.

4. Note-taking이 허용된다.

시험 내내 Note-taking을 할 수 있는 별도의 용지가 제공된다. 따라서 평소에 공부할 때도 기억력보다는 이해력과 논리력에 중점을 두고, 시험 중에 Note-taking을 위해 이를 최대한 활용할 수 있도록 충분히 연습해 두어야 한다.

5. Writing 영역의 답안 작성시에는 타이핑만 가능하다.

종이에 답안을 작성할 수 없으므로 능숙한 영자 타이핑 실력이 필요하다. 시험 도중 서투른 타이핑으로 시간을 낭비하는 일이 없도록 시험 전에 많은 연습을 해두도록 한다.

6. 인터넷으로 성적을 확인할 수 있다.

인터넷 기반 시험인 만큼 시험일로부터 15일 후에 인터넷으로 성적 확인이 가능하다.

iBT TOEFL 구성

영역	시간	문항 수	점수	특징
Reading	60~100분	지문 수 : 3~5개 문제 수 : 각 12~14개	0~30점	• 지문은 약 700자로 구성되어 있다. • 일부 지문에는 그림이 등장한다. • 지문의 종합적인 이해를 요구하는 표 채워넣기 문제(Summary, Category chart)가 출제된다.
Listening	60~90분	대화 지문 수 : 2~3개 대화 문제 수 : 각 5개 강의 지문 수 : 4~6개 강의 문제 수 : 각 6개	0~30점	• 대화는 약 400~500자로 구성되어 있고, 강의는 약 500~800자로 이루어져 있다. • 대화는 3분간 들려주고 강의는 3~5분간 들려준다. • 화자의 억양과 발음이 다양화되어 미국식, 영국식, 호주식 발음을 들려준다.
Break (휴식)	10분			
Speaking	20분	독립형 문제 수 : 2개 통합형 문제 수 : 4개	각 문제 : 0~4점 총점 : 0~30점	• 독립형은 개인적 경험을 말하는 문제 1개와 두 가지 선택사항 중 하나를 선택하여 말하는 문제 1개로 구성되어 있다. • 통합형은 지문을 읽고 강의나 대화를 들은 후 말하는 문제 2개와 강의나 대화를 듣고 말하는 문제 2개로 이루어져 있다. • 헤드셋과 연결되어 있는 마이크에 대고 답을 녹음하며, 이는 디지털화되어 채점 기관으로 전송된다.
Writing	55분	통합형 문제 수 : 1개 독립형 문제 수 : 1개	각 문제 : 0~5점 총점 : 0~30점	• 통합형 문제는 먼저 독해 지문을 읽고 강의를 들은 후 강의 내용을 독해 지문과 연계하여 요약해야 한다. • 독립형 문제는 주어진 주제에 대해 개인적 경험이나 생각에 기초하여 글을 작성해야 한다. • 답안은 타이핑으로 작성해야 한다.

iBT TOEFL 시험 등록

1. www.ets.org/toefl 웹사이트를 방문하여 인터넷 접수를 한다. 상시 등록이 가능하며 응시일로부터 최소 7일 전까지 등록을 해야 한다. 응시료는 신용카드로 결제한다.

2. 한미교육위원단으로 전화를 하여 시험을 접수한다. 응시일로부터 최소 7일 전까지 등록을 해야 하며 응시료는 신용카드로 결제한다. 전화번호는 02-3211-1233.

3. 한미교육위원단으로 우편접수를 한다. 등록 신청서(registration form)를 작성하고 수표나 우편환을 동봉하여 보낸다. 응시일로부터 최소 4주 전까지 등록을 해야 한다. 주소는 서울특별시 마포구 염리동 168-15 한미교육위원단(121-874).

4. 응시료는 US $140, 시험일자 변경 비용은 US $40, 취소한 성적 복원 신청 비용은 US $20, 성적 추가 리포팅 비용은 US $170이다.

5. 등록한 시험을 취소하기 위해서는 직접 등록 센터를 방문하거나 웹사이트에 접속하여 절차를 밟아야 한다. 우편으로는 등록 취소가 불가능하다. 응시일로부터 최소 4일 전까지 등록 취소가 가능하며 US $85를 환불 받을 수 있다.

6. 시험 당일에는 반드시 신분증(주민등록증, 운전면허증, 여권 중 택일)을 지참해야 하며 등록 번호(registration number)를 알고 있어야 한다.

7. 시험은 약 4시간 동안 진행되고 두 영역이 끝난 후 10분간의 휴식시간이 주어진다.

8. 성적은 응시일로부터 15일 후 인터넷으로 확인 할 수 있다. 시험 당일에 원하는 4개 기관으로 성적 리포팅이 가능하다.

9. 성적표에는 영역별 점수와 함께 총점이 기재되며 각 영역별로 수험자의 실력을 진단해주는 feedback이 들어있다. 성적표의 유효 기간은 2년이다.

10. 시험 당일 날 시험을 마치면서 성적을 취소할 수 있으며 취소한 성적을 복원하기 위해서는 응시일로부터 10일 이내에 시험주최측에 연락을 해야 한다. 앞서 언급한 대로 성적 복원 신청 비용은 US $20이다.

학습 계획표

	Day 1	Day 2	Day 3	Day 4	Day 5	Day 6	Day 7
Week 1	Ch. 1 Overview, Preview	Ch. 1 OH	Ch. 1 SE	Ch. 1 Lectures	Ch. 1 Practice, Review	Ch. 2 Overview, Review	Ch. 2 OH
Check							
Week 2	Ch. 2 SE	Ch. 2 Lectures	Ch. 2 Practice, Review	복습	Ch. 3 Overview, Preview	Ch. 3 OH	Ch. 3 SE
Check							
Week 3	Ch. 3 Lectures	Ch. 3 Practice, Review	Ch. 4 Overview, Review	Ch. 4 OH	Ch. 4 SE	Ch. 4 Lectures	Ch. 4 Practice, Review
Check							
Week 4	복습	Ch. 5 Overview, Preview	Ch. 5 OH	Ch. 5 SE	Ch. 5 Lectures	Ch. 5 Practice, Review	복습
Check							

* OH: Office Hours   SE: Service Encounters

주제
Main Idea

Overview

Preview

Office Hours

Service Encounters

Lectures

Practice

Review

Main Idea

주제

Overview

- Main Idea 유형은 대화와 강의의 주제가 무엇인지를 고르는 문제
- 대화와 강의 모두 첫 번째 문제로 항상 출제됨
- 대화의 경우, 대화 첫 머리에 보통 주제가 드러남: 교수가 학생을 부른 이유, 학생이 교수를 찾아간 이유, 학생이 가지고 있는 문제, 학생이 교내 여러 부서를 찾아간 이유 등
- 강의의 경우, 대화와 마찬가지로 전반부에 주제가 제시되지만 오늘 배울 내용이 무엇인지 잘 구분해서 들어야 할 때가 자주 있음: 지난 시간에 배운 내용을 간략히 언급하고 넘어가는 경우, 앞으로 배울 큰 토픽을 먼저 언급한 후 그 중에서 특히 오늘은 어떤 것을 중점적으로 알아보겠다라고 말하는 경우 등
- 주제 찾기 문제는 항상 앞부분을 집중해서 듣는 것이 가장 중요하지만, 대화와 강의가 진행되면서 주제와 관련된 키워드가 여러 번 반복해서 등장하므로 앞부분의 내용을 놓쳤다고 해도 끝까지 흐름을 따라가며 듣는 것이 더 중요함

Sample Questions

- What are the speakers mainly talking about?
- Why does the man talk to the woman?
- Why does the man go to see his professor?
- What is the man's problem?
- What problem does the woman have?
- What is the professor mainly discussing?
- What are the speakers mainly discussing?
- What is the main topic of the lecture?
- What is the lecture mainly about?

Preview

What are the speakers mainly talking about?

Ⓐ The importance of the course guidelines
Ⓑ Older forms of music
Ⓒ Great jazz musicians
Ⓓ The types of music the course will cover

Listen to part of a conversation between a student and a professor.

W : Um, do you mind if I ask about <u>the musicians we'll be discussing in this</u>
대화 토픽 : 강의 시간에 다룰 음악가
<u>course</u>?

M : Sure, what do you want to know?

W : Well, I've noticed that there's <u>so much focus on old music</u> like classical,
강의 초점 : 옛날 음악
baroque, and so on. <u>What about newer music like jazz and rock</u>?
학생이 알고 싶은 것 : 최신 음악

M : Well, were you in class on the first day, when I went over the course
guidelines?

W : Actually, no. I added the class in the second week of the semester.

M : All right, I think you missed some important information. This is an
<u>introductory class</u>, but there are <u>two different classes</u>. <u>Mine covers older</u>
개론 수업   2개의 다른 강의   교수의 수업: 옛날
<u>musical traditions</u>, and if you were <u>looking for jazz and rock, that's a</u>
음악 양식을 다룸   재즈, 록: 다른 강의에서 다룸
<u>different course</u>. Students get them mixed up sometimes.

W : Oh, I didn't know that. Thanks for clearing that up!

M : Sure, no problem.

여 : 이 강좌에서 다룰 음악가들에 관해 여쭤봐도 될까요?
남 : 그래, 알고 싶은 것이 무엇이지?
여 : 음, 강의를 듣다 보니 클래식이나 바로크 음악 같은 옛날 음악을 주로 다루시는 것 같아서
　　요. 재즈나 록 음악처럼 좀더 최신 음악은 안 배우나요?
남 : 강의 첫 날 강의 계획서를 함께 살펴볼 때 수업에 참석했니?
여 : 아뇨. 학기가 시작하고 나서 2주째에 수강 신청을 했거든요.
남 : 그렇다면 중요한 내용을 못 들은 것 같구나. 이 수업은 개론 수업이고, 2개의 다른 강의가
　　있단다. 내 수업은 더 오래된 음악 양식을 다루고, 재즈나 록 음악에 관해 배우는 수업을
　　찾는 거라면, 그건 다른 강의야. 학생들이 가끔 혼동하기도 한단다.
여 : 아, 그건 몰랐어요. 명쾌하게 알려주셔서 감사합니다!
남 : 그래.

W : Um, do you mind if I ask about <u>the musicians we'll be discussing in this course</u>?
M : Sure, what do you want to know?
W : Well, I've noticed that there's <u>so much focus on old music</u> like classical, baroque, and so on. <u>What about newer music like jazz and rock</u>?

여자의 첫 번째 말을 다른 말로 바꾸어 표현한 것이 보기 ⓓ이다. 보기 ⓐ는 스크립트에 언급된 course guidelines란 표현을 이용하여 만든 오답이고, 보기 ⓑ 역시 스크립트에 언급된 old music과 older musical traditions란 표현을 이용하여 만든 오답이다. 스크립트에 jazz란 말은 언급되었지만 위대한 재즈 음악가에 관해서는 언급된 바가 없으므로 보기 ⓒ 역시 오답이다.

해석 | 화자들은 무엇에 관해 이야기하고 있는가?
　　ⓐ 강의 계획서의 중요성
　　ⓑ 더 예전의 음악 양식
　　ⓒ 위대한 재즈 음악가
　　ⓓ 강의에서 다룰 음악의 종류

어휘 | musician 음악가 | notice 알아채다 | focus 초점 | baroque 바로크 음악 | go over 검토하다, 설명을 되풀이하다 | add 더하다, 추가하다 | mix up 혼동하다, 착각하다 | clear up (의문을) 풀다

정답 | ⓓ

Office Hours

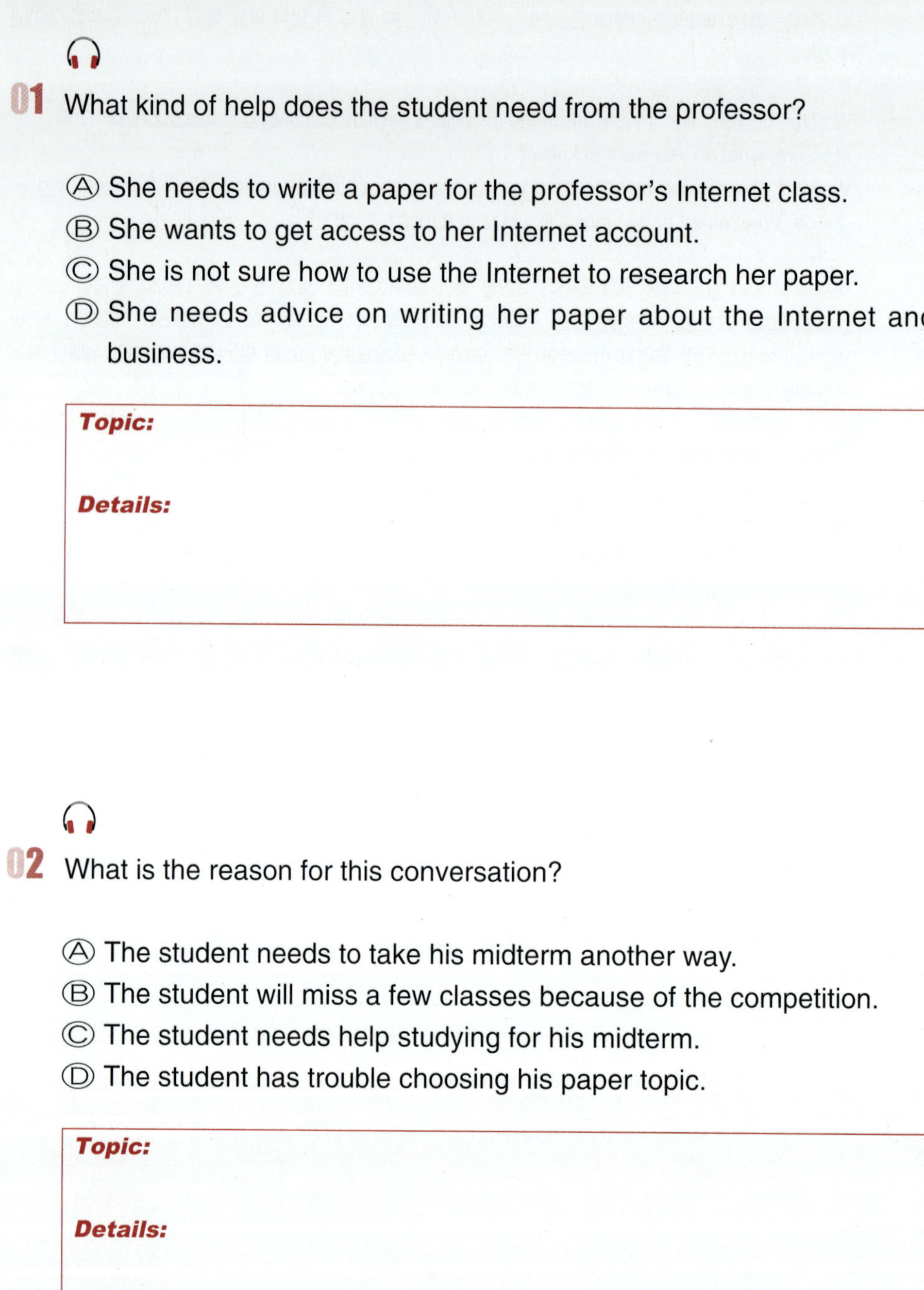

01 What kind of help does the student need from the professor?

    Ⓐ She needs to write a paper for the professor's Internet class.
    Ⓑ She wants to get access to her Internet account.
    Ⓒ She is not sure how to use the Internet to research her paper.
    Ⓓ She needs advice on writing her paper about the Internet and business.

> **Topic:**
>
> **Details:**

02 What is the reason for this conversation?

    Ⓐ The student needs to take his midterm another way.
    Ⓑ The student will miss a few classes because of the competition.
    Ⓒ The student needs help studying for his midterm.
    Ⓓ The student has trouble choosing his paper topic.

> **Topic:**
>
> **Details:**

03 What is the situation the student is discussing with the professor?

Ⓐ The student has a family emergency and needs a replacement.
Ⓑ The student needs articles because a couple of reporters are absent.
Ⓒ The student has asked the professor to write news stories.
Ⓓ The student wants some information about the journalism program.

Topic:

Details:

Dictation : Office Hours

01

> W : Um, are you busy? I'm writing a paper, and maybe I could use
> ① ______________ .
>
> M : Sure, have a seat.
>
> W : Thanks, um, I'm writing about the Internet and ② ______________ the
> business world, but I don't know ③ ______________ .
>
> M : It sounds like a very broad topic. Were you thinking about ④ ______________ ,
> or is that as far as you'd gotten?
>
> W : That's all I've ⑤ ______________ . I guess I need to ⑥ ______________ ,
> don't I?
>
> M : That would be a good way to start. Choose a very focused topic. For
> example, you can look at the history of the Internet, and focus on one or
> two businesses that adopted web technology early. Or compare one
> industry before and after.
>
> W : Oh, now I ⑦ ______________ in my head.

M : Thanks for seeing me, professor Powter. The reason I'm here is that I'm on the archery team, and the state competition is scheduled ① ______________ the midterm. The competition is really important······.

W : You mean missing the midterm? Um, you know that's ② ______________ than you think.

M : I know, but is there any way I can ③ ______________ ?

W : The thing is sometimes students are dishonest in situations like yours.

M : So that means I can't take the midterm later?

W : I'm afraid so. I've been too busy to prepare a backup test. I'm going to have to ask you to write a paper, instead.

M : Oh, that sounds good. Thank you. Um, do I choose the topic?

W : Well, let me sleep on it for a couple of days, and ④ ______________ after the next class. I'll be able to tell you more at that time.

M : OK, ⑤ ______________ . Thank you so much!

M : Um, you're the faculty advisor for the student newspaper, so I need some advice, please!

W : Sure, what's going on?

M : Well, two of the reporters have had problems ① ________________. One is sick, and one has had a family emergency. I still have 3 pages to fill, and no articles!

W : All right, let's think about it. Uh, have you spoken to the head of the journalism program?

M : Not yet. Oh, should I?

W : Yes. Tell her ② ____________. You've still got a week ③ ____________, so there's time to recruit a couple of students to write articles, I mean temporarily.

M : That's a good idea, and is there anything else I should do?

W : You should also meet with your current reporters and ④ ____________. They may be able to help, as well.

M : Great, thanks! I'll get right on it!

Service Encounters

01 Why is the student talking to the woman?

    Ⓐ He needs an extension on paying for his dorm room.
    Ⓑ He wants to apply for a scholarship for the summer course.
    Ⓒ He needs a recommendation letter from his professor.
    Ⓓ He wants to switch to a different dorm for the summer.

> *Topic:*
>
> *Details:*

02 What problem does the student have?

    Ⓐ She does not know how to use the library.
    Ⓑ She is unable to use the online book reservation system.
    Ⓒ She lost library books that she checked out.
    Ⓓ She doesn't have the receipt on her late fees.

> *Topic:*
>
> *Details:*

03 What is the reason for this discussion between the man and the woman?

Ⓐ The radio shows have been cancelled.
Ⓑ The thunder is too loud for the broadcast to be audible.
Ⓒ The lightning has disrupted the broadcast signal.
Ⓓ The broadcast equipment is not working.

Topic:

Details:

Dictation : Service Encounters

01

M : Hi, I have a question about ① __________ over the summer.

W : All right, what's your question?

M : The thing is I want a single room, but I can't ② __________ right now, and the deadline is tomorrow. I've gotten a scholarship from my department, though, and the disbursement date is next week. Um, if I bring documentation, can I ③ __________?

W : I see. That happens ④ __________. Here's what you need to do. Can you pay the basic housing fee now?

M : Yes.

W : Good. Do that, and then get a letter from your department head verifying the scholarship. We'll reserve one of the single rooms for you. Once you have the money, ⑤ __________, and the room is yours.

M : This is a lot easier than I thought it would be, thanks!

W : You're welcome.

W : I'm sorry, but ① _______________ isn't working. Could you help me with it, please?

M : Sure, let me check our central database first. May I have your student ID number?

W : Ah, here it is.

M : Hmm... OK, no wonder. Are you aware you have a book that is ② _______________ ?

W : What? I ③ _______________ a long time ago.

M : The computer says the book is still out. It also says you ④ _______________ on four others, too. Here, ⑤ _______________ .

W : No way! I paid the fees on those books when I returned them. I ⑥ _______________ , too. What should I do?

M : In that case, I need to see your receipts and make sure that the overdue book was returned. You won't be able to use the system until we've done that. I'm sorry.

W : All right.

M : Oh, no, our whole broadcasting system is down. This is ① ___________ !

W : It ② ___________ the thunderstorm. There was a lot of lightning. I bet that's the reason.

M : What are we going to do?

W : Let's be rational. OK, first, we can still stream over the Internet, even if we're ③ ___________ .

M : That's true. But what about the equipment?

W : For that, we should call the facilities department and ④ ___________ a technician. We need to know whether the equipment can be repaired, or whether we will have to replace it.

M : Then, what about tonight's radio shows?

W : They'll just have to be webcast-only. I doubt we'll have the equipment working again by tonight.

M : All right, I guess ⑤ ___________ !

Lectures

01 🎧 Business administration

1. What is the topic of the lecture?

    Ⓐ Competitors to German luxury cars
    Ⓑ The importance of marketing
    Ⓒ Mental space and automakers
    Ⓓ Product positioning

2. What can be inferred about Toyota, Honda, and Nissan from the lecture?

    Ⓐ Consumers currently recognize them as economy car makers.
    Ⓑ There is a great demand for their luxury car lines now.
    Ⓒ They failed to occupy the customers' mental space.
    Ⓓ Their cars are more reliable than those of BMW, Audi, or Mercedes-Benz.

Topic:

Details:

 🎧 **Asian studies**

1. What is the main topic of the lecture?

    Ⓐ Tea cultivation in Sri Lanka
    Ⓑ Sri Lanka, a former British colony
    Ⓒ Origins of the name Sri Lanka
    Ⓓ History of Ceylon and Sri Lanka

2. Which of the following is NOT true of Sri Lanka?

    Ⓐ It was once called Ceylon.
    Ⓑ James Taylor invented the unique process of preparing Ceylon tea.
    Ⓒ It is under British colonial rule.
    Ⓓ Its tea production accounts for 1/5 of the tea industry in the world.

Topic:

Details:

03 🎧 **Marine zoology**

1. What is the lecture mainly about?

    Ⓐ Reproduction of sea creatures
    Ⓑ Sexual and asexual reproduction
    Ⓒ Starfish's generative function
    Ⓓ Mating habits of starfish

Listen again to part of the lecture. Then answer the question.

2. What does the professor imply when he says this: 

    Ⓐ Starfish are poorly understood now.
    Ⓑ Most students already know what starfish are.
    Ⓒ The class focus is not on starfish.
    Ⓓ People are not usually interested in starfish.

3. Which of the following is true of starfish?

    Ⓐ They have caused problems throughout history.
    Ⓑ They are an excellent food source due to their reproductive abilities.
    Ⓒ They change to the other sex during the breeding season.
    Ⓓ Their arms grow again if destroyed.

> *Topic:*
>
> *Details:*

Dictation : Lectures

01

P(M): Marketing is something I think ① ________________ , since in today's world we are constantly exposed to it. But today, let's talk about one of the more subtle concepts, positioning. There are several ways to look at positioning a brand. It involves more than just ② ____________ a brand or an organization. If you're familiar with the term mental space, this is what marketers want the brand to occupy. It's ③ ____________ they want you to make, and it operates in comparison to other brands – the competitors. That's the crucial point: ④ ____________ . This means establishing a very clear idea of not just who the customers are, but who they ought to be.

In many cases, a company wants its products to be perceived one way, but the reputation is something different. You may not remember the late 1980s, when the car companies Toyota, Honda, and Nissan decided to ⑤ ____________ in North America: Lexus, Acura, and Infiniti. Previously, these three car makers had been known for building economy cars. All three had good reputations for being well-built, but no one could imagine paying $50,000 for a big Toyota. Nor could many people imagine consumers choosing one of these cars ⑥ ____________ like BMW, Audi, or Mercedes-Benz. However, these cars were carefully positioned when they were introduced to the market. The prices were a bit lower than their German competitors, well, actually, ⑦ ____________ , and the outstanding mechanical reliability was a big factor. And the cars were a hit!

P(W): When we think of Sri Lanka, it's perhaps a little difficult to come up with a specific image or association. But I guess all of you have probably heard of Ceylon tea. You might remember that it's the island nation ① _______________ of India, and was formerly known as Ceylon. Today, tea is one of Sri Lanka's main exports. ② _______________, most of the island's coffee crop was destroyed by blight and insect attacks. At the time, Ceylon was part of the British Empire, and much of the agriculture there was ③ _______________ British plantation owners. They realized they needed to be growing ④ _______________, so they wouldn't be so vulnerable.

Well, we should probably thank James Taylor for giving the world Ceylon tea, which is known to be some of ⑤ _______________ in the world today. In 1867 he planted 19 acres of tea. He already had some experience with tea cultivation, ⑥ _______________. When he harvested the leaves, he rolled them by hand and carefully fired them on clay stoves over charcoal. The result was ⑦ _______________ in London, and the Ceylon tea industry was born ⑧ _______________. In 1880, less than 23 pounds of tea had been harvested. By 1890, almost 23,000 tons of it was harvested! Today, the British ⑨ _______________ the Sri Lankan tea industry. The country is now ⑩ _______________ of tea, and it exports about 20% of the world's market.

P(M): Yesterday we were talking about some of the interesting sea creatures. I'd like to continue that talk today by discussing starfish and their amazing reproductive abilities. The starfish needs very little introduction. If you don't know what one is, ① ________________. You probably already know that starfish have ② ______________ regenerate themselves. This is a very sensible survival mechanism, since they are brittle creatures. They move slowly and have very little means of defending themselves. If a starfish loses an arm, ③ ______________. But that's not all: if the arm is attached to a piece of the central disc, then asexual reproduction may take place. ④ ______________, a new starfish grows from that smaller piece. This is possible because certain vital organs are kept in the arms of the starfish. This sounds great, doesn't it? Like everything, ⑤ ______________, also. Well, starfish used to be a problem for fishermen who harvested clams and oysters, which are what starfish eat. In order to increase a haul of clams and oysters, they'd catch starfish, chop them up, and ⑥ ______________ into the sea. Did that solve the problem? No, it resulted in lots more starfishes!

OK, uh, reproduction occurs sexually, as well. Individual starfish are male or female. When the time comes for reproduction, they release sperm and egg cells into the water round them. Fertilized starfish embryos are a form of plankton until they are older. Some starfish follow ⑦ ______________ to know when it's time to release sperm and eggs, and others actually pair up. So, thanks for coming, and I hope you've enjoyed the slideshow.

Practice

01 Why is the student talking to her professor?

   Ⓐ She is not sure about getting her teaching credential.
   Ⓑ She is not sure which graduate school is best for her.
   Ⓒ She is not sure what to choose as her major.
   Ⓓ She is not sure what to do after graduation.

02 What does the student imply about acquiring teaching credentials from the state?

   Ⓐ Education majors with the credentials have better job opportunities.
   Ⓑ The students who do not have the credentials are not allowed to graduate.
   Ⓒ The credentials are required when the students apply for jobs overseas.
   Ⓓ Graduate schools prefer the applicants with the credentials.

03 In the conversation, the professor mentions several good reasons for the student to consider teaching English overseas. Indicate in the table below whether each of the following is mentioned by the professor. Click in the correct box for each phrase.

	Mentioned	Not Mentioned
Ⓐ The demand for English teachers is pretty high.		
Ⓑ It is a good opportunity to learn another language.		
Ⓒ English teachers in some countries are paid well.		
Ⓓ Living in another culture will be a new experience.		
Ⓔ The student can get along with many local neighbors.		

04 What can be inferred about the professor's former student in Taiwan?

    Ⓐ She will return to her country soon.
    Ⓑ She is considering moving to Europe.
    Ⓒ She has several years of teaching experience.
    Ⓓ She had debts at the time she graduated.

Listen again to part of the lecture. Then answer the question.

05 What does the professor mean when he says this: 🎧

    Ⓐ It's better to teach in Asia than in Eastern Europe or Latin America.
    Ⓑ Going to Asia is a turning point in many people's lives.
    Ⓒ Many English teachers get started in Asian countries.
    Ⓓ People in Asia are more likely to welcome native English teachers.

   ALL ABOUT JUNIOR TOEFL

06 What is the professor mainly discussing?

    (A) Geography of the Great Lakes region
    (B) How snow is formed
    (C) Weather patterns of North America
    (D) A phenomenon of lake-effect snow

Listen again to part of the lecture. Then answer the question.

07 What does the professor imply when she says this:

    (A) The Great Lakes are the most well-known lake in North America.
    (B) The students are familiar with the geography around the Great Lakes.
    (C) The lake-effect snow only occurs in the Great Lakes.
    (D) The Great Lakes are undergoing unusual weather changes.

08 Which of the following is NOT mentioned as a main area that receives lake-effect snow?

    (A) Rochester
    (B) Detroit
    (C) Buffalo
    (D) Cleveland

09 What are two primary ingredients that determine the amount of lake effect snow? Click on 2 answers.

    (A) Cooler air than the lake water temperature
    (B) Low elevation
    (C) A great deal of water vapor
    (D) The area of the lakes

10 What does the lecture imply about the cities along the southeast shores of the Great Lakes?

Ⓐ They need help during the winter.
Ⓑ They have the smallest population in the U.S.
Ⓒ They are on the windward side of the lakes.
Ⓓ They have the accurate weather research craft.

11 In the lecture, the professor discusses several causes that lead to heavy snowfall in the Great Lakes region. Indicate in the table below whether each of the following is one of the causes. Click in the correct box for each phrase.

	Yes	No
Ⓐ The depth of the lakes		
Ⓑ The way in which the wind moves		
Ⓒ The relative location of the cities		
Ⓓ The size of the cities		
Ⓔ The frequency of strong winds		

Review

01 영어는 우리말로, 우리말은 영어로 바꾸어 써보자.

1. effect ______________	11. 연체의 ______________
2. broad ______________	12. 영수증 ______________
3. adopt ______________	13. 이성적인 ______________
4. reasonable ______________	14. 수리하다 ______________
5. temporarily ______________	15. 장비 ______________
6. philosopher ______________	16. 행사, 경우 ______________
7. explore ______________	17. 예약하다 ______________
8. encouraging ______________	18. 점유하다 ______________
9. disbursement ______________	19. 평판 ______________
10. extension ______________	20. 출시하다 ______________

02 숙어와 맞는 뜻을 연결해 보자.

1. come up with	•	• 이따금
2. narrow down	•	• 폐쇄하다
3. make up	•	• 들르다
4. sleep on	•	• ~에 뒤떨어지지 않다
5. stop by	•	• 제안하다, 생각해내다
6. at the last minute	•	• 당연하다
7. keep up with	•	• ~에 대해 시간을 가지고 생각하다
8. once in a while	•	• 보충하다, 만회하다
9. no wonder	•	• 마지막 순간에
10. close down	•	• 범위를 좁히다

tremendous	destroyed	replace
exports	relatively	means

1. In the 1800s, most of the island's coffee crop was ____________ by blight and insect attacks.

2. They move slowly and have very little ____________ of defending themselves.

3. As far as I'm concerned, there's a ____________ demand for English teachers in East Asia, Eastern Europe, and Latin America.

4. But why do those cities in New York get so much snow when Toronto and Hamilton, on the north side of the lake, in Canada, get ____________ little?

5. The country is now the 3rd largest producer of tea, and it ____________ about 20% of the world's market.

6. We need to know whether the equipment can be repaired, or whether we will have to ____________ it.

세부사항
Detail

Overview

- Detail 유형은 들려주는 대화와 강의의 세부적인 내용까지 정확히 이해하고 있는지를 확인하는 문제
- 대화에서는 1~2 문항, 강의에서는 2문항 이상이 출제됨
- 대화의 경우, 육하원칙(who, when, where, what, how, why)과 관련된 문제가 자주 출제됨: 왜 학생이 수업에 빠졌는지, 교수가 학생의 문제 해결을 위해 제안하는 것이 무엇인지, 학생이 어떻게 문제를 처리할 것인지, 행사가 언제 어디서 열리는지 등
- 강의의 경우, 주제에 관한 진술 중 맞는 것(true)과 맞지 않는 것(NOT true)을 고르는 문제와 주제를 뒷받침하는 세부적인 내용을 묻는 문제가 주로 출제됨
- 아주 세세한 부분까지 기억해야 풀 수 있는 문제는 거의 등장하지 않지만, 긴 대화와 강의를 들으면서 중요한 내용을 체계적으로 이해하고 기억하는 것이 쉽지 않으므로 지문을 들으면서 중심 내용들은 메모를 해두고(note-taking) 문제를 풀 때 이를 활용하도록 함
- 답을 고를 때 들려준 내용과 똑같은 표현이 들어있는 보기는 오히려 오답일 가능성이 크고, 정답은 대부분 비슷한 의미를 가진 다른 표현으로 paraphrase(바꾸어 쓰기) 되어 있음
- 답을 2개 고르는 (click on 2 answers) 문제도 가끔씩 출제되는데, 하나만 고르면 오답 처리되므로 문제를 풀 때 반드시 확인해야 함

Sample Questions

- What is ~?
- Why is ~?
- Where will ~?
- Who will ~?
- When will ~?
- How will ~?
- Which of the following is true of ~?
- Which of the following is NOT true of ~?
- What does the professor suggest the student do?
- What are two reasons for ~? Click on 2 answers.

Preview

Why can't the man help the student with the fridge?

Ⓐ He doesn't know how to fix mechanical problems.
Ⓑ The school is not responsible for it.
Ⓒ It is too expensive to repair it.
Ⓓ It is better to throw it out.

🎧 Listen to part of a conversation at a housing office.

W : Hello. Um, is this the right place for me to ask about <u>a mechanical problem in the dorm</u>?
기숙사의 기계 결함 / 학생이 찾아온 이유:

M : Sure. If we can't help you here, I can suggest where you should go next.

W : That's great. Um, so...

M : What seems to be the problem?

W : It's <u>the refrigerator in my room, it died</u>. It shut off yesterday, and all the ice
문제 원인 : 냉장고 작동이 멈춤
around the little freezer compartment is melting. There's <u>water on the floor</u>, and...
바닥에 물이 차 있음

M : Oh, so you're not staying in one of the suites with a kitchenette?

W : No, I'm <u>in a regular dorm room</u>.
학생은 일반 기숙사에 거주하고 있음
M : <u>So the refrigerator isn't school property</u>.
일반 기숙사에 있는 냉장고는 학교에서 제공해 주는 것이 아님
W : I guess not. I <u>bought it from another student</u> at the beginning of the
다른 학생이 쓰던 것을 산 것임
semester.

M : <u>I'm afraid we can't help in that case</u>. I'm sorry.
학교 기물이 아니라면 도움을 줄 수 없음

여 : 안녕하세요. 음, 기숙사에 있는 기계에 문제가 있는데 제가 제대로 찾아온 것이 맞나요?

남 : 맞아요. 여기서 도와줄 수 없으면, 어디로 가야 하는지 알려줄게요.

여 : 잘됐네요. 그게 말이죠...

남 : 어떤 문제죠?

여 : 제 방에 있는 냉장고가 멈춰버렸어요. 어제 전원이 나가버렸는데, 작은 냉동칸에 붙어있는 얼음들이 전부 녹아버렸어요. 바닥에 물이 흥건해요...

남 : 아, 그럼 학생은 간이 부엌이 있는 기숙사에 있는 것이 아니군요?

여 : 아니에요, 일반 기숙사에 있어요.

남 : 그럼 냉장고가 기숙사에 비치되어 있던 것이 아니겠네요.

여 : 아닐 거에요. 학기 초에 제가 다른 학생한테 샀거든요.

남 : 그런 경우에는 도움을 줄 수가 없겠네요. 미안해요.

해설 | 학생은 기숙사 방에 있는 냉장고가 고장 나서 기숙사 사무실을 찾아 왔다. 학생은 냉장고가 작동을 멈춰 얼음이 모두 녹아 바닥에 물이 흥건하다고 문제를 호소하였는데, 직원은 일반 기숙사에 있는 냉장고는 학교에서 제공해주는 것이 아니기 때문에 도움을 줄 수가 없다고 하였다. 대화의 끝부분에 문제 해결의 단서가 있다.

W : No, I'm in a regular dorm room.
M : <u>So the refrigerator isn't school property</u>.
W : I guess not. I bought it from another student at the beginning of the semester.
M : <u>I'm afraid we can't help in that case</u>. I'm sorry.

문제에서 남자가 도움을 줄 수 없는 이유를 묻고 있으므로, 남자의 말을 주의 깊게 들어야 한다. 남자의 말을 연결해보면, '일반 기숙사에 있는 냉장고는 학교 기물이 아니다 → 그런 경우라면 도움을 줄 수가 없다' 이다.

M : So the refrigerator isn't school property.
↓
보기 ⓑ : The school is not responsible for it.

해석 | 왜 남자는 학생에게 냉장고 문제를 해결할 도움을 줄 수 없는가?
Ⓐ 기계 문제를 고칠 줄 모른다.
Ⓑ 학교 측의 책임이 아니다.
Ⓒ 비용이 너무 많이 들어 수리할 수 없다.
Ⓓ 내다버리는 것이 더 낫다.

어휘 | mechanical 기계의 | refrigerator 냉장고 | shut off 끄다, 잠그다 | freezer compartment 냉동실 | melt 녹다 | floor 바닥 | kitchenette 간이 부엌 | property 자산

정답 | Ⓑ

Office Hours

🎧

01 Which of the following is true of the student?

(A) She's majoring in Physics.
(B) She will raise a fund for the Physics department.
(C) She doesn't know who Dr. Kovacs is.
(D) She has knowledge of organic compounds.

> **Topic:**
>
> **Details:**

🎧

02 Which of the following is true of Cinema and Drama 441?

(A) Only Polish students are allowed to take the course.
(B) It requires students to take the placement test.
(C) Students should watch the movies with no subtitles during the
class.

> **Topic:**
>
> **Details:**

03 Why does the student want to interview his friend's grandfather?

Ⓐ He might give some interesting stories for the paper.
Ⓑ He lived in New York in the 1950s.
Ⓒ He's now playing at the New York jazz clubs.
Ⓓ He teaches students jazz at a college.

Topic:

Details:

Dictation : Office Hours

01

W : I noticed that the lab assistant position isn't ① _____________ now... did the department hire someone?

M : As a matter of fact, we did.

W : Oh, no, I was going to ② _____________ . Is that the only lab assistant job? Do you know of any other jobs opening up?

M : Well, it's the only lab assistant we're going to hire, but I do know that the assistant in the physics department ③ _____________ . You're a physics minor, aren't you?

W : Yes, I am. Do you think I'd have a chance?

M : I don't see why not. You should also check with Dr. Kovacs. One of his grad students ④ _____________ some new organic compounds, and he'll need to get a couple of assistants.

W : That's great! Thanks for ⑤ _____________ !

M : Uh, ① ________________ one of the Polish courses, but the catalog says it's

by permission only⋯⋯.

W : Which one?

M : Cinema and Drama. The course number is 441.

W : Ah, I see. Do you speak Polish, or have you studied it? It's just... um, I

don't believe ② ________________ , because I don't recognize you.

M : Well, my father is working in Krakow, and I've visited him a few times, so I

speak it a little. I, uh, I want to ③ ________________ , and the class seems

interesting, so...

W : That's not bad, but the problem is that the films shown in the class are not

subtitled. That means you need ④ ________________ to really benefit from

the class. May I ⑤ ________________? Why don't you take the placement

test, and study the language itself?

M : I guess you've got a point. Thanks!

M : Mind if I ask you a few questions about my paper? I've learned something interesting, and it's going to ① ____________ .

W : Chris, that sounds mysterious. What's the topic of your paper?

M : Um, it's about New York jazz culture in the 1950s.

W : That's pretty broad, considering ② ____________ . Had you thought about focusing only on one musician?

M : Well, that's exactly what I'm doing. I found out one of my friends' grandfather played the jazz club circuit in the 50s, and I want to interview him. But the paper's due Friday and I won't be able to speak to him by then. He's ③ ____________ .

W : Well, it would be quite interesting if you put his story on your paper. OK, tell you what: why don't you give me an outline and ④ ____________ on Friday? Then I'll give you another week to finish it. How's that?

M : That would be really great!

Service Encounters

01 Which of the following does the man NOT ask to replace the student's ID card?

Ⓐ Social Security Number
Ⓑ Other forms of ID with a picture
Ⓒ Recent photos
Ⓓ Replacement fees

Topic:

Details:

02 How much time is left until the student's *Incomplete* semester grade becomes an F?

Ⓐ 2 days
Ⓑ 10 days
Ⓒ 14 days
Ⓓ 30 days

Topic:

Details:

03 Why does the student have to stay at her friend's house tonight?

Ⓐ The technician will clean up the mess.
Ⓑ The leak won't stop until tomorrow.
Ⓒ A new radiator is not available.
Ⓓ The maintenance person is busy.

Topic:

Details:

Dictation : Service Encounters

01

W : Uh, I need to replace my student ID card. I lost it.

M : All right. Do you remember the number?

W : Well, no... can you use ① _______________ ?

M : Yes. Write down your full name and your Social Security Number on this piece of paper, and ② _______________ your driver's license or some other kind of picture ID.

W : OK. Can I... uh, will you be able to issue a new card ③ _______________ ?

M : It seems we can't do that right now. We're short-handed now. ④ _______________ or so.

W : That's not good. Anyway, do I need to give you a new photo? I brought one with me, ⑤ _______________ .

M : That's all right. Everything is digital now, so the image is already in our system. But you should pay the $5 replacement fee to get started.

W : Great, here you go.

M : So I got an e-mail asking me to call or ① ______________ ?

W : Yes, it seems that you got an *Incomplete* last semester in your biology class, and you're ② ______________ to complete the course. If your professor doesn't ③ ______________ within two weeks, the *I* will become an *F*. Did you know that?

M : Oh, no, I thought I had a little more time. I needed to redo an experiment, so she let me take an *Incomplete* for the semester... I guess I need to talk to her about it ④ ______________ .

W : Yes, the sooner you can do that, the better.

M : Is there any way to extend the deadline a little, though?

W : You can request one 10 day extension. After that, you need to ⑤ ______________ .

M : The dean? Wow... anyway, thanks for letting me know. You're ⑥ ______________ .

W : Look, I've got a big problem with the radiator in my room. Is a maintenance person free? It's really bad.

M : OK, ① _______________. Tell me what's going on, all right? I need to know what the problem is, so I know which technician to send.

W : It sprang a leak last night and there was ② _______________ on the floor this morning. It was like a pond, and ③ _______________!

M : Sounds like ④ _______________. I'll send someone over right now. But you should probably plan to stay somewhere else tonight.

W : Why?

M : The technician can stop the leak, but ⑤ _______________. We're getting more new radiators tomorrow afternoon.

W : I guess I can stay at my friend's apartment... anyway, thanks for your help! I need to get to class now.

Lectures

01 🎧 **Earth Science**

1. Which of the following is NOT true of orographic lift?

    Ⓐ Cool air cannot hold the moisture.
    Ⓑ Air rises along the mountain range.
    Ⓒ Air expands and cools at high altitudes.
    Ⓓ The windward side of the mountain is dry.

2. What cities are located in a region where there are many clouds formed by the presence of mountains?

    Ⓐ Seattle and San Francisco
    Ⓑ Portland and Toronto
    Ⓒ Vancouver and Seattle
    Ⓓ Los Angeles and Portland

Topic:

Details:

1. According to the discussion, what is true of geysers?
Click on 2 answers.

Ⓐ The word geyser has its origins in Icelandic.
Ⓑ It is not difficult to find one from all parts of the world.
Ⓒ The hottest water underground erupts because of the increased pressure.
Ⓓ They usually gush out hot water and steam on an irregular basis.

2. Where can people see more than 50% of the world's geysers?

Ⓐ Iceland
Ⓑ New Zealand
Ⓒ America
Ⓓ Japan

Topic:

Details:

1. What are the speakers mainly discussing?

  Ⓐ How to overcome the recession
  Ⓑ Different theories about an economic boom
  Ⓒ The cycle of boom and bust
  Ⓓ How long boom days last

2. Which of the following is NOT a characteristic of an economic boom?

  Ⓐ Outturn is increased.
  Ⓑ More people have jobs.
  Ⓒ Goods and services are high in demand.
  Ⓓ Prices tend to be lower.

3. Which of the following is true of American politicians these days?

  Ⓐ They feel it is important for the government to implement a solid economic policy.
  Ⓑ Most of them think the government should stand out of the economic situation.
  Ⓒ They think the government should invest more money in research in economics.
  Ⓓ Most of them feel the government is incapable of improving uncertain economic conditions.

Topic:

Details:

Dictation : Lectures

01

P(M) : Moving on, I want to take a brief look at clouds and how they form. Well, this is essential in understanding ①______________ , and how moisture is distributed in the atmosphere. So what are clouds, I mean, ②______________ ?

S(W): I love a cloud-capped mountain! Oh, sorry, um, clouds, of course, are visible clusters of water vapor. This can be water in liquid form, or it can be ③______________ .

P : As you said, the typical droplet of water in a cloud is 1/100 of a millimeter in diameter. Think about that, in relation to the size of the cloud... how many billions of them there must be, ④______________ . In mountain areas, clouds form through a process called orographic lift. Can anyone tell me the process?

S : As far as I know, air mass is forced up ⑤______________ , and when that happens, ⑥______________ . The cooler air makes its moisture condense at condensation level, so clouds form.

P : That is the reason you see such sharply different weather patterns on the windward and leeward sides of mountains. Think of Seattle and ⑦______________________ in America: Seattle, Portland, Vancouver, and the other cities in that region are east of the Cascades. Warm, moist winds from the Pacific rise along the mountainsides, cool, and ⑧______________ in the form of rain and snow. The other side of that mountain range is famously dry. The entire process is much more complicated than that, and there are different cloud formations that result from it, but that's all we have time for now...

P(M) : All right, you know what a hot spring is. Depending on what country you're from, or where you've gone on vacation, ① _______________. Personally, I went to Japan on my winter vacation last year, and ② _______________ dipping my feet in the hot water. You wouldn't want to bathe in geysers, though, because...

S(W) : They erupt!

P : Yes, they do. And when they do, they send a spray of steam and very hot water into the air. The word *geyser* comes from the Icelandic word for *to gush*, and ③ _______________. I'm pretty sure not many of you have seen them spouting out. They're quite rare. They only occur in a few places on Earth, ④ _______________. To give you an idea how few there are, well, there are only about 1000 total, and more than half can be found in Yellowstone National Park, in the U.S.

S : I've once seen one in New Zealand, and it was, um, what can I say... spectacular!

P: Yeah, sometimes it's ⑤ _______________. You can also see one in Iceland. Now, how it forms... uh, for a geyser to form, groundwater has to seep downward until it meets rock that has been heated by magma. Because there's ⑥ _______________ pressing down on the hot water below, pressure builds up, and periodically the hot water erupts upward. That explains why geysers burst out ⑦ _______________. Water sinks down and heats up, more water piles up on top of it, ⑧ _______________, and then the hottest water at the greatest depth... well, it blows its top. One thing to remember: if you're visiting a geyser, remember to ⑨ _______________, and don't even think about pouring or throwing anything into the water!

P(W) : Let's get started about the boom-and-bust cycle in economic theory. Many economists feel that economic systems are cyclical, with naturally-occurring, ①______________. This means exactly what it sounds like. Who wants to tell me what it's like in an economic boom?

S(M) : Well, it is ②______________, higher demand, lower unemployment, and so on.

P : Right. People are working, the economy's going strong, and money is being made. Unfortunately, these boom periods are often accompanied by inflation, which is ③______________. And – also unfortunately – all good things must ④______________. Then, what is a bust?

S : From what I read on the text, a bust is another name for a recession. I hear the word in the news a lot nowadays.

P : Good, well, the government is always worried about a recession. That means consumer demand is low, people lose their jobs, and the nation overall is earning less money. Ever since the Great Depression, the boom-bust cycle has been studied intensively. Governments around the world – not just the American government – want to ⑤______________, if they can. Some economic theories believe that these cycles can be ⑥______________. Some feel that the government should ⑦______________, and others feel that government intervention only makes the problem worse. The latter school of thought is what most modern-day American politicians believe. We are living ⑧______________, so... let's hope someone knows the answer to all these questions!

Practice

01 What is the reason for this conversation between the man and the woman?

(A) The woman wants to hire a personal fitness trainer.
(B) The woman wants to sign up for the gym.
(C) The woman wants to know the schedule for the pool.
(D) The woman wants to work as a student trainer.

02 What kind of information does the gym employee ask the student to provide?

(A) Her fitness and exercise history
(B) Her height, weight, and health information
(C) Her contact information in case there is an emergency
(D) Her clothing sizes for renting clothes at the gym

03 What does the man imply when he says this: 🎧

    Ⓐ The trainer is better than him.
    Ⓑ He's not able to show the student around.
    Ⓒ He has to do a desk work.
    Ⓓ He doesn't know much about exercise.

04 In the conversation, the man makes several recommendations to the student. Indicate in the table below whether each of the following is mentioned by the man. Click in the correct box for each phrase.

	Mentioned	Not Mentioned
Ⓐ Schedule a time with the trainer		
Ⓑ Take exercise with the swim team		
Ⓒ Prepare the right kind of clothes and shoes		
Ⓓ Take good care of the exercise equipment		

05 What is likely to happen right after this conversation?

    Ⓐ The student will buy a gym suit.
    Ⓑ The student will swim in the pool.
    Ⓒ The student will make an appointment with the man.
    Ⓓ The student will take a tour of the gym.

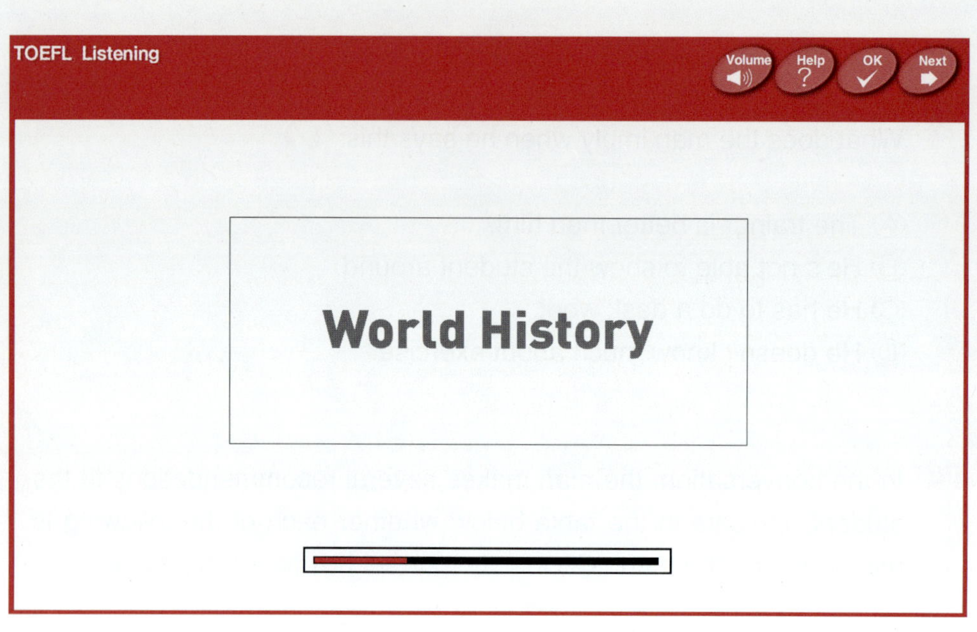

TOEFL Listening
Volume
Help
OK
Next
World History

TOEFL Listening
Volume
Help
OK
Next

06 What is the professor mainly talking about?

   Ⓐ The invention of vulcanization
   Ⓑ The use of rubber by the Central Americans
   Ⓒ History and development of rubber
   Ⓓ The rubber industry

07 The Para rubber tree is indigenous to what country?

   Ⓐ Indonesia
   Ⓑ Brazil
   Ⓒ Portugal
   Ⓓ Nigeria

08 In the lecture the professor mentions several early uses of rubber by the Central and South Americans. Indicate in the chart below whether each of the following is mentioned as one. Click in the correct box for each phrase.

	Yes	No
Ⓐ Balloons		
Ⓑ Water-resistant fabric		
Ⓒ Footwear		
Ⓓ Tires		
Ⓔ Balls		

09 What does the professor imply when he says this: 🎧

Ⓐ Most European technology was based on the inventions of the Mesoamericans.

Ⓑ The Europeans were great technological pioneers and open to new technology of other civilizations.

Ⓒ The Europeans often thought new inventions were the result of supernatural forces.

Ⓓ The Europeans usually stole technology from other civilizations and took credit for it.

10 What can be inferred about rubber according to the lecture?

Ⓐ One of its characteristics gave rubber its name.

Ⓑ Crude rubber is superior to synthetic rubber.

Ⓒ The use of rubber is on the wane.

Ⓓ Rubber was first discovered by the Europeans.

11 What is the name of the process in which rubber is heated and hardened with chemicals?

Ⓐ Vulcanization

Ⓑ Piercing

Ⓒ Harvesting

Ⓓ Coagulating

01 영어는 우리말로, 우리말은 영어로 바꾸어 써보자.

1. quit ______________
2. permission ______________
3. fluency ______________
4. outline ______________
5. mysterious ______________
6. wage ______________
7. statistics ______________
8. issue ______________
9. short-handed ______________
10. submit ______________

11. 실험 ______________
12. 녹슨 ______________
13. 참고 도서 ______________
14. 대기 ______________
15. 지름 ______________
16. 팽창하다 ______________
17. 분출하다 ______________
18. 드문 ______________
19. 주기적으로 ______________
20. 필연적인 ______________

02 숙어와 맞는 뜻을 연결해 보자.

1. as a matter of fact •
2. benefit from •
3. come by •
4. run out of •
5. out of print •
6. result from •
7. beyond expression •
8. so to speak •
9. come to an end •
10. work out •

• 운동하다
• ～에서 이득을 얻다
• 절판된
• ～을 다 써 버리다
• 형용할 수 없는
• 끝나다
• 실은
• ～에서 생겨나다
• 들르다
• 이를테면

| intervention | accompanied | subtitled |
| accusations | proper | compare |

1. Well, you ought to make sure you have ____________ clothes for the gym.

2. When samples of this waterproof cloth were brought back to Portugal, there were ____________ of witchcraft!

3. Unfortunately, these boom periods are often ____________ by inflation, which is a rise in prices of goods and services.

4. Some feel that the government should actively involve itself in the economy, and others feel that government ____________ only makes the problem worse.

5. Well, what I want to do is to look at wages in America's smaller cities, and I want to ____________ them to the cost of real estate.

6. That's not bad, but the problem is that the films shown in the class are not ____________.

추론
Inference

Chapter 3

Overview

- Inference 유형은 들려주는 대화와 강의를 통해 미루어 짐작할 수 있는 것, 또는 추론할 수 있는 것을 고르는 문제
- 대화와 강의 모두 1문항 정도가 출제됨
- 언급된 사실을 답으로 고르는 Detail 문제와 달리, Inference 유형은 지문에 제시된 사실 정보들 사이에 암시되어 있는 내용을 유추하여 답으로 고르는 문제임
- 지문의 일부 사실만을 근거로 추론할 수 있는 문제와 여러 정보를 종합하여 일반화 또는 새로운 결론을 도출하는 문제로 이루어져 있음
- 사실 관계를 올바르게 이해하고 논리적으로 사고하는 능력을 갖추어야 함
- 문제 해결의 단서는 들려주는 내용에 모두 들어있으므로 상식 동원과 억측은 금물
- 지문의 내용과 표현이 그대로 등장하는 보기는 오답일 가능성이 높음

Sample Questions

- What can be inferred about ~?
- What does the man imply about ~?
- What will the woman probably do next?
- What can be concluded about ~?
- What would be a similar example of ~?
- Which of the following is probably true about ~?

Preview

What can be concluded about the Olmec culture, based on the carvings of the enormous heads?

Ⓐ The carving technique had influence on the statues on Easter Island.
Ⓑ Olmec people are thought to have had big square heads.
Ⓒ Ballgames and ballplayers had an important role in the Olmec society.
Ⓓ The stones used for carving were readily available.

Listen to part of a lecture in an archaeology class.

P : In our discussion about the ancient cultures of Mesoamerica, we've talked
토픽: 중앙아메리카의 고대 문명
about the Aztecs and the Maya. Today I'd like to turn our focus on the
강의 주제: 올멕 문명
Olmec. Their homeland was in the tropical coastal areas of south-central
올멕 문명이 꽃피운 곳
Mexico, in the area that is now the states of Veracruz and Tabasco. They
were one of the first advanced Mesoamerican civilizations, from about
1200 B.C. until 400 B.C. In fact, many historians believe they were the
올멕 문명의 발생 시기와 소멸 시기
forebears to many of the later civilizations that flourished in that area.
후대 문명의 시조
What makes the Olmec stand out the most for us today was perhaps their
올멕 문명의 압권   예술
art. They were highly skilled artisans, and they left behind a number of
interesting artifacts. They were known for producing enormous
거대 조각상, 특히
monumental statues – particularly of heads. It seems they liked to carve
거석 두상이 유명함
gigantic heads... not tall and narrow like the ones of Easter Island, but
모양: 이스터섬의 높고 폭이 좁은 석상과 달리 쪼그리고 앉아 있는 모습
more squat. They range in height from 1.5 to 3.5 meters, and in weight
높이: 1.5 ~3.5 미터   무게: 20 ~ 40 톤
from 20 to 40 tons. The heads were thought to be those of famous rulers
통치자 또는 공놀이 선수의 두상
or ballplayers. They were carved from basalt, which surprisingly is not
석상의 재료는 현무암인데, 그 지역에 많지 않은 돌이라
abundant in the area. So far, only 17 have been discovered, 14 of which
놀라움
were found in 1936.

P : 고대 중앙아메리카 문명에 관해 알아보면서, 아즈텍 문명과 마야 문명에 대해 먼저 이야기
나누어 보았죠. 오늘은 올멕 문명에 초점을 맞춰봅시다. 올멕 문명은 멕시코 중남미의 열대
해안 지방에서 꽃피웠는데, 이 지역은 현재 베라크루스(Veracruz) 주와 타바스코(Tabasco)
주에 해당하죠. 올멕 문명은 중앙아메리카의 최초의 선진 문명 가운데 하나로, 기원전 1200
년 ~ 기원전 400년 사이에 존재했어요. 사실, 많은 역사가들이 올멕 문명이 그 지역에서 번
성했던 많은 후대 문명의 시조라고 믿고 있어요.
오늘날 우리가 봤을 때 올멕 문명이 월등하게 두드러지는 이유는 바로 그들의 높은 예술적
경지에 있어요. 올멕인들은 높은 공예 수준을 지니고 있었고, 사람들의 관심을 끌만한 공예품
을 많이 남겼죠. 그들은 거대 조각상을 만든 것으로 유명한데, 그 중에서도 특히 두상을 많이

해설 | 스크립트는 약 3000년 전 경 중앙아메리카에서 발달한 올멕 문명의 예술에 관한 강의이다. 올멕인들이 남긴 많은 예술품 중 거대 조각상, 특히 거대한 바위에 사람의 머리를 조각한 거석 두상에 관해 주로 이야기하고 있다. 질문지에서 거석 두상에 비추어 올멕 문명에 관해 결론 내릴 수 있는 것을 고르라고 하였는데, 이는 강의의 주제와 밀접한 관련이 있는 부분이다. 그럼, 각 보기와 지문의 해당 부분을 비교하여 정답이 무엇인지 확인해보자.

보기 Ⓐ : 이스터섬(Easter Island)은 스크립트의 2단락 4번째 문장에 올멕 두상과의 모양 비교를 위해 언급되었다. 이스터섬에 있는 조각상이 올멕인들의 조각 기술의 영향을 받아 만들어졌는지는 알 수 없다. 따라서 보기 Ⓐ의 내용은 오답이다.

보기 Ⓑ : 올멕인들이 거대한 두상을 조각했다고 해서 올멕인들의 머리가 크고 네모난 모양이었다고 생각할 근거는 없다. 따라서 보기 Ⓑ 역시 오답이다.

보기 Ⓒ : 공놀이 선수(ballplayers)가 언급된 스크립트의 2단락 6번째 문장을 보면, 올멕인들이 조각한 두상이 통치자 또는 공놀이 선수의 모습을 본떠 만들어진 것으로 여겨졌다고 했다. 거대한 석상을 조각하면서 통치자의 두상과 함께 공놀이 선수의 두상을 선택했다는 사실을 통해 그만큼 올멕 사회에서 공놀이 선수의 위상이 높았거나 중요했다고 짐작할 수 있다. 따라서 보기 Ⓒ가 정답이다.

보기 Ⓓ : 석상의 재료가 언급된 부분은 스크립트의 2단락 7번째 문장이다. 현무암을 깎아 만들었다고 했는데, 석상이 세워진 지역에 현무암이 많지 않기 때문에 놀라운 일이라고 하였다. 따라서 조각 재료로 쓰인 돌을 쉽게 구할 수 있었다는 보기 Ⓓ의 내용은 오답이다.

해석 | 거석 두상에 비추어 생각해 볼 때, 올멕 문명에 관해 결론 내릴 수 있는 것은 무엇인가?
Ⓐ 조각 기술은 이스터섬의 조각상에 영향을 끼쳤다.
Ⓑ 올멕인들은 크고 네모난 얼굴을 가졌던 것 같다.
Ⓒ 공놀이와 공놀이 선수는 올멕 사회에서 중요한 역할을 지니고 있었다.
Ⓓ 조각 재료로 쓰인 돌은 쉽게 구할 수 있었다.

어휘 | ancient 고대의 | Mesoamerica 중앙 아메리카(Central America) | homeland 본국, 조국 | tropical 열대의 | advanced 고등의, 뛰어난 | civilization 문명 | historian 역사가 | forebear 선조 | flourish 번성하다 | stand out 두드러지다, 뛰어나다 | artisan 장인 | artifact 공예품, 인공 유물 | enormous 거대한 | monumental 기념비의 | statue 조각상 | carve 조각하다 | gigantic 거대한 | narrow 좁은 | squat 쪼그리고 앉은 | range 범위가 ~에 이르다 | height 높이 | weight 무게 | ruler 통치자 | ballplayer 공놀이 하는 사람 | basalt 현무암 | abundant 풍부한 | so far 지금까지

정답 | Ⓒ

Office Hours

01 What will the student probably do after this conversation?

   Ⓐ He will ask the professor for more advice before deciding.
   Ⓑ He will look for ways to pay for his expenses.
   Ⓒ He will postpone the internship by one semester.
   Ⓓ He will do more part-time jobs.

> *Topic:*
>
> *Details:*

02 Which of the following can be inferred about the student?

   Ⓐ She will be absent from today's class.
   Ⓑ Her ankle has not healed properly and will require surgery.
   Ⓒ She has to rewrite her paper because it's overdue.
   Ⓓ She will reschedule her appointment with the doctor.

> *Topic:*
>
> *Details:*

03 What can be inferred about the student from the conversation?

(A) He is not interested in getting extra credit.
(B) He thought he had written a good paper.
(C) He hasn't done many presentations in public.
(D) He never thought he had performance anxiety.

> *Topic:*
>
> *Details:*

Dictation : Office Hours

01

M : I'm ① _______________, um, would you mind giving me some advice?

W : Sure, what's up?

M : Well, I've been offered an internship at the National Gallery in Washington D.C., but ② _______________. It's really a good opportunity, but I'm not sure how I can afford to live there and pay for ③ _______________.

W : Wow, that's very prestigious, though. I know you were hoping to get that internship.

M : Yes, I was, but now I don't know what to do. It would really help my career later, but I'm worried about the money.

W : I think you should ④ _______________. Talk to your family, the financial aid office, and the Gallery's human resources people. Maybe you can explain your situation, and ask for some... ⑤ _______________?

M : Well, I don't think that's ever going to happen.

W : You won't know until you try.

M : You're right, ⑥ _______________. Thanks!

W : Professor Banks, ① ______________ for just a moment?

M : Sure, come on in. What do you need?

W : I just stopped by ② ______________. It's due in today's class.

M : Yes, it is. Um, why don't you give it to me then?

W : The thing is I have to go to the hospital this afternoon, so I won't be able to ③ ______________.

M: Oh... you're not sick, are you? Is everything OK?

W : It's fine. I broke my ankle last semester and now that ④ ______________, it's been aching. I want to get another X-ray to make sure ⑤ ______________.

M : I see. I hope it's nothing serious!

W : It's probably one of those things I'll just ⑥ ______________.

M : All right. Good luck.

W : Thanks for staying after class to see me. I'll ① ____________ .

M : That sounds scary.

W : Scary? No, your paper about performance anxiety was really great, and I'd like you to ② ____________ next time.

M : Oh, well... thanks! ③ ____________ , but... a presentation? I'm not sure I'd do a very good job.

W : Do you have performance anxiety?

M : Of course! That's why I wrote the paper.

W : So maybe you ought to try giving a presentation in class. You can use some of the techniques you wrote about. It'll be ④ ____________ .

M : Well, it's just... scary!

W : I think you should ⑤ ____________ . For extra credit, as well as for the experience. Just ten minutes. How does that sound?

M : Um... all right, I guess.

Service Encounters

01 What can be concluded about the student from the conversation?

    Ⓐ She will turn to other areas aside from Europe.
    Ⓑ She is likely to choose the program in Albania.
    Ⓒ She will go to Moldova where many subjects are available.
    Ⓓ She will request more information from the office.

Topic:

Details:

02 What can be inferred about the student from the conversation?

    Ⓐ She will give up taking BIO221 class.
    Ⓑ She will ask the man to put her on the waiting list.
    Ⓒ She will sign up for Dr. Yuen's class.
    Ⓓ She will not take any biology classes.

Topic:

Details:

03 What can be concluded about the records in the database based on this conversation?

Ⓐ There seems to be some mistakes.
Ⓑ The database has been updated since fall break.
Ⓒ The records are for a different dorm.
Ⓓ The records are absolutely correct.

> **Topic:**
>
> **Details:**

Dictation : Service Encounters

01

W : Excuse me, hi, uh, I'd like to know ① _______________ in Europe?

M : Sure, there are two. Well, it's not like a vacation in the South of France. I want to make sure you know that.

W : I know. I do ② _______________ . I understand one program is in Albania, right?

M : Yes, ③ _______________ in the capital, Tirana. The volunteers work with middle school and high school students, tutoring them in English.

W : That sounds interesting. What's the other one?

M : It is ④ _______________ . It's in Moldova, in Chisinau – the capital – as well as in small cities and towns.

W : Well, I'm ⑤ _______________ English and education, so the English literacy program might be a good opportunity. Do you have any brochures?

M : Here you are.

W : Thanks!

W : I'm trying to ① _______________ Dr. Winerock's conservation biology class,

but the computer says it's full.

M : What's the course number?

W : BIO338.

M : Oh, yes, it's full and ② _______________ of 5 students ahead of you.

W : Not good. Is there anything I can do?

M : Um, there's an environmental science course – BIO221 – that covers a lot

of similar material. That's taught by... let me see... Dr. Yuen?

W : I know him. One of my friends took his class before, and I've heard he's a

great teacher. I think I could take that. Are there any openings?

M : Yes, ③ _______________, and it'll ④ _______________ .

W : I'm going to be ① _______________ for the semester. What's ② _______________ ?

M : All I need to do is inspect the room once it's empty, and collect your card

key. I also need to check the computer to make sure ③ _______________ ...

in fact, why don't I do that now? The computer's on. May I have your

name?

W : My name is Blair Waldorf.

M : OK, ④ _______________ ...

W : Is everything OK?

M : Well, it looks like you have an outstanding fee here. It says there's a chair

missing.

W : We talked about that ⑤ _______________ , remember? My roommate and I

were both here? We never had that chair.

M : Really?

W : Yes. Do you want to ask her when we ⑥ _______________ the room? I

promise, we never even saw that chair!

M : All right, ⑦ _______________ . I believe you!

Lectures

01 🎧 Ornithology

1. Which of the following is probably true about bowers?

    Ⓐ One bower differs from another because of each bird's personal taste.
    Ⓑ The arrangement of objects in bowers must be random.
    Ⓒ Most of the objects used for decoration are edible.
    Ⓓ Almost all of the bowers have complex structures.

2. According to the lecture, what can be inferred about male bowerbirds?

    Ⓐ They keep quiet during the mating rituals.
    Ⓑ Their feathers are brightly-colored.
    Ⓒ They have a good visual memory.
    Ⓓ All of them are selected by females.

Topic:

Details:

1. What does the professor imply about Napoleon's relationship with modern Italy?

Ⓐ He modernized Italy's military systems.
Ⓑ He caused a great deal of bloodshed that could have been avoided.
Ⓒ He was responsible for uniting Italy.
Ⓓ He was much less important than the Pope.

2. Which of the following does the professor NOT imply about Napoleon?

Ⓐ He thought gathering information was essential in winning a war.
Ⓑ He was renowned for making a surprise attack.
Ⓒ He knew the importance of both the artillery and the infantry.
Ⓓ He led the wars against Britain, Russia, and Austria to the victory.

Topic:

Details:

03 🎧 Drama

1. What is the professor mainly talking about?

    Ⓐ An early death of Sidney Howard
    Ⓑ The subjects Sidney Howard mainly dealt with
    Ⓒ Sidney Howard's life as a playwright
    Ⓓ Sidney Howard's many talents

Listen again to part of the lecture. Then answer the question.

2. What does the professor mean when he says this: 

    Ⓐ Students should have known better about Sidney Howard.
    Ⓑ Sidney Howard did not write many plays during his lifetime.
    Ⓒ Many students are not familiar with Sidney Howard and his plays.
    Ⓓ Sidney Howard was not given a favorable reception.

3. What can be inferred about Sidney Howard?

    Ⓐ He was better-known for writing movie screenplays.
    Ⓑ He had a great command of French.
    Ⓒ He won the Pulitzer Prize and an Academy Award during his lifetime.
    Ⓓ He was much interested in a comic play.

Topic:

Details:

Dictation : Lectures

01

P(W) : The bowerbirds are not a species you're likely to have heard much about, but they are ① ________________ while we talk about animal courtship rituals. What these birds do is truly unique... and a little bit weird! The bowerbirds are ② ________________ of Australia and Papua New Guinea, although some species can also be found in more southerly parts of Australia. You remember I said they are unique, well, the peculiar thing about them is ③ ________________. The male bowerbird will build a bower, or a highly decorated nest, to attract a mate. Um, each bower has ④ ________________. Some bowerbird males build fairly simple bowers: a circle of plain earth with some twigs in the center. But some of them can be very ⑤ ________________. Some males will stack twigs into statue-like arrangements. They bring brightly-colored objects into the bower and decorate it with those like flowers, berries, shells, feathers, or rocks. Not only that, uh, if you ⑥ ________________ in a specific place before the male bowerbird knows, it will notice, and it will put the object back where it was before! When it's time for mating, the female ⑦ ________________, with some males making strange sounds and dancing. They are all ⑧ ________________. So, who's going to be the lucky guy?

P(M): No discussion of ① ___________ would be complete without spending some time on Napoleon Bonaparte of France. Among the Europeans, few other leaders can ② ___________. Perhaps only Alexander the Great rivals or surpasses Napoleon in that regard. When Napoleon was a general for France, his early military genius quickly elevated him to prominence. He was born in Ajaccio, Corsica, ③ ___________ before his birth. ④ ___________ that Napoleon first focused on Italy. He led France's invasion of Italy, and defeated the Austrians – who had occupied Lombardy – as well as the armies of the Papal States.

Remember: in the late 1700s, Italy was not the unified country that we think of now. At that time, it was a number of independent, and much smaller, states. After this victory, he ⑤ ___________ into a single country called the Cisalpine Republic, which was the predecessor of today's unified Italy. In this series of battles, Napoleon showed ⑥ ___________, and was able to use it creatively. He kept his artillery forces mobile, and used them to support the infantry. He also ⑦ ___________ information-gathering than other military leaders had. He was known for ⑧ ___________ when his enemies were least prepared. When he returned to France, he embarked on attempted invasions of Egypt and Syria. Neither attempt was successful, although he did ⑨ ___________ Malta, and on his return, he became France's emperor ⑩ ___________. This led the way for ⑪ ___________ Britain, Russia, and Austria, in which the French Empire expanded and contracted over and over.

P(M): When you think about the great American playwrights, Sidney Howard probably isn't the first name ① _______________ , is it? Ah, I'd like to talk a little bit about... about this author today, because his is not a household name, and ② _______________ . He lived from 1891 until 1939, and was the first person to win both the Pulitzer Prize and an Academy Award. Howard was ③ _______________ , and later became a translator. In particular, well, he was fond of the French playwrights Charles Vildrac and um... Rene Fauchois, and he enjoyed some success with his English-language adaptations of their work. By then, he was ④ _______________ because of his own work, though. Ah, plays like *They Knew What They Wanted* in 1924 had begun attracting notice. Howard tended to ⑤ _______________ in a warm-hearted, sympathetic way. Instead of ⑥ _______________ , he tended to take the larger view, and to see them as flawed human beings – just like we all are. He enjoyed a great deal of popular success for his plays in the late 20s and throughout the 30s, with sold-out productions on Broadway and in London. Tragically, his life ended in an accident in 1939... the same year he was posthumously awarded an Academy Award for his screenplay adaptation of *Gone with the Wind*. The lives of many talented, important writers and artists end too soon, and Sidney Howard is a great example of one of these people. The American theater is a little poorer ⑦ _______________ .

Practice

01 What problem does the man have?

Ⓐ He has lost some valuables in the classroom.
Ⓑ Some of his and his roommate's things in the dorm have been stolen.
Ⓒ His roommate has stolen some of his belongings.
Ⓓ He has been arrested for stealing things from the dorm.

Listen again to part of the lecture. Then answer the question.

02 What does the man imply when he says this: 

Ⓐ Reporting in person is faster than calling.
Ⓑ The officer should have come by the dorm.
Ⓒ He doesn't have to remember the number.
Ⓓ He doesn't use his cell phone much.

03 Which of the following was NOT stolen?

    Ⓐ Personal computers
    Ⓑ Music player
    Ⓒ Cell phones
    Ⓓ Books

Listen again to part of the conversation. Then answer the question.

04 How does the woman seem to feel about the situation when she says this:

    Ⓐ She thinks the campus did everything to protect the students.
    Ⓑ She isn't interested in helping the students.
    Ⓒ She thinks the students are at fault to some degree.
    Ⓓ She feels regretful, and a little bit responsible.

05 In the conversation, the campus security officer tells the student that several things will happen next. Indicate in the table below whether each of the following is mentioned by the woman.

Click in the correct box for each phrase.

	Mentioned	Not Mentioned
Ⓐ City police officer will talk to the man and his roommate		
Ⓑ Campus security officer will call the student's professors		
Ⓒ The man and his roommate will need to stay with their family		
Ⓓ Families will need to file insurance claims		
Ⓔ Locks will be changed		

TOEFL Listening
Volume
Help
?
OK
Next

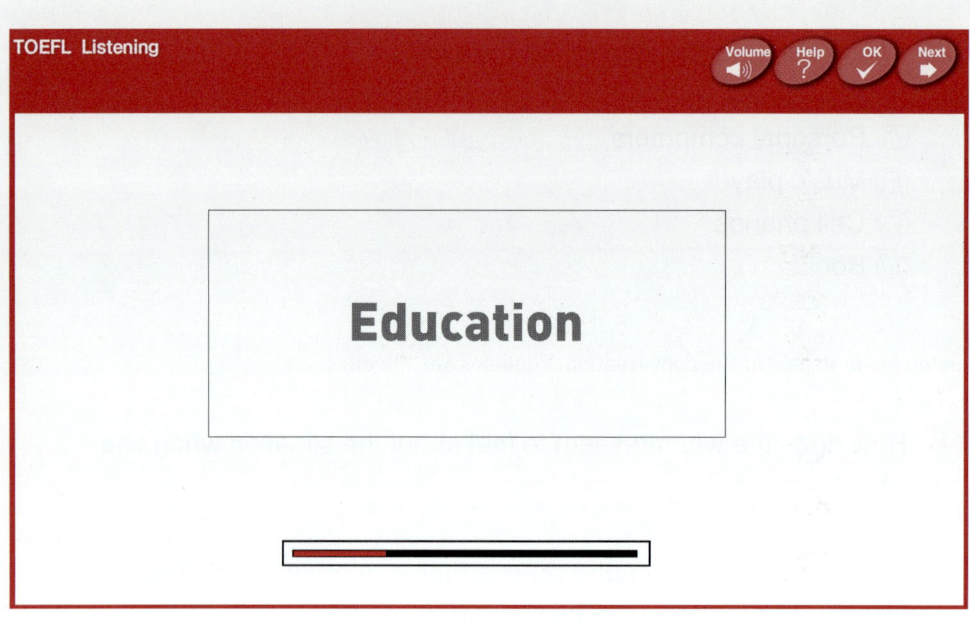

Education

TOEFL Listening
Volume
Help
?
OK
Next

06 What is the professor mainly discussing?

    Ⓐ Life of Maria Montessori
    Ⓑ Italian education methods
    Ⓒ Early childhood education
    Ⓓ The Montessori Method of education

Listen again to part of the lecture. Then answer the question.

07 What does the professor mean when she says this:

    Ⓐ The method is an old outdated educational philosophy.
    Ⓑ The method is considered interesting but not very useful.
    Ⓒ The method is underestimated by many critics.
    Ⓓ The method has become very influential.

08 In the lecture, the professor mentions a number of principles of Montessori education. Indicate in the table below whether each of the following is one of those principles.

Click in the correct box for each phrase.

	Yes	No
Ⓐ All lessons are taught in Italian.		
Ⓑ Teachers observe and provide feedback.		
Ⓒ Students have longer play time than regular students.		
Ⓓ Students direct their own learning.		
Ⓔ All the five senses are incorporated into learning activities.		

Listen again to part of the lecture. Then answer the question.

09 What does the professor imply when she says this:

Ⓐ The method works well with students of higher intelligence.
Ⓑ Montessori educators tend to stick to its principles.
Ⓒ The method adapted itself to certain educational settings.
Ⓓ More American schools are turning to the Montessori programs.

10 Which of the following is NOT true of Maria Montessori?

Ⓐ She believed the approach to child and adult education was alike.
Ⓑ She conceived her unique educational method in the early 20th century.
Ⓒ She was interested in educating little children.
Ⓓ She is a person of an Italian origin.

11 Which of the following is probably true about the Montessori Method?

Ⓐ Its organization is based in Rome, Italy.
Ⓑ Each country has its own standards of Montessori education.
Ⓒ Anyone can use the Montessori name and method.
Ⓓ There is an international organization that certifies Montessori teachers.

Review

01 영어는 우리말로, 우리말은 영어로 바꾸어 써보자.

1. prestigious _______________
2. opportunity _______________
3. heal _______________
4. anxiety _______________
5. disrupt _______________
6. volunteer _______________
7. literacy _______________
8. conservation _______________
9. procedure _______________
10. fine _______________

11. 검사하다 _______________
12. 넘쳐나다 _______________
13. 의식 _______________
14. 장식하다 _______________
15. 배열 _______________
16. 업적 _______________
17. 침략 _______________
18. 전임자 _______________
19. 동정적인 _______________
20. 극작가 _______________

02 숙어와 맞는 뜻을 연결해 보자.

1. in a predicament •
2. look into •
3. turn in •
4. give it a try •
5. make an appointment •
6. figure out •
7. ahead of •
8. take a rest •
9. turn down •
10. worthy of note •

• 휴식을 취하다
• 주목할만한
• 소리를 줄이다
• 제출하다
• 약속을 정하다
• ~에 앞서
• 조사하다
• 시도해보다
• 곤경에 처한
• 이해하다

03 문장의 빈 칸에 들어갈 단어를 보기 박스에서 골라 넣어 보자.

obstacles	attract	flawed
groundbreaking	assignments	emphasis

1. And we'll give you notes for your professors, in case you've lost any _______________ when your PCs were stolen.

2. Her interest was in educating the children with the most challenges and _______________.

3. Another unique and _______________ principle of the Montessori Method was its incorporation of elements of all the five senses.

4. Instead of passing moral judgment on his characters, he tended to take the larger view, and to see them as _______________ human beings – just like we all are.

5. He also put more _______________ on information-gathering than other military leaders had.

6. The male bowerbird will build a bower, or a highly decorated nest, to _______________ a mate.

정보 연결
Connecting Information

Overview
Preview
Office Hours
Service Encounters
Lectures
Practice
Review

Chapter 4 — Connecting Information 정보 연결

Overview

- Connecting information 유형은 대화와 강의가 어떤 방식으로 전개되는지를 파악하고 주제와 관련된 세부 정보들 사이의 관계를 이해하여 질문에서 요구하는 대로 재구성할 수 있는지를 묻는 문제
- 대화와 강의 모두 1문항 정도가 출제됨
- 들려주는 내용에 대한 총체적인 이해가 필수
- 들으면서 대화와 강의의 구성 방식을 이해하고 그 구성 방식에 맞추어 note-taking 을 해두면 문제를 풀 때 유리함

전개 방식과 note-taking

학생이 리포트 작성에 관해 교수의 조언을 구하는 대화 내용

이런 내용의 대화에서는 교수가 학생에게 딱 한가지가 아니라 여러 가지 가능성을 제시해주는 경우가 대부분이므로, 교수의 조언으로 제시된 것(Suggested)과 제시되지 않은 것(Not Suggested)을 구분하는 문제를 예상할 수 있다. 새로운 제안이 나올 때마다 차례대로 내용을 간단히 적는다.

> Topic: Writing a paper
>
> Suggestion
> 1. Good outline
> 2. Focus on specific ideas
> 3. Have a classmate review it

∷ 교수가 두 종류의 사회 집단에 관해 설명하는 강의 내용

◐ 각 보기가 어떤 사회 집단의 특징인지를 분류하는 문제를 예상할 수 있다. 두 범주의 특징을 비교(공통점, 차이점) 및 대조(차이점)하여 설명하는 강의에서는 각 범주 별 특징을 분류하는 문제가 빠지지 않고 출제되는 편이다. 강의를 들으면서 각 범주의 특징을 구분해서 적는다.

Topic: Two types of social groups

In-group
1. Family members
2. Membership in the group
3. Some color shirts

Out-group
1. Feel a desire to compete
2. Unfriendly

∷ 교수가 메이플 시럽을 만드는 과정을 설명하는 강의 내용

◐ 메이플 시럽을 만드는 순서를 올바르게 배열하라는 문제를 예상할 수 있다. 역사적 사건이 일어난 순서, 사물의 제작 순서 등을 중심으로 강의가 전개되면 대개 보기를 순서에 맞게 배열하는 문제가 출제된다. 강의를 들으면서 선후 관계를 구분하여 차례대로 내용을 적는다.

Topic: Making maple syrup

Step
1. Collect the syrup
2. Boil the sap down right away
3. Skim off the top scum or froth
4. Remove the pan from heat

Sample Questions

- The speakers discuss several ways to predict when volcanoes will erupt. Indicate on the chart below whether each of the following is mentioned as one of the ways. Click in the correct box for each phrase.

화자들은 화산이 언제 폭발할지를 예측하는 여러 방법들에 대해 이야기 하고 있다. 아래의 각 보기가 이러한 방법들 중 하나로 언급되었는지 아래 표에 표시하시오. 각 보기에 맞는 칸에 클릭하시오.

	Mentioned	Not Mentioned
Ⓐ Earth quakes	V	
Ⓑ Flooding		V
Ⓒ Strange animal behavior	V	

- In the lecture, the professor discusses two types of social groups. Indicate on the chart below to which group each of the following is attributed. Click in the correct box for each phrase.

강의에서, 교수는 두 가지 종류의 사회 집단을 설명하고 있다. 아래의 각 보기가 어떤 집단의 특징인지 아래 표에 표시하시오. 각 보기에 맞는 칸에 클릭하시오.

	In-group	Out-group
Ⓐ A desire to compete		V
Ⓑ Family members	V	
Ⓒ Same color shirts	V	

- The professor describes the procedure of making maple syrup. Put the steps in correct order. Drag each sentence to the space where it belongs.

교수는 메이플 시럽을 만드는 과정을 설명하고 있다. 각 단계를 순서대로 배열하시오. 보기를 해당되는 표의 빈 칸으로 드래그하시오.

	Making maple syrup
Step 1	
Step 2	
Step 3	

- Ⓐ Boil the sap down
- Ⓑ Collect the sap from trees
- Ⓒ Remove the syrup from heat

Preview

In the conversation, the professor makes several recommendations for the student in order to help him revise his proposal. Indicate whether each of the following is mentioned by the professor. Click in the correct box for each phrase.

	Mentioned	Not Mentioned
Ⓐ Check misspelt words		
Ⓑ Put the reasons for the grant at the beginning		
Ⓒ Take out the information about the student		
Ⓓ Add more information to the section with the research topics		
Ⓔ Make contact with the Chicago Transit Authority		

🎧 Listen to part of a conversation between a student and a professor.

M : So you wanted to talk about my <u>grant proposal</u>?
대화 주제: 학생의 연구보조금 제안서

W : Yes, it's a good proposal, and the topic about <u>Chicago's transportation system</u> is interesting. But before you submit it to the foundation, <u>you need to edit it</u>.
제안서 주제: 시카고 대중교통 시스템
교수의 조언: 제안서 수정

M : OK, what should I do?

W : <u>First, you should explain why you need the grant.</u> <u>Move the justification to the beginning</u>, ahead of the background.
수정 사항 1 : 보조금이 필요한 이유 설명
왜 학생이 보조금을 받아야 하는지를 앞쪽으로 옮기기

M : Sure, let me write this down... what else?

W : <u>Next, your background information should relate to the work you've already done, and how your project will enable you to continue.</u> You should also <u>include more information when you explain the study topics.</u> The foundation may not know much about the Chicago Transit Authority.
수정 사항 2 : 자기 소개 부분은 그 동안의 연구와 관련이 있어야 함
이 프로젝트가 앞으로의 연구에 어떤 도움을 줄 것인가
연구 주제를 자세히 쓰기

M : Great, anything else?

W : Well, just one simple thing: <u>use spell check!</u>
수정 사항 3: 철자법 검사 프로그램 사용

M : Oops – I guess I forgot about that. Thanks, I'll get on it tonight!

남 : 제 연구보조금 제안서에 관해 하실 말씀이 있으시다고요?

여 : 그래, 제안서를 아주 잘 썼더구나. Chicago(시카고)의 대중교통 시스템에 관한 토픽도 흥미롭고. 그런데 재단에 제안서를 제출하기 전에 한 번 더 손을 봐야 할 것 같구나.

남 : 네, 무엇을 해야 하죠?

여 : 먼저, 왜 보조금이 필요한지를 설명해줘야 해. 왜 네가 보조금을 받아야 하는지를 앞쪽으로 옮기도록 해, 배경 정보 앞에 말이야.

남 : 네, 좀 적도록 할게요... 그리고요?

여 : 그리고 네 소개 부분은 그 동안 네가 해온 일이나 연구와 관련이 있어야 하고, 어떻게 이 프로젝트가 앞으로 네 연구 분야를 계속 이어가게 해줄 수 있는지를 보여주어야 해. 그리고 연구 주제를 설명할 때 좀 더 상세히 쓰도록 하렴. 재단에서 시카고 교통 당국에 관해서 잘 모를 수도 있으니까.

해설 | 교수와 학생은 시카고 대중교통 시스템을 연구하는 학생의 연구보조금 제안서에 관해 대화를 나누고 있다. 학생의 제안서를 검토한 후 교수는 재단에 제안서를 제출하기 전에 몇 가지 사항을 수정하라고 일러주고 있다. 대화를 들으면서 제안서의 구체적 수정 방향이 언급될 것이라는 걸 예상하고 핵심 부분은 간단히 적어두는 것이 좋다. 각 보기와 지문의 해당 부분을 확인하여 보자.

보기 Ⓐ : 대화의 마지막에 교수가 학생에게 철자법 검사 프로그램을 이용해 철자가 틀린 단어가 있는지 확인하라고 하였으므로 보기 Ⓐ는 정답이다.

보기 Ⓑ : 교수의 첫 번째 조언이 학생이 왜 보조금을 받을 자격이 있는지를 앞쪽에서 설명하라는 것이었다. 따라서 보기 Ⓑ도 정답이다.

보기 Ⓒ : 자기 소개는 그 동안의 연구 성과와 관련 지어 하라고 한 것이지, 보기 Ⓒ처럼 학생에 대한 이야기는 완전히 빼라는 내용은 아니었다.

보기 Ⓓ : 재단 심사위원들이 시카고의 대중교통 시스템에 관해 잘 모를 수도 있으니 연구 주제를 좀 더 자세히 쓰라고 조언하였으므로 보기 Ⓓ는 정답이다.

보기 Ⓔ : 시카고 교통 당국에 연락을 취해보라는 말은 전혀 언급되지 않았다.

해석 | 대화에서, 교수가 학생이 제안서를 수정하는데 도움을 주기 위해 여러 제안을 하고 있다. 다음 보기가 교수가 언급한 내용에 속하는지 표시하시오. 각 보기에 맞는 칸에 클릭하시오.

	Mentioned	Not Mentioned
Ⓐ 철자가 틀린 단어 확인하기	V	
Ⓑ 보조금을 받아야 하는 이유를 앞쪽에 배치하기	V	
Ⓒ 학생에 대한 소개는 빼기		V
Ⓓ 연구 주제를 소개하는 부분에 더 많은 내용을 담기	V	
Ⓔ 시카고 교통 당국에 연락을 취하기		V

어휘 | grant 보조금 | submit 제출하다 | foundation 재단 | edit 편집하다, 수정하다 | justification 정당화 | relate to ~와 관련이 있다 | spell check 철자법 검사 프로그램

정답 | Mentioned – Ⓐ, Ⓑ, Ⓓ   Not Mentioned – Ⓒ, Ⓔ

Office Hours

01 In the conversation, the professor informs the student about his scholarship status, asking the student to provide several documents. Indicate in the table below whether each of the following is one of the documents. Click in the correct box for each phrase.

	Yes	No
Ⓐ A personal essay on related academic issues		
Ⓑ A studies plan		
Ⓒ A letter to the Dean of the student's department		
Ⓓ A certificate of volunteer work		
Ⓔ A copy of the student's transcript		

02 In the conversation, the student gives several reasons for choosing to major in both music and chemistry. Indicate the reasons of each subject in the chart below. Click in the correct box for each phrase.

	Music	Chemistry
Ⓐ The student is truly fond of doing this.		
Ⓑ The student can earn a steady income.		
Ⓒ The student's father is in this profession.		
Ⓓ The student displays her talent.		

Topic:

Details:

03 The speakers discuss inviting the dance troupe to the class. Indicate in the table below whether each of the following is suggested by the professor as an alternative plan. Click in the correct box for each phrase.

	Suggested	Not Suggested
Ⓐ Change the place for the performances		
Ⓑ Consider changing the time of Ghana dancers' performance		
Ⓒ Ask other groups available to perform		
Ⓓ Cancel the prearranged dance performances		

Topic:

Details:

Dictation : Office Hours

01

W : Thanks for coming by. I just wanted to tell you about ① __________ ...
you're a finalist!

M : Are you serious?

W : Yeah, there are a number of additional documents you'll need to submit,
though.

M : Oh? Sure, I'll do ② __________ !

W : Uh, you need to write a letter to the Dean of the Department of
Humanities explaining why you think ③ __________ .

M : All right.

W : You also need to write ④ __________ .

M : What's that? What should it say?

W : You've not heard of that? Well, it should ⑤ __________ like your
qualifications for and commitment to your chosen field. The letter I
mentioned should be more about ⑥ __________ , and the SOP is
more about academics.

M : I see. That's a little confusing, but I'll try. Anything else?

W : Finally, you need to hand in one official copy of your transcript.

M : OK, well, I'll try my best!

W : I wish you ⑦ __________ !

W : May I ask for some advice? I need to ① _____________ when I register
for next semester's classes, and I'm running out of time.

M : Sounds like you haven't decided your major yet.

W : Uh, I'm between music and chemistry...

M : Those aren't very similar!

W : I know, well, I want to major in music because I enjoy it. I have played the
piano all my life, and I'd like to do it professionally.

M : You ② _____________!

W : Actually, I've won some awards. I guess that means I'm good, which is
another reason to consider music, after all. If I were terrible, then
chemistry ③ _____________.

M : Are you good in chemistry?

W : Um, so-so, but my father's a research chemist, and he wants me to
④ _____________.

M : And do you want to be a chemist?

W : I think ⑤ _____________.

M : Well, have you considered double-major?

W : How are things going with the traditional dance troupe from Ghana? Have you heard from them? Will they be able to make it?

M : Actually, I was going to talk to you about this. Um, their director is very nice, and he always ① _______________, but he told me their schedule's crazy now. They don't have much time.

W : That might be a problem. There's still ② _______________ in the semester, so why don't you reschedule, then?

M : Is that all right? I thought ③ _______________ ... Anyway, I'll look at the calendar.

W : Also, you might want to look around for other groups. I know there's at least one other African dance troupe touring the country right now, as well as a couple of European ones. You could even invite more than one! ④ _______________, you really should ⑤ _______________.

M : I'll remember that. Thanks!

Service Encounters

01 In the conversation, the woman cites several groups of people who will be able to use the new parking place for free. Indicate in the table below whether the groups include each of the following. Click in the correct box for each phrase.

	Yes	No
Ⓐ Freshmen and sophomores		
Ⓑ All full-time students		
Ⓒ Professors and university staff		
Ⓓ The third and fourth year full-time students		
Ⓔ The general public		

Topic:

Details:

02 In the conversation, the postal service employee mentions several reasons why the student's airmail might have been returned undelivered. Indicate whether each of the following in the table is mentioned as the reasons. Click in the correct box for each phrase.

	Mentioned	Not Mentioned
Ⓐ The postal workers might not have been able to read the student's handwriting.		
Ⓑ The new employee might have stuck down the envelope carelessly.		
Ⓒ There might not have been enough postage.		
Ⓓ The postal service might not deliver mail to that country without permission.		
Ⓔ There might have been a security issue with the packing materials.		

Topic:

Details:

03 In the conversation, the financial aid officer explains the process of withdrawing the student's loan applications. Indicate in the table below whether each of the following is mentioned by the man. Click in the correct box for each phrase.

	Mentioned	Not Mentioned
Ⓐ Complete a form to delay the beginning of the payments.		
Ⓑ Write a thank you letter to the dean of the student's department.		
Ⓒ Fill out a form to cancel the current loan applications.		
Ⓓ Bring the office a copy of the award letter.		
Ⓔ Get all As from his classes from now on.		

Topic:

Details:

Dictation : Service Encounters

01

M : I'd like to ask a parking question.

W : Are you ① _______________ ?

M : No, I just want to know about parking in the new zone when it opens. How much is a permit going to cost, if I want to park there?

W : Well, ② _______________ . Four floors are reserved for faculty and staff. Are you faculty or staff?

M : No, I'm not. I'm a student. Can't students use the lot, too?

W : They can, but ③ _______________ . Only full-time juniors, seniors, and grad students will be issued permits.

M : Oh, I see. But I thought there was going to be a paid section ④ _______________ _______________ ?

W : Yes, but we ⑤ _______________ . All I can say is that it'll be high enough to discourage daily student to use.

M : It looks like I won't be able to drive to school that often.

M : Look, the airmail that I sent to my friend ① ______________ was returned today, and I can't figure out why. Can you help me?

W : Sure, let me take a look.

M : Actually, I left it at the dorm. I ② ______________ with me.

W : All right. I'll tell you the usual causes, then.

M : Thanks. What are they?

W : Sometimes mail is rejected ③ ______________ . Postal security in the U.S. is very strict. If you spilled some kind of white powder on it, that might be the reason.

M : Well, ④ ______________ .

W : It's also possible that the mail handlers couldn't read the address. Was it handwritten?

M : Yes, and I've got awful handwriting. I bet that's the reason.

W : It might be, but you can't ⑤ ______________ that it wasn't sealed correctly. We just hired a new guy, and he has been a little sloppy with the tape. If you'll bring me your mail, I'll help you figure out what to do.

W : I've just won the scholarship... what do I need to do about my financial aid?

M : Congratulations! I guess you won't need student loans for the rest of your time here, will you?

W : No, I guess not.

M : Then, ①________________. First, you need to provide us with a copy of your award letter. Then you need to fill out a form to indicate that you ②________________.

W : Is that all?

M : Almost. You don't want to start paying for your existing loans yet, so you'll need to fill out a separate deferment form.

W : Deferment form... OK, and ③________________?

M : And ④________________, you need to keep your grades up once you get the scholarship, because you don't want to lose it! Oh, sorry, I sometimes ⑤________________.

W : No! You're absolutely right. I'll be sure to do that... thanks!

Lectures

01 🎧 **Herpetology**

1. In today's lecture, the professor is talking about what subject?

    Ⓐ Pit organs in snakes
    Ⓑ Snakes' habitats
    Ⓒ Snakes of many species
    Ⓓ Biological adaptations

2. In the lecture, the professor discusses several functions of the snake's pit organs. Indicate in the table below whether each of the following is one of the functions. Click in the correct box for each phrase.

	Yes	No
Ⓐ Regulating temperature		
Ⓑ Emitting infrared radiation		
Ⓒ Finding and avoiding predators		
Ⓓ Locating preys		
Ⓔ Communicating with other snakes		

Topic:

Details:

1. Why are forested lands being lost? Click on 2 answers.

    Ⓐ Cutting down trees for commercial uses
    Ⓑ Cattle grazing
    Ⓒ The sea level going up
    Ⓓ Expanding residential areas

2. In the lecture, the professor discusses the consequences that result from deforestation. Indicate in the table below whether each of the following is one of the consequences. Click in the correct box for each phrase.

	Yes	No
Ⓐ Soil erosion		
Ⓑ Loss of biological diversity		
Ⓒ Decrease in the amounts of ultraviolet light		
Ⓓ Flooding		
Ⓔ Global warming		

Topic:

Details:

 🎧 **Business administration**

1. Which of the following costs the highest?

    Ⓐ Radio commercials
    Ⓑ TV commercials
    Ⓒ Subway posters
    Ⓓ Magazine ads

2. The professor discusses two forms of advertising. Indicate on the chart below to which form each of the following is attributed. Click in the correct box for each phrase.

	Print Ads	TV/Film Ads
Ⓐ Advertised products are used by characters		
Ⓑ Pamphlets are included		
Ⓒ These ads are the most expensive		
Ⓓ People will pick those up when walking		

Topic:

Details:

Dictation : Lectures

01

P(M) : Ah, why don't we take a few moments to look at the pit organs of certain snake species? Pit vipers have these organs, and so do some pythons and boas. They're truly ① ______________. Um, before I began studying reptiles, I was surprised to learn that pit vipers don't live in pits. Yeah, as you guess cleverly, the name relates to their sense organs, ② ______________. They are usually ③ ______________ between the eyes and the nose. So what these pit organs do? ④ ______________, the pit organ allows the snake to detect infrared radiation... otherwise known as heat. In action movies, you've probably seen characters ⑤ ______________ that allow the wearers to "see" in the dark by showing the heat profile of living creatures around them. For the snake, ⑥ ______________. Warm-blooded animals emit thermal radiation, and the snake recognizes this heat by comparing the temperatures in the outside and inside of the pit organs. Scientists ⑦ ______________ they evolved to detect predators, or to detect prey. It's possible that there were multiple environmental reasons for pit organs to evolve. Whatever their origin, they allow snakes to strike their prey ⑧ ______________. The prey such as rodents and birds gives off its body heat, and the pit organ detects it. They also have a thermoregulation function. This allows snakes to locate warmer and cooler places — for example, if they are trying to ⑨ ______________. Experiments have confirmed this, too.

P(W) : We're all aware that the Earth is ① ______________ , and it's really important to understand it so that we can ② ______________ . With that being said, today I'd like to talk about, well, deforestation. What it means is the conversion − either ③ ______________ , or as a consequence of environmental degradation − of forest land to other uses. Sometimes it is cleared for farming or for livestock farming. You know, those large fast food chains are looking to buy beef for hamburgers. Sometimes it's developed ④ ______________ . Logging obviously is an issue, like for ⑤ ______________ paper or chopsticks. And some forests simply ⑥ ______________ , unfortunately.

Now, the results of this devastating activity vary. Of course, the environment itself is harmed. There is less biodiversity, because the forest simply cannot support the same number of species. In fact, ⑦ ______________ at such a rapid rate that the present day has been referred to as a period of mass extinction. But the effects don't stop there. There is ⑧ ______________ . Soil erosion is also a big issue. Soil is not kept in place because all the trees in the area are cut down, and then essential soil nutrients, well, they are gone. In the end, ⑨ ______________ , which means less food available for both animals and humans. And there's one last thing to mention, and this ⑩ ______________ that I mentioned earlier: climate change. As the trees that could convert carbon dioxide into healthy oxygen have been lost, less oxygen is produced for the atmosphere. As you already know, carbon dioxide is one of the greenhouse gases that will increase Earth temperature. Accordingly, weather patterns are affected and sea levels rise, you know, global warming. It goes without saying that this will need to ⑪ ______________ .

P(M): Let's talk a bit about advertising this morning. I think we all know what advertising is, since we see it every day. We see ① _____________ daily, from the time we open our eyes in the morning until the time we go to bed. When we use the Internet, when we watch TV, when we walk down the street... ads are everywhere. Advertising is ② _____________. You might not have thought of it that way, but it is simply a type of communication from someone who has paid to ③ _____________. The information in that message is ④ _____________.

Now, advertising comes in different forms. Print media are one form of advertising. Ads in magazines and newspapers, on subway trains and in stations, on little cards that are distributed... these all ⑤ _____________ of print advertising. They are generally placed in places where large numbers of people will see them, or large numbers of copies are placed in individual items. ⑥ _____________, TV and film include different types of advertisements. Commercials on TV are considered ⑦ _____________ and therefore the most important ads. This means they are also the most expensive. A single commercial in a football game with a large audience may ⑧ _____________. Product placement is another form of advertisement in which characters in TV shows or movies use – or mention – certain items. This is ⑨ _____________ the things being placed. This is increasingly common in major Hollywood films and popular American TV shows.

Practice

01 What are the speakers mainly talking about?

    Ⓐ The student's practicum is not going well.
    Ⓑ The professor wants the student to start her practicum.
    Ⓒ The student has hard time getting along with little kids.
    Ⓓ The professor is making suggestions for revising the student's paper.

02 What can be inferred about the student?

    Ⓐ She might switch her area of specialization to classroom management.
    Ⓑ She is not acquainted with Joanna Smith.
    Ⓒ She had a teaching practice at an elementary school.
    Ⓓ She can't figure out what to put in her paper.

03 What area of education has the student been having difficulty in according to the professor?

    Ⓐ Early childhood education
    Ⓑ Special education
    Ⓒ Child psychology
    Ⓓ Classroom management

04 In the conversation, the professor mentions several ways the student could improve her paper. Indicate in the chart below whether each of the following is mentioned as one of them. Click in the correct box for each phrase.

	Mentioned	Not Mentioned
Ⓐ Do some research on learning disabilities and emotional disorders		
Ⓑ Include tips from a fellow student who's specializing in special education		
Ⓒ Talk less about the theories and more about personal experience		
Ⓓ Spend more time with children who need special care		
Ⓔ Narrow the focus down to some specific areas		

Listen again to part of the lecture. Then answer the question.

05 What does the student imply when she says this:

    Ⓐ She clearly loves all her students equally.
    Ⓑ She knows nothing about special-needs kids and is embarrassed.
    Ⓒ She doesn't want to look further into special education areas.
    Ⓓ She thought she was dealing with special-needs kids well.

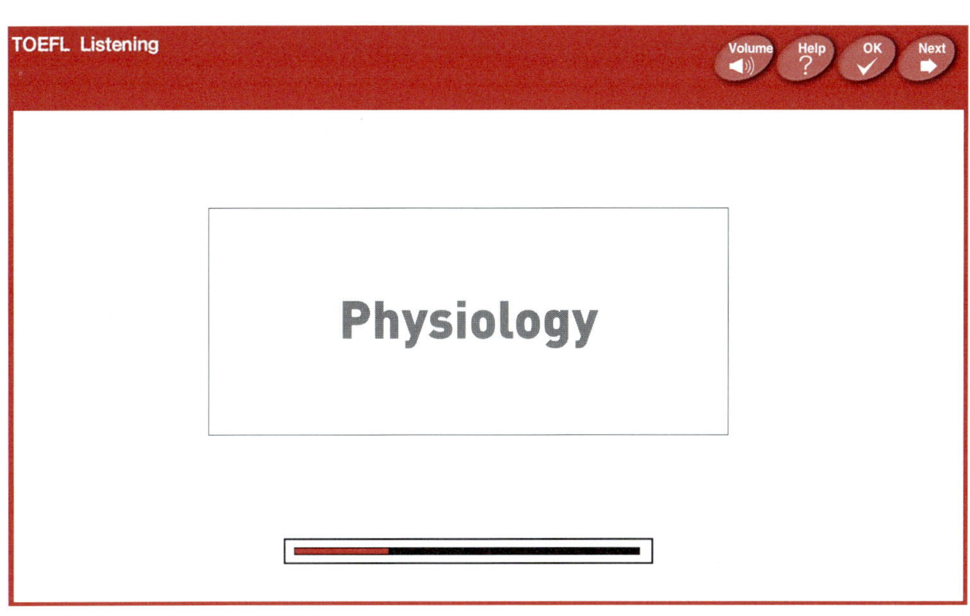

Physiology

06 What is the topic that the lecturer is covering today?

    Ⓐ The spread of infectious diseases
    Ⓑ The immune system of vertebrates
    Ⓒ Chemical immune defenses
    Ⓓ Skin and its protection against disease

Listen again to part of the lecture. Then answer the question.

07 Why does the professor say this: 🎧

    Ⓐ To help the students understand the role of specialized organs in the immune system
    Ⓑ To provide an example of the internal organs of humans
    Ⓒ To emphasize the significance of the liver in the body's functioning
    Ⓓ To point out that people don't understand how the liver works

08 According to the lecture, why should people treat cuts and punctures on the skin with caution?

    Ⓐ It takes too long for the skin to heal by itself.
    Ⓑ Too much blood will spurt from the wounds.
    Ⓒ The scar will remain on the skin.
    Ⓓ The skin is the first route of infection.

09 Immunization against diphtheria, smallpox, and tetanus operates via what bodily process?

Ⓐ Cleansing
Ⓑ Mutation
Ⓒ Enzymes
Ⓓ Immunological memory

10 In the lecture, the professor discusses several different ways in which the immune system functions. Indicate in the table below whether each of the following is mentioned. **Click in the correct box for each phrase.**

	Mentioned	Not Mentioned
Ⓐ Enabling our DNA to mutate in helpful ways		
Ⓑ Creating special new cells to protect against disease		
Ⓒ Recognizing which cells and tissues are healthy and which ones are harmful		
Ⓓ Purging the body of germs and viruses		
Ⓔ Remembering and attacking foreign substances that once entered into the body		

11 Which of the following is NOT the process by which the immune system removes pathogens?

Ⓐ Sneezing
Ⓑ Coughing
Ⓒ Spitting
Ⓓ Blowing your nose

Review

01 영어는 우리말로, 우리말은 영어로 바꾸어 써보자.

1. nomination _____________	11. 엄격한 _____________
2. candidate _____________	12. 밀봉하다 _____________
3. commitment _____________	13. 흘리다 _____________
4. income _____________	14. 연기 _____________
5. interrupt _____________	15. 환불 _____________
6. backup _____________	16. 저자 _____________
7. restore _____________	17. 서식지 _____________
8. hectic _____________	18. 탐지하다 _____________
9. rate _____________	19. 먹이 _____________
10. discourage _____________	20. 결과 _____________

02 숙어와 맞는 뜻을 연결해 보자.

1. hand in •	• 배제하다
2. follow in a person's footsteps •	• 방출하다, 내뿜다
3. rule out •	• 제출하다
4. fill out •	• ~는 말할 나위도 없다
5. bring back •	• 나눠주다
6. give off •	• 조처를 취하다
7. take action •	• 작성하다
8. It goes without saying that •	• ~에 속하다
9. fall into •	• ~의 뒤를 잇다
10. give out •	• 반환하다

qualifications	accuracy	audience
referred	harmful	collapsed

1. Even bacteria have enzymes that protect them against _______________ viruses.

2. A single commercial in a football game with a large _______________ may cost millions of dollars.

3. In fact, species are dying off at such a rapid rate that the present day has been _______________ to as a period of mass extinction.

4. Whatever their origin, they allow snakes to strike their prey with terrific _______________ .

5. Well, as you probably know, there was the campus French club, but it _______________ last year when the university ran out of funds.

6. Well, it should explain your academic goals like your _______________ for and commitment to your chosen field.

태도/발화 목적
Stance/Function

Overview

- Stance/Function 유형은 화자가 어떤 말을 왜 했는지 발화 목적과 의도를 파악하고 그런 말을 할 때 무슨 생각을 하고 있었는지 화자의 태도를 알아내는 문제
- 대화와 강의 모두 1문항 정도가 출제됨
- 주로 대화와 강의의 일부를 다시 들려주고(Replay) 그 특정 부분의 말을 통해 알 수 있는 화자의 태도, 감정, 목적과 그 말 속에 함축되어 있는 의미를 이해하고 있는지를 확인함
- 일부를 다시 듣고 푸는 문제라 해도, 전체적인 흐름 속에서 그 말의 의미와 숨은 뜻을 생각하는 것이 중요함
- Stance(태도) 문제는 겉으로 드러나 있는 문장의 사전적 의미보다는 화자의 말투 등을 통해 드러나는 화자의 속마음을 알고 있는지를 물으며, 주로 화자가 놀라거나, 부러움을 표시하거나, 의심을 하거나, 확인을 하거나, 강조를 하거나, 반어적으로 말하는 상황 등에서 문제가 출제됨
- Function(발화 목적) 문제는 왜 그 말을 한 것인지 이유와 목적을 물으며, 제안을 하거나, 요청을 하거나, 확인 및 재확인을 하거나, 확신 및 불확신을 나타내거나, 예를 들거나, 강조하거나, 불평하는 상황 등에서 문제가 출제됨

Sample Questions

- Listen again to part of the conversation. Then answer the question.
  What does the woman mean when she says this: 🎧
- Listen again to part of the lecture. Then answer the question.
  Why does the professor say this: 🎧
- Listen again to part of the lecture. Then answer the question.
  What does the professor imply when she says this: 🎧
- Why does the professor mention ~?
- What is the man's stance toward ~?
- How does the student seem to feel about ~?

Preview

Listen again to part of the conversation. Then answer the question.

What does the man imply when he says this: 

Ⓐ The fax machine is out of order now.
Ⓑ The student should've known how to use the machine.
Ⓒ Other people have had the same problems.
Ⓓ The fax machine has been much of service.

🎧 Listen to part of a conversation at a library.

W : Uh, can you come over here, please?

M : Sure, I'm coming.

W : Thank you. <u>I need to send a fax but I think it's broken</u>.
여자의 문제 : 팩스를 보내고 싶은데 고장 난 것 같음
M : *That thing can be tricky sometimes.*
가끔 말썽을 부릴 때가 있음
W : Yeah. I put the paper in, dialed the number, and pressed the SEND button. The paper went through and I heard some sounds, but then the fax machine beeped and printed out an error sheet.

M : That's nothing serious. <u>I'll show you what to do</u>. If you don't press the
남자의 제안: 어떻게 해야 하는지 보여줄 것임
buttons at the right time, the thing won't work. After all those years of troubles, I've learned that. I don't know who designed it and manufactured it, but they need to get down to new jobs.

W : So, <u>the fax machine's not actually broken</u>?
사실은 고장 난 것이 아님?
M : <u>No</u>, but between you and me I wish someone would break it, so we could
고장 난 것이 아님
get a new one!

Listen again to part of the question. Then answer the question.
W : Thank you. I need to send a fax but I think it's broken.
M : That thing can be tricky sometimes.

What does he imply when he says this: 🎧
M : That thing can be tricky sometimes.

여 : 잠깐 이쪽으로 와 주실 수 있으세요?

남 : 네, 가고 있어요.

여 : 감사합니다. 제가 팩스를 보내야 하는데요, 기계가 고장 난 것 같아요.

남 : 가끔 팩스기가 말썽을 일으킬 때가 있어요.

여 : 네. 제가 종이를 넣고, 번호를 누르고, 전송 버튼을 눌렀어요. 종이가 안으로 들어가더니 이상한 소리가 나는 게 들리다가, 삑 소리가 나면서 오류 종이가 인쇄되어 나왔어요.

해설 | 학생과 도서관 직원은 팩스기 사용에 관해 대화를 나누고 있다. 팩스기가 제대로 작동하지 않자 학생이 직원
에게 도움을 요청하는데, 이 때 직원이 '가끔 팩스기가 말썽을 일으킬 때가 있어요.' 라고 말하는 것을 통해
미루어 짐작할 수 있는 내용을 고르는 문제이다. 가끔 제대로 작동하지 않을 때가 있다는 말은 학생 이전에
다른 사람들에게도 똑같은 문제가 발생했었음을 암시한다.

W : Thank you. I need to send a fax but I think it's broken.
M : That thing can be tricky sometimes.

....

W : So, <u>the fax machine's not actually broken</u>?
M : <u>No</u>, but between you and me I wish someone would break it, so we could get a new one!

직원이 학생에게 올바른 사용법을 알려준 후 대화의 마지막에 팩스기가 실제로는 고장 난 것이 아니라는 내용
이 나오고 있다. 따라서 팩스기가 고장 났다는 보기 Ⓐ는 오답이다. 팩스기가 제대로 작동하지 않을 때가 있다
고 해서 보기 Ⓑ와 같이 학생이 사용법을 알고 있었어야 한다는 의미도 아니다. 팩스기가 너무 오래 사용되었
다는 보기 Ⓓ의 내용 역시 질문의 의도와는 직접적인 관련이 없다.

해석 | 대화의 일부를 다시 들으시오. 그리고 나서 질문에 답하시오.

여 : 감사합니다. 제가 팩스를 보내야 하는데요, 기계가 고장 난 것 같아요.
남 : 가끔 팩스기가 말썽을 일으킬 때가 있어요.

남자가 이것을 말할 때 암시하는 것은 무엇인가: 
남 : 가끔 팩스기가 말썽을 일으킬 때가 있어요.

Ⓐ 팩스기는 지금 고장 난 상태다.
Ⓑ 학생이 팩스기 사용법을 알고 있었어야 한다.
Ⓒ 다른 사람들도 같은 문제를 겪었다.
Ⓓ 팩스기가 꽤 오래 사용되어 왔다.

어휘 | tricky 고장이 잘 나는 | dial 전화를 걸다, 번호를 돌리다 | beep 삑 소리가 나다 | manufacture 제조하다

정답 | Ⓒ

Office Hours

Listen again to part of the conversation. Then answer the question.

01 What does the professor imply when she says this: 🎧

    Ⓐ She wants to reproach the student for being late.
    Ⓑ She was expecting the student would come to see her.
    Ⓒ She thinks the student's paper has a major problem.
    Ⓓ She has not the slightest idea of what the student is talking about.

Topic:

Details:

Listen again to part of the conversation. Then answer the question.

02 What does the student mean when she says this: 🎧

    Ⓐ Her group is in trouble due to John's insincerity.
    Ⓑ She asks the professor to tell her why John is in her group.
    Ⓒ She wants the professor to talk to John in person.
    Ⓓ Her group should add a new member.

Topic:

Details:

Listen again to part of the conversation. Then answer the question.

03 Why does the professor say this: 🎧

    Ⓐ To indicate that he doesn't understand what the student wants
    Ⓑ To hint that the student is mistaken about something
    Ⓒ To imply that he's too busy to answer the question
    Ⓓ To suggest that the student should find ways by herself

> *Topic:*
>
> *Details:*

Dictation : Office Hours

01

M : Professor Frist, I was hoping to ask you about my paper for your child psychology 305.

W : ① _______________. You're here because you didn't get your paper back, aren't you?

M : That's exactly why I'm here! Um, everyone else got theirs back today, and I didn't……．

W : Actually, I wanted to talk to you about it. Well, you ② _______________, really excellent on your paper about play therapy. I was wondering ③ _______________.

M : A model?

W : Yes, for future classes. I'll ④ _______________, of course. I keep sample reports so that students can see what an A+ paper should look like, an A, a B+, and so on. Would that be all right with you?

M : Of course! I'm really flattered!

M : Please come in, Penelope. Have a seat here.

W : Tanks for taking your time to see me, Professor Wahlberg.

M : You seem to be ① ______________ . What seems to be the problem?

W : Well, it's about John. He's in our group, but he has missed about half of the meetings.

M : That must be causing a problem for your group.

W : ② ______________ . More than that, we just found out ③ ______________ . He says he's behind because he has to work a lot, but we're ④ ______________ . Apparently, we have jobs, too.

M : Yeah, that's not a reasonable excuse.

W : Um, so, could we have an extra week to ⑤ ______________ ?

M : I suppose that's fine, but I'll need to speak to John in the next class. Let me know if you have any other problems.

W : I know the semester's just started and things are a little crazy right now, but could I ask you about your filmmaking class?

M : Sure, do you have ①_______________?

W : Um, I'm wondering if you could suggest tips for writing screenplays. I've never done that before.

M : I'm not sure ②_______________.

W : Aren't the students supposed to write screenplays for the films we'll make in that class?

M : No, I think ③_______________ with a higher-level course. The 200-level one I teach focuses on ④_______________. It involves a lot of reading, and for your semester project, you have to read an entire novel and the screenplay adaptation.

W : Oh, wow, I was really mixed up, wasn't I?

M : If you actually want to ⑤_______________, you should check one of the 400-level classes.

Service Encounters

01 Why does the student say this: 🎧

    Ⓐ She is worried her film will be damaged.
    Ⓑ She wants a full refund when something happens to her film.
    Ⓒ She needs to make sure the photos are ready before the project deadline.
    Ⓓ She does not believe this is truly a free service.

> *Topic:*
>
> *Details:*

Listen again to part of the conversation. Then answer the question.

02 What does the woman imply when she says this: 🎧

    Ⓐ She doesn't think the ID photo resembles the student.
    Ⓑ She discovers that something funny has happened to the student.
    Ⓒ She can see that there is a problem on the computer record.
    Ⓓ She does not actually care about the student's problem.

> *Topic:*
>
> *Details:*

Listen again to part of the conversation. Then answer the question.

03 What does the student mean when he says this: 🎧

    Ⓐ He thought the storage room requires reservations.
    Ⓑ He thought there were no large tables in the storage room.
    Ⓒ He thought he's not allowed to use the storage room.
    Ⓓ He thought there were maps in the storage room.

Topic:

Details:

Dictation : Service Encounters

01

W : Hi, I heard you can get photos developed here ① _____________ ?

M : Yes, you've ② _____________ , if you're not afraid to let students develop your film!

W : I don't have much money, and my class project is due soon……．

M : So you don't have much of a choice, do you?

W : Nope! I sure don't.

M : All right. You just need to fill out this little form, and here's a bag for your film.

W : So... is there ③ _____________ with this?

M : Don't worry, I know what's on your mind right now. We only ④ _____________ film for this service. There's almost no chance something bad will happen to it. But it's free, so you're ⑤ _____________ . If it's for a class project, maybe you need to think twice.

W : No, it's fine. I guess you guys know what you're doing. When should I come back?

M : They'll be ready on Monday.

M : Can I ask you about my pay?

W : Sure, how can I help you?

M : Well, yesterday was payday, but ① _______________, the money hadn't been deposited. Can you find out what's going on?

W : All right. Let me have your ID card?

M : Here you are.

W : ... OK... um, that's interesting.

M : What is it?

W : It looks like ② _______________.

M : Go ahead, please?

W : The record says that none of your accounts exist. That can't be correct. This ③ _______________.

M : I promise, I still have the same bank account!

W : Oh, I believe you. Don't worry about that. I think we have a bigger problem on our hands. I need to speak to my manager about this.

M : Any idea when I can get paid?

W : Give us ④ _______________ to find out what went wrong.

M : Um, OK, that sounds fair.

M : I'm with a group of geography students now, and we'd like to know if there's a space with larger tables available.

W : What for?

M : It's ① _______________ . We need to ② _______________ in order to compare them.

W : I see. Unfortunately, it looks like all the private study rooms are booked tonight.

M : Oh. Is there any other place with big tables?

W : Actually, there is. If you ③ _______________ to the 7th floor and turn left at the water fountain, and you'll see an area the library uses for storage.

M : Is it OK to go up there? I mean taking the maps?

W : Yes. It's not like ④ _______________ without permission. There's ⑤ _______________ , but there's also a really big table. If you ⑥ _______________ , you're welcome to use it.

M : Cool, thanks!

Lectures

01 🎧 **Marine Biology**

Listen again to part of the lecture. Then answer the question.

1. What does the professor imply when he says this: 🎧

    Ⓐ Communication does not always involve a spoken language.
    Ⓑ Certain behavior patterns of animals are similar to those of humans.
    Ⓒ Animal communication is not difficult to interpret.
    Ⓓ Communication is a form of animal behavior.

Listen again to part of the lecture. Then answer the question.

2. What does the professor imply when he says this: 🎧

    Ⓐ Most people thought that fishes just had the ability to distinguish colors.
    Ⓑ Many people were not aware that fishes have a lateral line.
    Ⓒ It was widely known that fishes have a keen sense of hearing.
    Ⓓ Most people believed that fishes were deaf.

Topic:

Details:

Listen again to part of the lecture. Then answer the question.

1. Why does the professor say this: 🎧

    Ⓐ To imply understanding gestures and many other visual cues is stressful

    Ⓑ To indicate that she doesn't have much time to talk about gestures

    Ⓒ To emphasize gestures and visual cues play an important role in language acquisition

    Ⓓ To express she doesn't understand why visual cues are essential

Listen again to part of the lecture. Then answer the question.

2. What does the professor imply when she says this: 🎧

    Ⓐ The students can read more about this in their textbooks.

    Ⓑ The students have learned this in a previous lesson.

    Ⓒ The students don't have to know this information.

    Ⓓ The students should have gone over this concept.

Topic:

Details:

1. What is this lecture mainly about?

Ⓐ History of the lie detector
Ⓑ Uses and limitations of the polygraph
Ⓒ Lie detection techniques of the ancient Chinese
Ⓓ Accuracy of the lie detector

2. Which of the following is NOT measured by a polygraph?

Ⓐ Pulse rate
Ⓑ Salivation
Ⓒ Blood pressure
Ⓓ Respiration

Listen again to part of the lecture. Then answer the question.

3. What does the professor imply when he says this: 

Ⓐ The use of the polygraph needs to be expanded.
Ⓑ It is good to standardize the polygraph.
Ⓒ The polygraph is not a trustworthy tool.
Ⓓ The person operating the polygraph is clumsy.

> *Topic:*
>
> *Details:*

Dictation : Lectures

01

P(M) : To continue our discussion of important zoologists, I'd like to talk a little about Karl von Frisch. He is the one ① ____________ a number of ② ____________ . Does anyone want to describe his discoveries?

S(W) : Um, in fact, his discoveries won him the 1973 Nobel Prize. Some of his early work proved that fish and bees ③ ____________ and that bees ④ ____________ . He also was the first ⑤ ____________ in the waggle dance of bees.

P : Good. Well, ⑥ ____________ , of course, were monumental. His work showed the parallels between animal communication and human communication. As you know, animals do not communicate the way humans do, via language, but certain behavior patterns definitely occur for the purpose of communication.

S : But as far as I know, his discoveries were also met with ⑦ ____________ at the time?

P : Yes, as most great discoveries often are. As a matter of fact, the confirmation was relatively recent. Perhaps not as well known, but equally interesting, was his discovery that fish can hear. It is known that the lateral line of fishes functions as a sensory organ: ⑧ ____________ . However, fishes do have an ear – complete with an otolith, an internal ear bone similar to what can be found in the human ear.

P(W): Everybody take a seat... uh, OK, let's quickly get back to our conversation from last class. As you know, we have been talking a lot about speech patterns, which are especially important ① _______________. Well, there is one aspect of language that ② _______________ and that is gestures and other visual cues... these are, ah, these are essential – now, I can't stress this enough – to learning a language. Well, if you've ever learned another language, you know that it's one thing to read it on paper ③ _______________. And, it's another game altogether to try and figure out what people are saying, or rather, what they mean.

So, um, basically I want to look at the development of gesture from infancy, uh, I think this will give you a good understanding of ④ _______________. Because, as you know, language acquisition is both innate and learned... I don't have to go over this again, do I? Uh, in particular, it happens rapidly during the first 18 months. While it's true that ⑤ _______________ until about 12 months, they do have ways to ⑥ _______________ ... like, for example, a newborn can show ⑦ _______________ by moving its arms and legs around... maybe it will play with its toes if it is uncomfortable or, well, you get the idea.

P(M) : Everyone's seen movies that feature a person ①____________,
right? Who's going to tell me about it?

S(W) : Um, I've once read a novel in which the police connect electrodes
②____________, turn on the machine, and start asking questions.

P : Yes, and you'll exactly know ③____________. If he is lying, he will be
caught. The lie detector is often shown to be invincible, but the truth is a
little more complicated than that. Do you know which type of lie detector is
the most common in real life?

S : The polygraph?

P : You're right. While someone is being questioned, ④____________
certain physiological responses like heartbeat, blood pressure, pulse rate,
and respiration. These are all governed by the sympathetic nervous
system, which lies ⑤____________. Stress and anxiety cause changes in
these bodily processes. This fact has been known since ancient China –
back then, people would ⑥____________ by making a person hold rice in
his or her mouth. Salivation was believed to stop during times of anxiety, so
if the rice remained dry at the end of the questioning, the person was
believed to have been lying. A similar idea underpins modern lie detection.
Once a preliminary interview has established the person's normal readings,
the real questioning may begin, because ⑦____________ know what
changes to look for.

S : So, this polygraph is always perfect?

P : I was about to talk about that right now. In fact, there is evidence that it is
not reliable at all. One study from 1997 showed that its accuracy was only
61%. Other critics say that the polygraph is not a form of testing, which
means that ⑧____________. There are also famous examples of spies
managing to 'beat' the polygraph and ⑨____________. It's possible that
the polygraph may soon be a thing of the past.

Practice

01 What is the reason for the student's conversation with his professor?

   Ⓐ He is having difficulty writing his applications for graduate school.
   Ⓑ He is not sure where she wants to attend graduate school.
   Ⓒ He is trying to decide whether to stay at the university or get a job.
   Ⓓ He is asking the favor of helping him land a job.

Listen again to part of the conversation. Then answer the question.

02 What does the professor imply when she says this: 🎧

   Ⓐ She is trying to make up her mind about the student's situation.
   Ⓑ Her perspective is not neutral because she works here.
   Ⓒ She thinks the student has not made the right decision.
   Ⓓ She is not sure which program is best for the student yet.

03 What can be inferred about the student?

    Ⓐ He will acquire work experience during spring break.
    Ⓑ He can't afford to pay his school expenses.
    Ⓒ He is a microbiology major.
    Ⓓ His grade is below the average.

04 In the conversation, the professor gives the student several reasons for staying at the current university. Indicate in the table below whether each of the following is one of the reasons suggested by the professor. Click in the correct box for each phrase.

	Suggested	Not Suggested
Ⓐ His parents would live closer to him.		
Ⓑ Tuition would be cheaper because he is a resident of the state.		
Ⓒ The university has a renowned academic program.		
Ⓓ He is familiar with the professors.		
Ⓔ Living in the same place is better for finding a job in the community.		

05 Which of the following is true of the student?

    Ⓐ He is graduating this year.
    Ⓑ His parents want him to go to another state.
    Ⓒ He is not interested in studying abroad.
    Ⓓ He has friends in Maryland and New York.

TOEFL Listening
Volume
Help
?
OK
Next
English Literature

TOEFL Listening
Volume
Help
?
OK
Next

06 What is the professor mainly discussing?

(A) The heritage of English literature
(B) The comparison of neoclassical and romantic poetry
(C) The writings of William Wordsworth
(D) The works of famous romantic poets

Listen again to part of the lecture. Then answer the question.

07 Why does the professor say this:

(A) To make a joke about young couples
(B) To clarify a common misunderstanding about a term
(C) To suggest that many people write poetry as tokens of love
(D) To explain that romanticism is indirectly related to romance

08 Why did critics dislike the works of Wordsworth?

(A) They included depictions of countryside and people that were considered too perfect.
(B) They challenged the belief that wealthier people were more interesting than the poor.
(C) They were published alongside the works of a lower-class man named Samuel Coleridge.
(D) They did not use a dialect of English that was recognizable to members of the elite class.

09 In the lecture, the professor compares neoclassical and romantic literature. Indicate on the chart below with which of the categories the following characteristics can be attributed. Click in the correct box for each phrase.

	Romanticism	Neoclassicism
Ⓐ Use of the language of the common people		
Ⓑ Admiration for the link between nature and humanity		
Ⓒ Suppression of expression of one's sentiments		
Ⓓ Complicated vocabulary		
Ⓔ A focus on the poor working class		

Listen again to part of the lecture. Then answer the question.

10 Why does the professor say this: 🎧

Ⓐ He wants to make sure the students don't judge Wordsworth's poetry unjustly.

Ⓑ He wants to explain that Wordsworth only published two works later in life.

Ⓒ He wants to apologize for criticizing Wordsworth's later works.

Ⓓ He wants to recognize the value of Wordsworth's later contributions.

11 According to the professor, why is Wordsworth's poetry important?

Ⓐ They represent all romantic authors working in America.

Ⓑ They are the connection between older and contemporary writing.

Ⓒ Their plain style is elegant and commanding.

Ⓓ They are perfect compared with traditional works.

Review

01 영어는 우리말로, 우리말은 영어로 바꾸어 써보자.

1. outstanding __________	11. 무료의 __________
2. remove __________	12. 타고난 __________
3. therapy __________	13. 습득 __________
4. guarantee __________	14. 복잡한 __________
5. deposit __________	15. 무죄 __________
6. stack __________	16. 증거 __________
7. interpret __________	17. 신뢰할만한 __________
8. implication __________	18. 유산, 전통 __________
9. vibration __________	19. 비평가 __________
10. scent __________	20. 시인 __________

02 숙어와 맞는 뜻을 연결해 보자.

1. sick and tired of	약속하다
2. give one's word	~할 수 있다
3. show up	복습하다, 되풀이 하다
4. take chances	시대에 뒤떨어지다
5. in charge of	~이 지긋지긋한
6. be capable of	주문하다
7. go over	나타나다
8. go out of date	~를 담당하고 있는
9. place an order	운에 맡기고 해보다, 위험을 무릅쓰다
10. make sense	이해가 되다

 문장의 빈 칸에 들어갈 단어를 보기 박스에서 골라 넣어 보자.

booked	rejected	adapted
storage	skepticism	invincible

1. He ______________ academic approaches to writing that removed the emotive expression, and emphasized the importance of natural human emotions.

2. The lie detector is often shown to be ______________, but the truth is a little more complicated than that.

3. If you go all the way up to the 7th floor and turn left at the water fountain, and you'll see an area the library uses for ______________.

4. The 200-level one I teach focuses on how books are ______________ for film.

5. But as far as I know, his discoveries were also met with a great deal of ______________ at the time?

6. Unfortunately, it looks like all the private study rooms are ______________ tonight.

iBT Find TOEFL Series

iBT Find TOEFL [Reading]

Steven Oh 저
4×6배판
본책 600쪽(별책 156쪽)
22,000원(mp3 CD포함)

리딩 고득점을 위한 테마별, 레벨별 공략 프로그램 제시!

- 방대하고 다양한 독해지문
- iBT 토플유형에 대한 친절한 해설
- 복습을 위해 활용할 수 있는 Vocabulary Check-Up
- 지문별 주요 어휘 영영한 사전식 설명
- 권말 실전 테스트 수록
- 문제를 풀기 전에 들어야 할 원어민이 녹음한 CD제공

iBT Find TOEFL [Listening]

Rebecca Hardy, Naomi Kim 저
4×6배판
368쪽
19,000원(mp3 CD포함)

리스닝 고득점을 위한 최적의 전략과 문제 제공!

- 유형공략에 앞서 풀어보는 샘플문제
- 체계적인 문제유형 학습
- 미니 테스트의 핵심내용을 적는 노트 테이킹 박스 마련
- 어휘와 표현에 대한 정확한 발음과 스펠링 훈련
- 유형공략 학습 후 풀어보는 실전문제
- 실전과 유사한 문제 난이도와 형식 반영

iBT Find TOEFL [Speaking]

Rebecca Hardy, Naomi Kim 저
4×6배판
379쪽
15,000원(mp3 CD포함)

스피킹 고득점을 위한 6주간 프로그램 제시!

- 스피킹 섹션의 각 파트별 문제유형 상세 분석
- 논리적 문장전개를 위한 센텐스 오더링 훈련
- 문제유형별로 답안작성에 도움이 되는 표현정리
- 문제해결에 필수인 노트 테이킹 훈련
- 실전감각을 익히기 위한 실전 테스트
- 문제와 해답 내용 mp3 CD 제공

iBT Find TOEFL [Writing]

Jack Betts, Naomi Kim 저
4×6배판
332쪽
15,000원(mp3 CD포함)

라이팅 고득점을 위한 공략 프로그램 제시!

- 라이팅 섹션의 각 파트별 문제유형 상세 분석
- 각 문제마다 문제 해결에 필수인 노트 테이킹 훈련
- 문장전개를 위한 아이디어 채집을 돕는 브레인스토밍 훈련
- 문제유형별 답안작성에 도움이 되는 표현정리
- 실전감각을 익히기 위한 실전 테스트
- 문제와 해답 내용 mp3 CD 제공

JUNIOR
iBT TOEFL®

Answer / Script / Explanation

L₂

Bansok Junior

ALL ABOUT JUNIOR TOEFL [LISTENING]

Intermediate Course

Answer / Script / Explanation

Bansok Junior

Chapter 1 Main Idea

1. ⒟   2. ⒜   3. ⒝

1. 학생은 교수에게서 어떤 도움을 필요로 하는가?
　ⓐ 학생은 교수의 인터넷 강의 시간 과제인 리포트를 써야 한다.
　ⓑ 학생은 자신의 인터넷 계좌를 이용하기를 원한다.
　ⓒ 학생은 리포트 자료 조사를 위해 어떻게 인터넷을 이용해야 하는지 잘 모르고 있다.
　ⓓ 학생은 인터넷과 비즈니스를 주제로 하는 리포트 작성에 대한 조언을 구하고 있다.

Dictation | ① a few recommendations　② its effects on　③ where to start　④ some specific aspect　⑤ come up with　⑥ narrow it down　⑦ have the pictures

여 : 바쁘신가요? 제가 지금 리포트를 쓰고 있는데요, 교수님의 의견을 좀 구할 수 있을까 해서요.
남 : 그래, 여기 앉도록 해.
여 : 감사합니다. 지금 인터넷과 인터넷이 비즈니스 세상에 끼친 영향에 관한 내용을 쓰고 있는데, 어디서 부터 시작해야 할지 잘 모르겠습니다.
남 : 아주 광범위한 토픽인 것 같구나. 구체적으로 다루고 싶은 내용이 있는 거니, 아니면 아직 거기까지 밖에 생각을 못해본 거니?
여 : 거기까지만 생각해봤어요. 토픽의 범위를 좀 더 구체적으로 줄여야겠죠?
남 : 그렇게 시작하는 것이 좋지. 한 가지 구체적인 주제를 집중적으로 다룰 수 있는 것으로 정하도록 하렴. 예를 들면, 인터넷의 역사를 알아보고 남들보다 먼저 웹 기술을 도입한 한 두 기업에 대해 중점적으로 조사를 해 볼 수도 있지. 혹은 한 산업 분야를 선정해서 인터넷 기술 도입 이전의 상황과 이후의 변화에 대해서 비교해볼 수도 있고.
여 : 아, 이제 머릿속에 뭔가 그림이 그려지네요.

어휘 | recommendation 추천 | effect 영향 | broad 광범위한 | specific 구체적인 | aspect 국면 | come up with ~를 생각해내다 | narrow down 줄이다 | adopt 채택하다 | compare 비교하다 |

2. 학생과 교수가 이 대화를 나누는 이유는 무엇인가?
　ⓐ 학생은 중간고사를 다른 방식으로 보아야 한다.
　ⓑ 학생은 대회 때문에 몇 시간의 수업을 빠질 것이다.
　ⓒ 학생은 중간고사 공부를 하는데 도움이 필요하다.
　ⓓ 학생은 리포트 주제를 고르는데 어려움이 있다.

Dictation | ① the same day as　② a little more complicated　③ make it up　④ stop by again　⑤ that's reasonable

남 : 시간을 내주셔서 감사합니다, Powter 교수님. 제가 교수님을 찾아온 이유는 제가 양궁 팀에 있는데요, 주 대항전 날짜랑 중간고사 날짜가 겹칩니다. 이번 대회가 정말 중요해서요…….

여 : 그럼 중간고사를 못 치른다는 말이니? 사실 그 문제는 네가 생각하는 것보다 좀 더 복잡하단다.

남 : 알고 있어요, 그렇지만 제가 보충 시험을 치를 수 있는 방법이 있을까요?

여 : 문제는 가끔 너와 같은 상황에 있는 학생들이 부정행위를 할 때도 있다는 거야.

남 : 그럼, 제가 나중에 중간고사를 따로 치르지 못한다는 말씀이세요?

여 : 그럴 것 같구나. 내가 그 동안 너무 바빠서 추가 시험 준비도 못했고. 대신, 리포트를 제출하는 게 좋
겠구나.

남 : 아, 그게 좋을 것 같습니다. 감사합니다. 제가 리포트 주제를 선택하는 건가요?

여 : 음, 내가 이틀 정도 생각해보고 다음 수업 시간이 끝나고 들르면 알려주도록 할게. 그 때 더 자세히
이야기 하도록 하자.

남 : 네, 알겠습니다. 정말 감사합니다!

어휘 | archery competition 경기, 대회 | miss 빠지다 | complicated 복잡한 | make up 보충하다 |
dishonest 정직하지 못한 | backup test 추가 시험 | paper 리포트 | choose 선택하다 |
sleep on ~ ~에 대해 시간을 가지고 생각하다, 즉답하지 않다 | stop by 들르다 | reasonable 합리적인 |

3. 학생과 교수가 이야기 나누고 있는 상황은 무엇인가?

Ⓐ 학생의 집에 급한 일이 있어서 그를 대신할 사람이 필요하다.

Ⓑ 기자 2명이 빠지게 되어서 기사가 필요하다.

Ⓒ 학생은 교수에게 신문 기사를 써달라고 요청하고 있다.

Ⓓ 학생은 신문방송학에 관한 정보를 얻기를 원한다.

Dictation | ① at the last minute ② what's going on ③ before going to press ④ get their
suggestions

남 : 교수님께서 학생 신문 지도 교수시잖아요, 그래서 꼭 교수님의 조언이 필요해요!

여 : 그래, 무슨 일이지?

남 : 그게 말이죠, 저희 기자 2명이 마지막 순간에 문제가 생겼어요. 한 명은 아프고 또 한 명은 집에 급
한 일이 생겼어요. 아직 3 페이지나 더 채워야 하는데, 실을 기사가 없어요!

여 : 그렇구나, 한 번 방법을 생각해보자. 신문방송 학과장님께 문제를 말씀 드려보았니?

남 : 아직이요. 아, 말씀 드려야 하는 건가요?

여 : 그렇단다. 무슨 일인지 말씀 드려. 신문이 발행되려면 아직 1주일이 남아있으니, 기사를 작성할 학생
을 두 명 정도 모집할 시간이 있을 거야, 당분간 말이야.

남 : 좋은 생각이네요, 그리고 또 제가 해야 할 일이 있을까요?

여 : 지금 같이 일하고 있는 기자들을 만나서 그 학생들의 의견도 들어보렴. 도움을 줄 수도 있을 테니.

남 : 네, 감사합니다! 지금 바로 알아볼게요!

어휘 | faculty advisor 지도 교수 | reporter 기자 | at the last minute 마지막 순간에 | emergency 긴급한 일 |
fill 채우다 | article 기사 | go to press recruit 모집하다 | temporarily 일시적으로, 임시로 | current 현재의 |
suggestion 제안 | as well 또한 |

1. Ⓐ **2.** Ⓑ **3.** Ⓓ

1. 왜 학생은 여자와 이야기 하고 있는가?
　Ⓐ 기숙사비 납부 기한을 연장하고 싶어 한다.
　Ⓑ 여름 학기 장학금을 지원하고 싶어 한다.
　Ⓒ 교수님의 추천서가 필요하다.
　Ⓓ 여름 동안 다른 방으로 옮기고 싶어 한다.

Dictation | ① staying in the dorm　② pay for the whole thing　③ have an extension　④ once in a while　⑤ bring us the difference

남 : 안녕하세요, 여름에 기숙사에서 생활하는 것에 대해 질문이 있습니다.
여 : 그래요, 무엇이 궁금하죠?
남 : 제가 1인실을 사용했으면 하는데요. 지금으로서는 기숙사 비를 전부 낼 수가 없는데 납부 마감일은 내일이에요. 이번에 학과 장학금을 받게 되었는데 지급일은 다음 주입니다. 제가 증명 서류를 가져오면, 납부 기한을 연장할 수 있을까요?
여 : 무슨 일인지 알겠군요. 이따금 그런 일이 있어요. 이렇게 하도록 해요. 지금 기본적인 비용은 낼 수 있나요?
남 : 네.
여 : 좋아요. 그럼 그걸 먼저 내고, 학생이 장학금을 받았다는 것을 입증해 줄 학과장님의 추천서를 받아 오도록 해요. 학생이 사용할 1인실을 하나 남겨 놓을게요. 장학금을 지급 받고 나면, 차액을 납부하세요. 그럼 그 방은 학생 방이 되는 겁니다.
남 : 제가 생각했던 것보다 훨씬 간단하네요, 감사합니다!
여 : 천만에요.

어휘 | dorm 기숙사 | whole 전체의 | scholarship 장학금 | department 학과 | disbursement 지불, 지출 | documentation 서류 | extension 연장, 연기 | once in a while 이따금 | fee 요금, 이용료 | department head 학과장 | verify 증명하다 | reserve 남겨두다, 확보해 두다 | difference 차액

2. 학생이 가지고 있는 문제는 무엇인가?
　Ⓐ 도서관 이용 방법을 모른다.
　Ⓑ 온라인 도서 예약 시스템을 이용할 수 없다.
　Ⓒ 전에 대출한 도서관 책들을 잃어버렸다.
　Ⓓ 연체료를 냈다는 영수증을 가지고 있지 않다.

Dictation | ① the online reservation system　② two months overdue　③ brought it back　④ have unpaid late fees　⑤ take a look　⑥ kept my receipts

여 : 죄송한데요, 온라인 예약 시스템이 제대로 되지 않아요. 좀 도와주시겠어요?

남 : 네, 먼저 중앙 데이터베이스를 확인해보죠. 학생증 번호를 알려주겠어요?

여 : 여기 있습니다.

남 : 음... 아, 무슨 일인지 알겠네요. 학생이 두 달간 반납하지 않고 있는 책이 있다는 걸 알고 있나요?

여 : 네? 오래 전에 반납했는데요.

남 : 컴퓨터 기록에는 책이 아직 대출 상태로 되어 있어요. 그리고 다른 4권의 책에 대한 연체료를 아직 내지 않았군요. 자, 여길 봐요.

여 : 그럴 리가 없어요! 책을 반납하면서 연체료를 모두 냈어요. 영수증도 가지고 있어요. 전 어떡해야 하죠?

남 : 그렇다면, 영수증을 확인하고 연체된 책이 모두 반납되었다는 걸 확인해야겠군요. 확인이 끝날 때까지는 온라인 시스템을 이용할 수가 없습니다. 미안하군요.

여 : 알겠습니다.

어휘 | reservation 예약 | central 중앙의 | database 데이터베이스 | no wonder 당연하다 | aware ~을 알고 있는 | overdue 연체의 | unpaid 미납의, 지불하지 않은 | receipt 영수증 |

3. 남자와 여자가 이 대화를 나누고 있는 이유는 무엇인가?
    Ⓐ 라디오 방송이 취소되었다.
    Ⓑ 천둥소리가 너무 커서 방송이 잘 들리지 않는다.
    Ⓒ 번개가 쳐서 방송 신호가 잘 잡히지 않는다.
    Ⓓ 방송 장비가 작동하지 않고 있다.

Dictation | ① a nightmare ② must have been ③ not on the air ④ have them send ⑤ I'd better get busy

남 : 이런, 방송 시스템 전체가 다운되었네요. 완전 악몽 같아요!

여 : 뇌우 때문에 일어난 일이 틀림없어요. 번개가 많이 쳤잖아요. 그것 때문일 거예요.

남 : 그럼 이제 어떡해야 하죠?

여 : 차근히 생각해봅시다. 음, 먼저 생방송으로는 진행을 못하더라도 인터넷으로는 계속 방송을 내보낼 수 있어요.

남 : 그건 맞는 말이네요. 그렇지만 장비들은 어쩌죠?

여 : 그 문제라면, 설비 부서에 전화를 해서 기술자를 보내달라고 해야겠죠. 장비 수리가 가능한지, 새로 바꾸어야 하는지 알아야 하니까요.

남 : 그럼, 오늘 저녁 방송은 어쩌죠?

여 : 인터넷으로만 방송을 내보내야 할 거 같아요. 저녁까지 방송 장비가 다시 제대로 작동할 것 같지는 않아요.

남 : 그렇군요, 바쁘게 움직여야겠네요!

어휘 | broadcasting 방송 | nightmare 악몽 | thunderstorm 뇌우 | lightning 번개 | rational 이성적인 | on the air 방송 중인 | equipment 장비 | facilities department 설비부 | technician 기술자 | repair 수리하다 | replace 바꾸다, 대체하다 |

1. 1) Ⓓ 2) Ⓑ **2.** 1) Ⓐ 2) Ⓒ **3.** 1) Ⓒ 2) Ⓑ 3) Ⓓ

1. 경영학 수업

1. 강의 주제는 무엇인가?
   Ⓐ 독일 고급 승용차의 경쟁사
   Ⓑ 마케팅의 중요성
   Ⓒ 정신 공간과 자동차 제조회사
   Ⓓ 제품 포지셔닝

2. 도요타, 혼다, 닛산에 관해 강의에서 추론할 수 있는 것은 무엇인가?
   Ⓐ 소비자들은 현재 세 회사를 소형차 제조회사로 인식한다.
   Ⓑ 현재 이 세 회사의 고급 자동차 라인에 대한 수요가 높다.
   Ⓒ 세 회사는 고객의 정신 공간을 점유하지 못했다.
   Ⓓ 세 회사에서 제조하는 차량은 BMW, 아우디, 메르세데스-벤츠 차량보다 더 신뢰성이 높다.

Dictation | ① we're all familiar with ② creating an identity for ③ a series of associations ④ positioning is relative ⑤ launch their luxury car lines ⑥ instead of its competitors ⑦ more for the same

P : 오늘날의 세상에서는 사람들이 끊임없이 마케팅에 노출되고 있기 때문에 아마 우리 모두 마케팅이 무엇인지 잘 알고 있으리라 생각합니다. 오늘은 그 중에서도 보다 세부적이고 민감한 개념인 포지셔닝에 관해 이야기 하도록 하겠습니다. 소비자에게 브랜드를 인식시키는 작업은 여러 면에서 살펴볼 수 있어요. 브랜드 포지셔닝은 단순히 브랜드나 회사의 정체성을 만들어내는 것 이상의 개념을 포함하고 있어요. 여러분이 정신 공간(mental space)이란 용어를 알고 있다고 한다면, 마케팅 담당자들은 자사 브랜드가 바로 이 정신 공간을 차지하기를 원하는 겁니다. 그들은 소비자들이 브랜드를 보고 일련의 이미지를 떠올리기를 원하고, 이는 타 브랜드, 즉 경쟁 회사의 포지셔닝과 비교하여 작용하죠. 바로 이 점이 중요한데, 포지셔닝은 상대적이라는 거죠. 상대적이라는 것은 단순히 고객이 누구인가가 아니라, 누가 자사 브랜드의 고객이 되어야 하는가라는 명확한 아이디어를 정립하는 것을 말합니다. 기업은 대개 자사 상품이 한 방향으로 인식되기를 원하지만, 평판이란 것은 그와는 다른 것이죠. 여러분들이 1980년대 후반을 잘 기억 못 할 수도 있는데, 이 당시 자동차 회사인 도요타(Toyota), 혼다(Honda), 닛산(Nissan)은 고급 승용차 라인인 렉서스(Lexus), 아큐라(Acura), 인피니티(Infiniti)를 북미에서 출시하기로 했죠. 이전에는 이 세 자동차 회사가 소형차를 만드는 것으로 알려져 있었어요. 이 세 회사 모두 튼튼한 차를 만들어내는 것으로 유명하긴 했지만, 아무도 대형 도요타 차량을 구입하는데 50,000 달러를 낼 거라고는 상상도 못했죠. 사실 소비자들이 경쟁사인 BMW, 아우디(Audi), 메르세데스-벤츠(Mercedes-Benz)를 제치고 앞서 말한 세 회사의 자동차를 선택할 거라고 생각한 사람도 별로 없었어요. 하지만 이 차량들이 시장에 선보일 때, 신중하게 포지셔닝 전략이 실행되었죠. 독일 경쟁사에 비해 차량 가격은 약간 낮았고, 아니 실제로는 우수한 품질을 같은 가격으로 내놓았고, 기계적인 부분에 대한 높은 신뢰성 역시 소비자에게 접근하는데 큰 경쟁력이 되었어요. 그 결과 이 차종들은 큰 인기를 거두었죠!

2. 아시아 연구 수업

1. 강의의 주제는 무엇인가?
   Ⓐ 스리랑카의 차 재배
   Ⓑ 옛 영국 식민지인 스리랑카
   Ⓒ 스리랑카라는 국호의 유래
   Ⓓ 실론과 스리랑카의 역사

2. 다음 중 어느 것이 스리랑카에 관해 맞지 않는가?
   Ⓐ 한때 실론이라고 불렸다.
   Ⓑ James Taylor가 실론티를 만드는 특유의 비법을 창안했다.
   Ⓒ 영국의 식민 지배를 받고 있다.
   Ⓓ 스리랑카의 차 생산량은 전 세계 차 산업의 1/5을 차지한다.

Dictation | ① located just off the southeast coast   ② In the 1800s   ③ in the hands of   ④ a variety of crops   ⑤ the highest-quality tea   ⑥ fortunately for him   ⑦ a massive success   ⑧ almost overnight   ⑨ no longer control   ⑩ the 3rd largest producer

P : 스리랑카를 생각하면, 구체적인 이미지를 떠올리기가 쉽지 않죠. 하지만 여러분 모두 실론티에 대해서는 들어본 적이 있을 겁니다. 스리랑카는 인도의 남동쪽 인도양에 위치한 섬나라로, 과거에는 실론(Ceylon)이라고 불렸던 국가라는 것을 알고 있을 거예요. 오늘날 스리랑카의 주수출품 중 하나는 바로 차(茶)입니다. 1800년대에 스리랑카의 커피 작물이 병충해로 인해 거의 파괴되었어요. 당시 실론은 영연방 식민지였고, 농업은 영국인 농장주들이 거의 지배하고 있었어요. 그들은 재배작물을 다양화할 필요가 있다고 느꼈어요, 각종 재해에 취약하지 않도록 말이죠.
우리가 오늘날 전 세계적으로 최상품의 차로 이름난 실론티를 즐길 수 있게 된 데는 제임스 테일러의 공이 컸어요. 1867년에 그는 19에이커의 차를 재배했어요. 그는 그 이전부터 차 재배 경험을 가지고 있었는데, 그로서는 잘된 일이었죠. 그는 찻잎을 수확하면서, 손으로 잎을 말아 숯 위의 점토 화로에 올려놓고 정성들여 볶았어요. 결과는 런던에서 대성공이었고, 거의 하룻밤 사이에 실론티 산업이 탄생되었어요. 1880년에는 23 파운드에 채 못 미치는 차가 재배되었어요. 1890년에는 약 23,000 톤의 차가 재배되었죠! 오늘날에는 스리랑카의 차 산업을 영국인들이 지배하지 않아요. 이제 스리랑카는 세계 3위의 홍차 재배 국가이고 전 세계 시장의 약 20% 수출하고 있어요.

3. 해양 동물학 수업

1. 강의의 주제는 무엇인가?
    Ⓐ 해양 동물의 번식
    Ⓑ 유성 생식과 무성 생식
    Ⓒ 불가사리의 생식 기능
    Ⓓ 불가사리의 짝짓기 습성

강의의 일부를 다시 들으시오. 그러고 나서 질문에 답하시오.
오늘은 불가사리와 불가사리의 놀라운 생식 능력에 관해 이야기를 이어가 보겠어요. 불가사리에 대해 따로 소개할 필요는 없겠죠.

2. 교수가 이것을 말할 때 암시하는 것은 무엇인가: 🎧
    불가사리에 대해 따로 소개할 필요는 없겠죠.

    Ⓐ 현재 불가사리에 대해 잘 알려진 것이 없다.
    Ⓑ 대부분의 학생들이 불가사리가 무엇인지 이미 알고 있다.
    Ⓒ 강의 초점은 불가사리가 아니다.
    Ⓓ 사람들은 대개 불가사리에 관심이 없다.

3. 다음 중 어느 것이 불가사리에 관해 맞는가?
    Ⓐ 불가사리는 역사상 문제들을 유발시켰다.
    Ⓑ 불가사리는 생식 능력 덕분에 뛰어난 식량원이다.
    Ⓒ 불가사리는 번식기에 성전환을 한다.
    Ⓓ 불가사리의 팔은 손상되면 다시 생겨난다.

Dictation │ ① you probably need to get out more   ② remarkable abilities to   ③ it grows one back   ④ In other words   ⑤ there is a downside to it   ⑥ toss them back   ⑦ environmental signals

Listen again to part of the lecture. Then answer the question.
I'd like to continue that talk today by discussing the starfish and its amazing reproductive abilities. The starfish needs very little introduction.

What does the professor imply when he says this: 🎧
The starfish needs very little introduction.

P : 어제 수업에서는 흥미로운 해양 동물에 대해 살펴보았어요. 오늘은 불가사리와 불가사리의 놀라운 생식 능력에 관해 이야기를 이어가 보겠어요. 불가사리에 대해 따로 소개할 필요는 없겠죠. 불가사리가 뭔지 모른다면, 밖에 좀 더 자주 나가서 경험해보도록 해야겠군요. 불가사리에게는 자기 몸을 재생시키는 놀라운 능력이 있다는 것을 여러분이 알고 있을 겁니다. 불가사리는 몸에 상처를 입기 쉬운 생명체이기 때문에, 이러한 재생 능력은 매우 똑똑한 생존 메커니즘이죠. 불가사리는 느리게 움직이고, 방어 수단이 거의 없어요. 불가사리의 팔 하나가 떨어져 나가면, 하나가 다시 생겨납니다. 하지만 그게 다가 아니에요. 이 떨어져 나간 팔이 몸통 중앙의 체반에 붙어있다면, 무성 생식이 일어나게 됩니

다. 다시 말하면, 새로운 불가사리가 이 작은 부분에서 생겨나게 되는 거죠. 불가사리의 중요 기관이
팔에 남아있어서 가능한 일이에요. 굉장하죠? 하지만 세상 모든 일이 그러하듯 이런 무성 생식에도
단점이 있어요. 불가사리는 이들의 먹이인 조개와 굴을 잡아 올리는 어민들에게 큰 문젯거리였어요.
조개와 굴 어획량을 늘리기 위해 어민들은 불가사리를 잡아서 몸을 잘라 바다로 던져버렸어요. 과연
문제가 해결되었을까요? 아니에요, 더 많은 불가사리가 생겨나게 되었어요!
자, 불가사리는 유성 생식도 합니다. 불가사리 한 개체는 남성이거나 여성이죠. 번식기가 되면, 불가
사리는 바닷물 속에 정자와 난자를 뿌려요. 수정된 배아는 성체가 되기 전까지는 플랑크톤 형태를 띠
고 있어요. 환경 신호를 따라 언제 정자와 난자를 방출해야 하는지를 알고 있는 불가사리가 있는가
하면, 짝짓기를 하는 불가사리도 있어요. 자, 참석해주어서 고맙고, 모두들 슬라이드 쇼를 재미있게
보았기를 바랍니다.

어휘 | starfish 불가사리 | amazing 놀라운 | reproductive 번식의, 생식의 | remarkable 놀라운 |
regenerate 재생시키다 | survival 생존 | mechanism 메커니즘 | brittle 상처 입기 쉬운, 부서지기 쉬운 |
means 수단 | defend 방어하다 | be attached to ~에 붙어있다 | asexual 성별 없는 | take place 일어
나다, 발생하다 | vital 중요한 | organ 기관 | downside 단점, 불리한 점 | fisherman 어민 | clam 조개 |
oyster 조개 | haul 어획량 | chop 자르다 | toss 던지다 | solve 해결하다 | release 방출하다 |
sperm 정자 | fertilize 수정시키다 | embryo 배아 | pair up 짝짓기 하다 |

Practice

[1-5] **1.** Ⓓ **2.** Ⓐ **3.** Mentioned – Ⓐ, Ⓒ, Ⓓ Not Mentioned – Ⓑ, Ⓔ **4.** Ⓓ **5.** Ⓒ
[6-11] **6.** Ⓓ **7.** Ⓑ **8.** Ⓑ **9.** Ⓐ, Ⓒ **10.** Ⓒ **11.** Yes – Ⓑ, Ⓒ, Ⓔ No – Ⓐ, Ⓓ

[문제 1–5] 학생과 교수 사이의 대화의 일부를 들으시오.

1. 학생은 왜 교수와 이야기 하고 있는가?
Ⓐ 교사 자격증을 따야 하는지 확신을 못하고 있다.
Ⓑ 자신에게 어느 대학원이 가장 적합한지 확신을 못하고 있다.
Ⓒ 전공을 무엇으로 선택해야 할지 확신을 못하고 있다.
Ⓓ 졸업 후에 무슨 일을 해야 할지 확신을 못하고 있다.

해설 교육학 전공자인 학생이 졸업을 한 학기 남겨두고 앞으로의 진로에 대해 교수와 상담을 하는 대화이다.
따라서 정답은 보기 Ⓓ.

2. 학생이 주 정부에서 인증하는 교사 자격증을 따는 것에 관해 암시하는 바는 무엇인가?
Ⓐ 자격증을 가지고 있는 교육학 전공자들은 더 나은 구직 기회를 갖는다.
Ⓑ 자격증을 가지고 있지 않은 학생들은 졸업을 할 수 없다.
Ⓒ 학생들이 해외 근무직에 지원할 때 자격증이 필수이다.
Ⓓ 대학원에서는 자격증을 가지고 있는 지원자들을 선호한다.

해설 학생은 학위를 받고 교사 자격증을 딸 계획이다. 졸업 후 사회생활을 할 때 자격증을 갖고 있는 것이 중
요하다고 생각해서 이 자격증을 따야 진짜로 졸업하는 것이라고 말할 정도이다. 정답은 보기 Ⓐ.

3. 대화에서, 교수는 추천위원회에서 학생이 해야 할 일을 언급하고 있다. 아래 표의 각 보기가 교수가 언급한 내용인지 표시하시오. 각 보기에 맞는 칸에 클릭하시오.

	Mentioned	Not Mentioned
Ⓐ 영어 강사에 대한 수요가 꽤 높다.		
Ⓑ 외국어를 배울 좋은 기회이다.		
Ⓒ 몇몇 국가에서 영어 강사는 보수가 높다.		
Ⓓ 외국 문화를 접하며 생활하는 것은 새로운 경험이 될 것이다.		
Ⓔ 학생은 많은 지역 사람들과 어울려 지낼 수 있다.		

해설 교수는 대만에서 영어 강사로 일하고 있는 자신의 제자를 언급하면서 외국에서 영어 강사로 일하게 되면 좋은 점을 몇 가지 들어주고 있다. 첫째가 외국 문화를 경험할 수 있다는 것, 둘째가 영어 강사를 필요로 하는 국가가 많다는 것, 셋째가 보수가 높다는 것이다. 따라서 언급된 것은 보기 Ⓐ, Ⓒ, Ⓓ.

4. 대만에 살고 있는 교수의 제자에 관해 추론할 수 있는 것은 무엇인가?
    Ⓐ 곧 고국으로 돌아올 것이다.
    Ⓑ 유럽으로 거주지를 옮기는 것을 고려하고 있다.
    Ⓒ 수년간의 강사 경력을 가지고 있다.
    Ⓓ 졸업할 당시 빚을 지고 있었다.

해설 추론 문제는 특히 보기 하나하나를 들려준 내용과 꼼꼼히 비교하여 답을 고르는 것이 중요하다. Ⓐ의 경우, 교수의 제자가 곧 대만에서 결혼한다고 했지만 그 곳에 계속 살지, 여자의 고국으로 돌아올지에 대해서는 알 수 없다. Ⓑ의 경우, 언급된 바가 없다. 대화에 언급되었던 Europe이란 단어를 이용해 만든 오답이다. Ⓒ의 경우, 교수의 제자가 작년에 졸업했다고 했으므로 사실과 다를 것임을 알 수 있다. Ⓓ의 경우, 교수의 제자가 대만에서 영어 강사로 일하면서 학자금 융자금을 다 갚았다고 했으므로 졸업할 당시에 빚을 지고 있었을 것임을 유추할 수 있다. 따라서 정답은 보기 Ⓓ.

대화의 일부를 다시 들으시오. 그러고 나서 질문에 답하시오.
남 : 외국에 살면서 그 지방의 문화를 경험하며 즐기는 것을 환영한다면 좋은 선택이 될 수도 있단다. 내가 알기로는 동아시아와 동유럽, 남미에서는 영어 강사 수요가 아주 높아. 그 중에서도 아시아에서 영어 강사 일을 시작하는 사람들이 가장 많지.

5. 교수가 이것을 말할 때 의미하는 것은 무엇인가? 🎧
    남 : 그 중에서도 아시아에서 영어 강사 일을 시작하는 사람들이 가장 많지.

    Ⓐ 동유럽이나 남미에서보다 아시아에서 가르치는 것이 더 낫다.
    Ⓑ 아시아로 가는 것이 많은 사람들의 인생에서 전환점이 된다.
    Ⓒ 아시아 국가에서 영어 강사 일을 시작하는 사람들이 많다.
    Ⓓ 아시아인들이 원어민 영어 강사를 더 잘 받아들이는 편이다.

해설 교수는 동아시아와 동유럽, 남미에서 영어 강사에 대한 수요가 높은데, 그 중에서도 아시아에서 강사 일을 시작하는 경우가 가장 많다고 하였다. 교수의 말을 다시 들려주는 부분에서 나온 'jumping-off point(출발점)'라는 표현의 의미를 알면 문제를 풀기가 더 쉽다. 정답은 보기 Ⓒ.

W : Thanks for taking the time to see me. I know you're really busy with final exams right now.

M : No worries. Is there something you want to talk to me about in particular?

W : Well, I'm trying to get an idea of what I should do after graduation. I'm an education major, and I know the job market's pretty good. I'm just not sure what my options are.

M : I see. Uh, are you graduating this semester?

W : No, next semester. I've still got some time.

M : It's good that you're starting now, then. What about getting your teaching credentials from the state?

W : I thought I should do that once I finish the degree. I'm looking at it as my real graduation, to be honest. I'll have the degree, but I can't do much with it until I have the credential.

M : I should say that's a very good attitude to have. It's very practical.

W : But I'm not sure I want to settle down in a teaching job right away... not here, at least. And I'm not sure I want to start graduate school yet.

M : Have you thought about going abroad? Actually, one of my students who graduated last year has been teaching English in Taiwan, and she's very happy with it.

W : Oh, really? I hadn't thought about that.

M : It's a good option if you're open to the idea of living in another country and having fun by experiencing the local culture. As far as I know, there's a tremendous demand for English teachers in East Asia, Eastern Europe, and Latin America. Asia is the most common jumping-off point, though.

W : Does your student like Taiwan?

M : Yes, she does, very much. In fact, she e-mailed me last week with good news. She has a boyfriend there, and they're going to get married. She also said that she's making very good money, and she has paid off her student loans already.

W : Wow, maybe I should consider that. Thanks!

M : No problem. Let me know if you want her e-mail address. I'm sure she'd be glad to help.

Now get ready to answer the questions. You may use your notes to help you answer.

Listen again to part of the conversation. Then answer the question.

M : It's a good option if you're open to the idea of living in another country and having fun by experiencing the local culture. As far as I know, there's a tremendous demand for English teachers in East Asia, Eastern Europe, and Latin America. Asia is the most common jumping-off point, though.

5. What does the woman imply when she says this: 🎧

M : Asia is the most common jumping-off point, though.

여 : 시간을 내주셔서 감사합니다. 지금 기말고사 때문에 매우 바쁘시잖아요.

남 : 괜찮단다. 특별히 하고 싶은 이야기가 있니?

여 : 음, 졸업 후에 무슨 일을 할 것인지를 생각 중이거든요. 교육학 전공이라 취업 전망이 꽤 좋다는 것은 알고 있어요. 그런데 제가 선택할 수 있는 길들이 무엇인지 잘 모르겠어요.

남 : 그렇구나. 이번 학기에 졸업하니?

여 : 아뇨, 다음 학기에 졸업해요. 아직 시간이 좀 있는 편이죠.

남 : 그럼 지금부터 알아보는 것은 참 바람직한 일이지. 주 정부에서 인증하는 교사 자격증을 따는 건 어떠니?

여 : 학위를 받고 나서 자격증을 따야 한다고 생각하고 있었어요. 실은 교사 자격증을 따야 진짜로 졸업하게 되는 거라고 생각하고 있어요. 교육학 학위는 받게 되겠지만, 교사 자격증을 따기 전까지는 할 수 있는 일이 많지 않으니까요.

남 : 그런 생각을 하고 있다니 아주 좋은 자세구나. 매우 실용적인 태도지.

여 : 그런데 제가 바로 교사 일을 하고 싶어 하는 건지는 잘 모르겠어요... 적어도 이곳에서는 아니에요. 대학원을 가고 싶은 건지도 잘 모르겠어요.

남 : 해외로 나가는 것에 대해 생각해본 적은 있니? 작년에 졸업한 제자 중 한 명이 대만에서 영어를 가르치고 있는데, 그 곳 생활에 아주 만족하고 있다더구나.

여 : 그래요? 그 쪽으로는 생각해본 적이 없었어요.

남 : 외국에 살면서 그 지방의 문화를 경험하며 즐기는 것을 환영한다면 좋은 선택이 될 수도 있단다. 내가 알기로는 동아시아와 동유럽, 남미에서는 영어 강사 수요가 아주 높아. 그 중에서도 아시아에서 영어 강사 일을 시작하는 사람들이 가장 많지.

여 : 교수님 제자가 대만을 좋아하나요?

남 : 그렇단다, 정말 좋아하더구나. 지난주에도 나에게 이메일을 보내서 좋은 소식을 알려왔어. 그 곳에 남자 친구가 있는데, 곧 결혼을 한다고 하더구나. 돈도 잘 벌어서 이미 학자금 융자금도 다 갚았다고 했지.

여 : 와, 그럼 한 번 고려해봐야겠네요. 감사합니다!

남 : 도움이 되었다니 다행이구나. 대만에 있는 내 제자의 이메일 주소를 원하면 알려주도록 할게. 그 아이도 도움을 줄 수 있어 좋아할 거야.

어휘 | in particular 특히 | graduation 졸업 | major 전공 | job market 구직 시장 | credential 자격 증명서 | state 주 | degree 학위 | to be honest 사실대로 말하면 | attitude 태도 | practical 실용적인 | settle down 정착하다 | at least 적어도, 최소한 | graduate school 대학원 | abroad 해외로 | open to ~에 개방적인 | experience 경험하다 | local 지역의 | culture 문화 | as far as I know 내가 아는 한 | tremendous 엄청난 | demand for ~에 대한 수요 | jumping-off point 출발점 | get married 결혼하다 | pay off 돈을 갚다 | loan 융자금 | address 주소 |

[문제 6-11] 기후학 강의의 일부를 들으시오.

6. 교수는 주로 무엇에 관해 이야기 하고 있는가?

Ⓐ 5대호 지역의 지형

Ⓑ 눈은 어떻게 만들어지는가?

Ⓒ 북미의 기후 패턴

Ⓓ 호수 효과 눈 현상

 교수는 5대호 지역의 '호수 효과 눈' 현상과 이러한 현상이 발생하는 원인을 설명하고 있다. 정답은 보기 ⑩.

강의의 일부를 다시 들으시오. 그러고 나서 질문에 답하시오.
오늘 강의에서는, 왜 매년 겨울 이런 기후 패턴이 반복되는지를 알아보겠어요. 이 현상을 설명하는 가장 일반적인 용어는 '호수 효과 눈'이에요. 이 '호수'라는 단어를 들으면 이 도시들 가까이에 있는 5대호가 떠오르겠죠.

7. 교수가 이것을 말할 때 암시하는 것은 무엇인가:
이 '호수'라는 단어를 들으면 이 도시들 가까이에 있는 5대호가 떠오르겠죠.

Ⓐ 5대호는 북미에서 가장 유명한 호수이다.
Ⓑ 학생들은 5대호 주변의 지리를 잘 알고 있다.
Ⓒ 호수 효과 눈은 5대호에서만 발생한다.
Ⓓ 5대호에 기후 이변이 일어나고 있다.

 교수는 학생들에게 뉴욕 주 북부 도시들을 생각하면 먼저 폭설이 내리는 모습이 떠오를 거라고 하면서, 이 현상을 설명하는 가장 일반적인 용어가 '호수 효과 눈'이라고 하였다. 이 '호수'라는 말을 들으면 앞서 언급된 도시들 근처에 있는 5대호가 생각날 거라 말한 것은 학생들이 5대호와 그 주변 지리를 이미 잘 알고 있다는 것을 가정하고 하는 말이다. 따라서 정답은 보기 Ⓑ.

8. 다음 중 어느 것이 호수 효과 눈이 내리는 주요 지역으로 언급되지 않았는가?
Ⓐ 로체스터
Ⓑ 디트로이트
Ⓒ 버팔로
Ⓓ 클리블랜드

 보기 Ⓑ의 디트로이트는 호수 효과 눈의 영향을 거의 받지 않는 지역으로 언급되었다. 정답은 보기 Ⓑ

9. 호수 효과 눈의 양을 결정짓는 주요인 2가지는 무엇인가? 2개의 답을 클릭하시오.
Ⓐ 호수 온도보다 차가운 공기
Ⓑ 낮은 고도
Ⓒ 많은 양의 수증기
Ⓓ 호수의 넓이

 북극 지역에서 불어오는 찬바람이 더 따뜻한 호수 위를 지나며 수분을 흡수하여 습한 공기가 된다. 따라서 정답은 보기 Ⓐ와 Ⓒ.

10. 5대호 남동쪽 호반 도시들에 관해 미루어 짐작할 수 있는 것은 무엇인가?
Ⓐ 겨울에 도움이 필요하다.
Ⓑ 미국에서 인구가 가장 적다.
Ⓒ 바람이 불어오는 쪽에 위치해 있다.
Ⓓ 정확한 기상 관측기를 갖추고 있다.

 밀워키, 토론토, 디트로이트는 호수 효과 눈 현상의 영향을 거의 받지 않는다고 했는데, 그 이유는 이 지역들이 5대호의 leeward side, 즉 바람이 불어가는 쪽에 위치해 있기 때문이라고 하였다. 이를 통해, 호수 효과 눈 현상이 두드러지는 5대호의 남동쪽 호반 도시들은 windward side, 즉 불어오는 바람의 영향을 받게 되는 쪽에 위치해 있음을 미루어 알 수 있다. 따라서 정답은 보기 ⓒ. 보기 ⓓ처럼 눈이 많이 내린다고 해서 정확한 기상 관측기를 가지고 있다고는 유추할 수 없다. 강의 내용만으로는 추론하기 힘든 내용이다.

11. 강의에서, 교수는 5대호 연안에 폭설을 내리게 하는 원인을 몇 가지 이야기 하고 있다. 아래 표의 각 보기가 이 원인들 중 하나인지 표시하시오. 각 보기에 맞는 칸에 클릭하시오.

	Yes	No
ⓐ 호수의 깊이		
ⓑ 바람이 부는 방향		
ⓒ 도시의 상대적인 위치		
ⓓ 도시의 크기		
ⓔ 강한 바람이 부는 빈도		

 강의에서 교수는 5대호 연안의 호수 효과 눈이 발생하는 원인으로 5대호 연안 도시의 방위에 따른 상대적 위치, 공기가 호수 물 위를 이동하는 거리, 바람의 방향, 강한 바람이 부는 빈도, 호수 물 온도 등을 언급하고 있다. 이 중 보기에 언급된 것은 보기 ⓑ의 바람이 부는 방향, 보기 ⓒ의 도시의 상대적 위치, 보기 ⓔ의 강한 바람이 부는 빈도이다.

🎧 [Questions 6–11] Listen to part of a lecture in a climatology class.

P(W) : When you think of Upstate New York – most notably, the cities of Buffalo, Syracuse, and Rochester – you probably think of heavy snow in winter, right? In today's lecture, we'll take a look at what causes those weather patterns each winter. The most common term for the phenomenon is lake-effect snow. The word lake should remind you of the nearby Great Lakes. But why do those cities in New York get so much snow when Toronto and Hamilton, on the north side of the lake, in Canada, get relatively little? The north side should be colder, right? Well, winds blowing from the Arctic regions move from north to south. Crossing over Lake Ontario and Lake Erie, these cold winds acquire significant amounts of moisture.

In freezing temperatures, this falls as snow. And under certain circumstances, these areas even experience thundersnow, which is exactly what it sounds like: thunderstorms with snow instead of rain. Also, for the sake of clarity, I should add that many regions get lake-effect snow. Upstate New York might be the best-known, but all the cities along the southeast shores of the Great Lakes – Cleveland, Pittsburgh, and Michigan's Upper Peninsula are also affected. Other cities such as Milwaukee, Toronto, and Detroit are generally sheltered from lake-effect weather patterns because of their location: they are on the leeward side of the lakes, not the windward side. In other words, where the wind is blowing from, not where it's blowing to.

There are actually several other factors involved in this phenomenon that contributes about 40% of the annual winter snowfall in these areas. Let's see: uh, the distance air with moisture has to travel over water, the direction of the prevailing wind, how often strong wind blows, and the degree in lake water temperatures, etc. There are also some other places in the world where these weather patterns are regular occurrences, but that's all we have time for today.

Now get ready to answer the questions. You may use your notes to help you answer.

Listen again to part of the conversation. Then answer the question.
In today's lecture, we'll take a look at what causes those weather patterns each winter. The most common term for the phenomenon is lake-effect snow. The word lake should remind you of the nearby Great Lakes.

7. What does the professor imply when she says this: 🎧
The word lake should remind you of the nearby Great Lakes.

P : 뉴욕 주 북부 지방, 그 중에서도 버팔로(Buffalo) 시와 시러큐스(Syracuse) 시, 로체스터(Rochester) 시를 생각하면, 가장 먼저 떠오르는 것이 바로 겨울철에 내리는 큰 눈이죠? 오늘 강의에서는, 왜 매년 겨울 이런 기후 패턴이 반복되는지를 알아보겠어요. 이 현상을 설명하는 가장 일반적인 용어는 '호수 효과 눈'이에요. 이 '호수'라는 단어를 들으면 이 도시들 가까이에 있는 5대호가 떠오르겠죠. 그런데 캐나다의 5대호 북쪽 지역의 토론토(Toronto)나 해밀턴(Hamilton)에는 상대적으로 적은 눈이 내리는데 반해, 왜 뉴욕 주의 이런 도시들에는 눈이 그렇게 많이 내리는 걸까요? 북쪽 지역이 더 추워야 하는데 말이죠, 그렇죠? 북극 지방에서 불어오는 바람은 북쪽에서 남쪽으로 향합니다. 온타리오 호(Lake Ontario)와 이리 호(Lake Erie)를 지나면서 이 찬 바람은 상당한 양의 수분을 흡수하게 됩니다.
얼어붙을 듯이 추운 날씨 속에 공기 중의 습기는 눈이 되어 내립니다. 그리고 어떤 때는, 이러한 지역에 '뇌설'이 강타하는데, 들리는 그대로 비대신 눈이 내리는 '뇌우'죠. 더 명확하게 설명하자면, '호수 효과 눈'은 많은 지역에 내려요. 뉴욕 주 북부 지역이 가장 잘 알려져 있지만, 5대호의 남동쪽 호반 도시들, 가령 클리블랜드(Cleveland), 피츠버그(Pittsburgh), 미시간(Michigan) 주 북부의 상부 반도 (Superior 호와 Michigan 호 사이의 반도) 역시 '호수 효과 눈' 현상의 영향을 받죠. 밀워키 (Milwaukee)나 토론토(Toronto), 디트로이트(Detroit) 등의 도시는 지리적 위치가 '호수 효과' 기상 패턴의 영향을 받는 것을 막아주는데, 바로 이 도시들은 호수의 바람이 불어오는 쪽(windward)이 아닌 바람이 불어가는 쪽(leeward)에 있기 때문이에요. 즉, 불어오는 바람의 영향을 받는 쪽이 아닌, 바람이 불기 시작하는 쪽에 있다는 것이죠.
이들 지역의 연간 겨울 강설량의 약 40%를 차지하는 이 현상을 일으키는 요인들이 더 있어요. 습기 찬 공기가 호수 위를 이동하는 거리, 우세한 바람의 방향, 강한 바람이 부는 빈도, 그리고 호수 물 온도 등이 있죠. 전 세계 이런 기후 패턴이 계속해서 발생하는 지역들이 또 있는데, 오늘은 여기까지만 하죠.

어휘 | upstate 북쪽의 | notably 특히, 그 중에서도 | term 용어 | remind A of B A에게 B를 상기시키다 | nearby 가까이에 있는 | relatively 비교적, 상대적으로 | blow 바람이 불다 | acquire 얻다 | significant 상당한 | moisture 수분 | freezing 얼어붙을 듯한 | circumstance 상황, 환경 | thunderstorm 뇌우 | for the sake of ~를 위하여 | shelter 보호하다, 막다 | leeward 바람이 불어가는 쪽 | windward 바람이 불

어오는 쪽 | in other words 즉, 다시 말하자면 | factor 요인 | contribute ~의 원인이 되다 | distance 거리 |
prevailing 우세한 | temperature 온도 | occurrence 발생 |

Review

1. 1. 효과, 영향 2. 광범위한 3. 채택하다 4. 합리적인 5. 임시로 6. 철학자 7. 탐험하다 8. 힘을 북돋아주는 9. 지불 10. 연기 11. overdue 12. receipt 13. rational 14. repair 15. equipment 16. occasion 17. reserve 18. occupy 19. reputation 20. launch

2. 1. come up with 제안하다, 생각해내다 2. narrow down 범위를 좁히다 3. make up 보충하다, 만회하다 4. sleep on ~에 대해 시간을 가지고 생각하다 5. stop by 들르다 6. at the last minute 마지막 순간에 7. keep up with ~에 뒤떨어지지 않다 8. once in a while 이따금 9. no wonder 당연하다 10. close down 폐쇄하다

3. 1. destroyed 2. means 3. tremendous 4. relatively 5. exports 6. replace
해석 | 1. 1800년대에 스리랑카의 커피 작물이 병충해로 인해 거의 파괴되었어요.
2. 불가사리는 느리게 움직이고, 방어 수단이 거의 없어요.
3. 내가 알기로는 동아시아와 동유럽, 남미에서는 영어 강사 수요가 아주 높아.
4. 그런데 캐나다의 5대호 북쪽 지역의 토론토(Toronto)나 해밀턴(Hamilton)에는 상대적으로 적은 눈이 내리는데 반해, 왜 뉴욕 주의 이런 도시들에는 눈이 그렇게 많이 내리는 걸까요?
5. 이제 스리랑카는 세계 3위의 홍차 재배 국가이고 전 세계 시장의 약 20%를 수출하고 있어요.
6. 장비 수리가 가능한지, 새로 바꾸어야 하는지 알아야 하니까요.

Chapter 2 Detail

Office Hours

1. Ⓓ 2. Ⓒ 3. Ⓐ

1. 다음 중 어느 것이 학생에 관해 맞는가?
Ⓐ 물리학 전공이다.
Ⓑ 물리학과에 쓰일 기금 모금을 할 것이다.
Ⓒ Kovacs 박사가 누구인지 모른다.
Ⓓ 유기화합물에 대한 지식을 가지고 있다.

Dictation | ① being advertised ② apply for that ③ is going to quit ④ got funding to study ⑤ the inside information

여 : 실험실 조교직이 아직 공고가 안 난 것 같던데요... 학과에서 벌써 조교를 채용했나요?
남 : 실은 그렇단다.
여 : 아, 그럼 안 되는데요, 제가 지원하려고 했거든요. 조교 모집은 그것 밖에 없나요? 혹시 자리가 날

만한 다른 조교 일을 알고 계신가요?
남 : 이번에 채용하기로 결정한 건 그 자리 밖에 없지만, 물리학과 조교가 그만둘 예정이란 건 알고 있지.
　　 네 부전공이 물리학이지?
여 : 네, 맞아요. 저에게도 기회가 있을까요?
남 : 안 될 이유가 없지. 그리고 Kovacs 교수에게도 알아보렴. Kovacs 교수가 가르치는 대학원생 한 명
　　 이 새로운 유기화합물 연구 보조금을 받았는데, 조교 몇 명을 구한다고 하더구나.
여 : 잘됐네요! 내부 정보를 알려주시니 감사합니다!

어휘 | assistant 조교 **|** hire 채용하다 **|** as a matter of fact 실은 **|** quit 그만두다 **|** physics 물리학 **|**
minor 부전공 **|** funding 보조금 **|** organic compound 유기화합물 **|**

2. 다음 중 어느 것이 영화와 연극 441 강의에 관해 맞는가?
　　 Ⓐ 폴란드 학생들만이 수강할 수 있다.
　　 Ⓑ 학생들이 그 수업을 들으려면 진단 고사를 봐야 한다.
　　 Ⓒ 학생들은 수업 시간에 자막이 없는 영화를 봐야 한다.
　　 Ⓓ 폴란드어 전공자들이 우선적으로 수강할 수 있다.

Dictation | ① I wanted to register for　② you're majoring in it　③ improve my Polish
　　　　　　 ④ a pretty high degree of fluency　⑤ make a suggestion

남 : 제가 폴란드어 강좌 중 하나를 들으려고 했는데, 수강책자에 보니 사전승인을 받아야 한다고 나와
　　 있어요...
여 : 어떤 강의죠?
남 : 영화와 연극이요. 강의 번호는 441번이에요.
여 : 알겠어요. 폴란드어를 할 줄 아나요, 아니면 공부해본 적이 있어요? 학생이 폴란드어를 전공하는 것
　　 같아 보이지는 않네요, 내가 학생 얼굴을 못 알아보는 걸로 봐서는.
남 : 음, 저희 아버지께서 지금 Krakow(크라쿠프)에서 근무하고 계셔서 몇 번 가본 적이 있어요. 그래서 폴
　　 란드어를 약간은 할 줄 알아요. 전 폴란드어를 더 잘하고 싶기도 하고, 수업도 재미있을 것 같아서요...
여 : 나쁘지는 않네요, 그런데 문제는 강의 시간에 보게 되는 영화에는 자막이 들어있지 않아요. 그러니까
　　 강의를 통해 뭔가를 배워려면 폴란드어를 수준급 이상으로 해야 하죠. 내가 제안 하나를 해줄까
　　 요? 진단 고사를 봐서 폴란드어를 따로 공부하는 것이 어때요?
남 : 그러는 게 좋겠네요. 감사합니다!

어휘 | register for ~를 신청하다, 등록하다 **|** permission 승인, 허가 **|** Polish 폴란드어 **|** recognize 알아보다 **|**
improve 향상시키다 **|** subtitle 자막 **|** degree 정도, 수준 **|** fluency 유창함 **|** benefit from ~에서 이득을
얻다 **|** placement test 반편성 시험 **|**

3. 왜 학생은 친구의 할아버지를 인터뷰하길 원하는가?
　　 Ⓐ 리포트 작성에 필요한 흥미로운 이야기를 들려주실 지도 모른다.
　　 Ⓑ 1950년대에 뉴욕에 거주하셨다.
　　 Ⓒ 현재 뉴욕 재즈 클럽에서 연주를 하고 계신다.
　　 Ⓓ 대학에서 학생들에게 재즈를 가르치신다.

남 : 리포트 과제에 대해 몇 가지 질문을 해도 될까요? 제가 좀 흥미로운 사실을 알게 되었는데, 그것 때문에 리포트 작성 방향이 바뀔 것 같아요.

여 : 무슨 일인지 궁금해지는구나, Chris. 리포트 주제는 무엇으로 정했니?

남 : 1950년대 뉴욕의 재즈 문화에 관한 내용이에요.

여 : 리포트 작성 분량을 고려하면 주제가 너무 광범위한 것 같구나. 음악가 1명만을 중점적으로 다루는 것에 대해서는 생각해보았었니?

남 : 지금 제가 하려는 것이 바로 그거에요. 제 친구 할아버지께서 1950년대에 재즈 클럽 순회공연을 다니셨는데요, 그 분을 인터뷰하고 싶어요. 리포트 제출일이 금요일인데, 그 때까지 그 분과 인터뷰를 못할 것 같아요. 지금 여행 중이시래요.

여 : 그 분의 이야기를 리포트에 언급하면 아주 재미있을 것 같구나. 그럼 이렇게 하도록 해. 금요일까지 리포트 아웃라인과 인터뷰 질문 목록을 제출하는 것이 어떠니? 그렇게 하면 리포트를 작성하도록 1주일을 더 줄게. 어떻게 생각하니?

남 : 그렇게 해주시면 정말 좋겠어요!

어휘 | affect 영향을 끼치다 | mysterious 수수께끼 같은 | length 길이 | circuit 순회 | cruise 순항 | outline 개요

Service Encounters

1. ⓒ   2. ⓒ   3. ⓒ

1. 다음 중 학생의 학생증을 바꾸기 위해 남자가 요구하는 것이 아닌 것은?
Ⓐ 주민등록번호
Ⓑ 사진이 들어있는 다른 신분증
Ⓒ 최근 사진
Ⓓ 재발급 비용

여 : 제 학생증을 새로 발급받아야 할 것 같아요. 잃어버렸거든요.

남 : 그래요. 학생증 번호는 기억하고 있어요?

여 : 아니요... 다른 신분증을 이용해도 될까요?

남 : 그래요. 이 종이에 성과 이름을 모두 적고 주민등록번호도 적으세요. 그리고 운전면허증이나 기타 사진이 있는 신분증을 보여주세요.

여 : 알겠습니다. 지금 바로 새 학생증을 발급해주실 수 있나요?

남 : 지금 당장 발급은 불가할 것 같군요. 사람이 부족해서요. 하루 정도는 걸릴 거예요.

여 : 별로 좋은 일은 아니네요. 음, 제가 새로운 사진을 드려야 하나요? 만약의 경우를 대비해서 하나 가져왔어요.

어휘 | identification 신분증 | write down ~을 적다 | driver's license 운전면허증 | issue 발급하다 |
short-handed 일손이 부족한 |

2. 언제 학생의 '미완' 성적이 낙제로 바뀌게 되는가?
ⓐ 2일 후
ⓑ 10일 후
ⓒ 14일 후
ⓓ 30일 후

Dictation | ① come by this office ② nearing the deadline ③ submit a new grade
④ as soon as possible ⑤ write a letter to the dean ⑥ my life saver

어휘 | come by 들르다 | biology 생물학 | near 가까워지다 | submit 제출하다 | redo 다시 하다 |
experiment 실험 | the sooner, the better 빠르면 빠를수록 좋다 | extend 연장하다 | dean 학장 |
life saver 곤경에서 구해주는 사람(것) |

3. 왜 학생은 오늘 밤 친구 집에서 지내야 하는가?
ⓐ 기술자가 청소를 할 것이다.
ⓑ 내일까지도 물이 계속 샐 것이다.
ⓒ 새 난방기가 없다.
ⓓ 관리인이 바쁘다.

Dictation | ① hold on ② a huge puddle of rusty water ③ it smelled awful
④ that's an emergency ⑤ we're out of replacements

어휘 | radiator 라디에이터, 난방기 | maintenance 유지, 보수, 관리 | leak 새는 물, 누출 | puddle 웅덩이 |
rusty 녹슨 | pond 연못 | awful 끔찍한 |

Lectures

1. 1) Ⓓ　2) Ⓒ　**2.** 1) Ⓐ, Ⓒ　2) Ⓒ　**3.** 1) Ⓒ　2) Ⓓ　3) Ⓑ

1. 지구 과학 수업

　1. 다음 중 어느 것이 산악성 공기 상승 작용에 관해 맞지 않는가?
　　Ⓐ 찬 공기는 습기를 계속 함유하지 못한다.
　　Ⓑ 공기가 산맥을 따라 상승한다.
　　Ⓒ 고도가 높아지면 공기가 팽창하여 냉각된다.
　　Ⓓ 산의 바람받이 사면은 건조하다.

　2. 산으로 인해 구름이 많이 생성되는 지역에 위치한 도시는 어디인가?
　　Ⓐ 시애틀과 샌프란시스코
　　Ⓑ 포틀랜드와 토론토
　　Ⓒ 밴쿠버와 시애틀
　　Ⓓ 로스앤젤레스와 포틀랜드

Dictation | ① how weather patterns work　② in scientific terms　③ in the form of ice crystals
④ in order for it to be visible　⑤ to higher elevations　⑥ it expands and it cools
⑦ its reputation for being the rainiest city　⑧ lose all their moisture

P : 학생이 말한 것처럼, 구름 속에 들어있는 물방울은 지름이 0.01 밀리미터에요. 한 번 생각해봐요, 구름의 크기와 비교해서 말이죠... 얼마나 많은 물방울이 한데 뭉쳐져야 눈에 보이게 될지. 산악 지역에서는 구름이 산악성 공기 상승(orographic lift) 작용을 통해 형성 되지요. 누가 이 작용에 대해 설명해 보겠어요?
S : 제가 알기로는, 고도가 높아짐에 따라 공기 덩어리가 상승하면 팽창하여 온도가 내려가게 되요. 냉각된 공기는 응결고도에서 수증기가 응결하게 하여 구름이 형성됩니다.
P : 바로 그게 산에서 바람이 불어오는 쪽과 바람이 불어가는 쪽의 기후 패턴이 큰 차이를 보이는 이유에요. 시애틀(Seattle)이 미국에서 비가 가장 많이 내리는 도시로 이름난 걸 생각해봐요. 시애틀, 포틀랜드(Portland), 밴쿠버(Vancouver), 그리고 그 지역의 기타 도시들은 캐스케이드 산맥(the Cascades)의 동쪽에 있어요. 태평양에서 불어오는 따뜻하고 습윤한 바람이 산허리를 따라 상승하여, 냉각되고, 비와 눈의 형태로 습기를 모두 잃어버리죠. 캐스케이드 산맥의 반대쪽은 건조한 것으로 유명하고요. 전체적인 과정은 그것보다 훨씬 더 복잡하고, 그로 인해 형성되는 구름의 종류도 다양한데요, 오늘은 시간이 다 되었군요...

어휘 | distribute 분포하다 | atmosphere 대기 | cloud-capped 구름으로 뒤덮인 | cluster 떼, 무리 | water vapor 수증기 | ice crystal 빙정 | droplet 작은 물방울 | diameter 직경, 지름 | billions of 수가 막대한 | elevation 고도 | expand 팽창하다 | condense 응결하다 | condensation level 응결고도(미포화 습윤 공기가 응결을 시작하는 고도) | sharply 급격하게 | windward 바람이 불어오는 쪽의 | leeward 바람이 불어가는 쪽의 | reputation 평판 | result from ~에서 생겨나다 |

2. 지질학 수업

1. 강의에 따르면, 간헐천에 관해 맞는 것은 무엇인가? 2개의 답을 클릭하시오.
   Ⓐ 간헐천(geyser)이란 단어는 아이슬란드어에 기원을 두고 있다.
   Ⓑ 세계 도처에서 간헐천을 찾아보기란 어렵지 않다.
   Ⓒ 지하에 있는 가장 뜨거운 물이 압력 증가로 분출한다.
   Ⓓ 보통 불규칙적으로 뜨거운 물과 증기를 뿜어낸다.

2. 어디에서 전 세계 50% 이상의 간헐천을 볼 수 있는가?
   Ⓐ 아이슬란드
   Ⓑ 뉴질랜드
   Ⓒ 미국
   Ⓓ 일본

Dictation | ① you've probably bathed in it ② I couldn't be happier ③ gush is exactly what they do ④ with exactly the right geological formations ⑤ beyond expression ⑥ a constant supply of cold water ⑦ on a cyclical basis ⑧ so to speak ⑨ keep a safe distance

P : 자, 여러분 모두 온천이 무엇인지는 알고 있겠죠. 여러분의 출신지나 휴가지에 따라 온천에 몸을 담가본 적이 있을 거예요. 개인적으로 지난겨울 휴가 때 일본에 갔었는데, 뜨거운 물에 발을 담그고 있으니 그보다 더 좋은 것이 없었죠. 하지만 간헐천에 몸을 담그고 싶지는 않을 거예요, 왜냐하면...

S : 분출하기 때문이에요!

P : 맞아요. 간헐천이 분출할 때, 스팀과 뜨거운 물이 공중으로 솟구쳐요. 간헐천(geyser)이란 단어는 '분출한다(to gush)'라는 뜻의 아이슬란드어에서 왔는데, 분출하는 것이 바로 간헐천이 하는 것이죠. 여러분 가운데 간헐천이 분출하는 것을 직접 본 사람은 많지 않을 거예요. 상당히 드물기 때문이죠. 지상에서 몇 군데 없는데, 지질조건이 맞아 떨어지는 곳에서만 찾아볼 수 있어요. 그 수가 얼마나 적은지 보자면, 글쎄요, 약 1000개 정도가 전부고, 그 중 절반 이상이 미국의 옐로스톤 국립공원(Yellowstone National Park)에 있어요.

S : 전에 뉴질랜드에서 간헐천을 본 적이 있는데요, 뭐라고 말해야 할까요... 굉장했어요!

P : 그래요, 형용할 수 없을 정도로 장관을 이룰 때도 있죠. 아이슬란드에서도 간헐천을 볼 수 있어요. 자, 그럼 간헐천이 어떻게 만들어지는가 하면... 간헐천이 만들어지려면, 지하수가 땅속 깊이 스며들어 마그마에 의해 뜨거워진 암석까지 흘러 들어가야 하죠. 찬 물이 계속해서 아래 있는 뜨거운 물을 내리누르기 때문에, 압력이 올라가고, 이 뜨거운 물이 간헐적으로 위로 솟구쳐 오르는 겁니다. 이게 바로 간헐천이 주기적으로 분출하는 이유죠. 이를테면, 물이 땅속으로 흘러 들어가 뜨거워지고, 그 위에 더 많은 물이 흘러 들어오고, 그렇게 되면 가장 깊은 곳에 있던 가장 뜨거운 물이 폭발하여 분출하는 거죠. 여러분이 반드시 명심해 두어야 할 것이 있어요. 간헐천을 보러 가면, 안전한 거리를 유지하도록 하고 물속으로 뭔가를 쏟아 붓거나 던져 버리는 일은 생각지도 말아요!

어휘 | hot spring 온천 | erupt 분출하다 | steam 증기 | gush 뿜어내다, 분출하다 | spout out 분출하다 | rare 드문 | geological 지리적 | spectacular 장관을 이루는, 눈부신 | beyond expression 형용할 수 없는 | groundwater 지하수 | seep 스며 나오다, 침투하다 | periodically 주기적으로, 간헐적으로 | so to speak 이를테면 | pour 붓다, 쏟다 | throw 던지다 |

3. 경제학 수업

1. 화자들은 주로 무엇에 관해 토론하고 있는가?
   Ⓐ 불황을 극복하는 방법
   Ⓑ 경제 호황에 관한 다양한 이론들
   Ⓒ 호황과 불황의 순환
   Ⓓ 호황 시대가 얼마나 오래 지속되는가

2. 다음 중 어느 것이 경제 호황의 특징이 아닌가?
   Ⓐ 생산량이 증대된다.
   Ⓑ 더 많은 사람들이 일자리를 갖는다.
   Ⓒ 재화와 용역 수요가 높다.
   Ⓓ 가격이 낮아지는 편이다.

3. 다음 중 어느 것이 오늘날의 미국 정치가들에 관해 맞는가?
   Ⓐ 그들은 정부가 견실한 경제 정책을 시행하는 것이 중요하다고 생각한다.
   Ⓑ 대부분은 정부가 경제 상황에 개입하지 말아야 한다고 생각한다.
   Ⓒ 그들은 정부가 더 많은 자금을 경제학 연구에 투자해야 한다고 생각한다.
   Ⓓ 대부분은 정부가 불확실한 경제 상황을 개선할 능력이 없다고 생각한다.

Dictation | ① inevitable ups and downs　② a period of increased output　③ a rise in prices of goods and services　④ come to an end　⑤ keep something like that from happening again　⑥ regulated or even eliminated altogether　⑦ actively involve itself in the economy　⑧ in a time of economic uncertainty

P : 경제학 이론에서 말하는 호황과 불황의 순환에 관해 수업을 시작해보죠. 많은 경제학자들은 경제 시스템에는 주기가 있어서, 호경기와 불경기가 자연적으로 발생하며 이는 불가피한 것이라고 말해요. 들리는 그대로죠. 경제 호황기에는 어떤지 누가 말해볼래요?
S : 음, 생산량이 증대되고, 수요도 높고, 실업률도 낮아요.
P : 맞아요. 사람들은 일하고, 경제가 살아나고, 돈이 만들어지죠. 안타깝게도 이런 호황기 뒤에는 재화의 가격이 인상하는 인플레이션이 뒤따르게 되요. 또한 좋았던 모든 것들은 결국 끝을 보게 되죠. 그렇다면, 불황은 무엇일까요?
S : 책에서 읽은 바에 따르면, 불황은 경기 후퇴(recession)를 나타내는 것과 같은 말이에요. 요즘 뉴스에서 많이 듣는 말이고요.
P : 잘 대답해 주었어요. 음, 정부는 항상 이 불경기에 관해 걱정의 끈을 놓지 않죠. 불경기 때는 소비자 수요가 낮고 사람들이 일자리를 잃고 국가 전체 수입이 적어지니까요. 세계대공황이 발생한 이래로 호황과 불황의 순환은 많은 연구의 대상이었어요. 미국 정부뿐만이 아닌 각국 정부에서 이런 일이 다시 발생하는 것을 막고 싶어 하죠, 그게 가능하다면 말이에요. 일부 경제학 이론에 따르면, 이러한 순환은 규제되거나 아예 제거될 수도 있어요. 일부에서는 정부가 경제 활동에 적극 개입해야 한다고 말하고, 또 다른 측에서는 정부의 개입이 상황을 더 악화시킬 뿐이라고 말하죠. 대부분의 현대 미국 정치가들은 이 후자 학파의 입장을 취하고 있어요. 우리는 현재 경제적 불확실성의 시대에 살고 있지요, 그러니까 이 모든 문제의 해결책을 알고 있는 누군가가 나타나기를 기다려 봅시다!

어휘 | bust 불황 | economist 경제학자 | occur 발생하다 | inevitable 필연적인, 피하기 어려운 | ups and downs 오르내림, 성쇠 | accompany 수반하다 | rise 증가 | come to an end 끝나다 | recession 불경기 | regulate 규제하다 | eliminate 제거하다 | intervention 개입 | politician 정치가 |

Practice

[1-5] 1. Ⓑ　2. Ⓒ　3. Ⓑ　4. Mentioned – Ⓐ, Ⓒ　Not Mentioned – Ⓑ, Ⓓ　5. Ⓓ
[6-11] 6. Ⓒ　7. Ⓑ　8. Yes – Ⓑ, Ⓒ, Ⓔ　No – Ⓐ, Ⓓ　9. Ⓒ　10. Ⓐ　11. Ⓐ

[문제 1-5] 체육관에서 일어난 대화의 일부를 들으시오.

1. 남자와 여자가 이 대화를 나누는 이유는 무엇인가?
　Ⓐ 여자는 개인 트레이너를 고용하고 싶어 한다.
　Ⓑ 여자는 체육관 이용 등록을 하고 싶어 한다.
　Ⓒ 여자는 수영장 이용 스케줄을 알고 싶어 한다.
　Ⓓ 여자는 학생 트레이너로 일하고 싶어 한다.

해설 대화의 첫 부분에 이 대화의 주제가 드러나 있다. 학생은 체육관을 처음 이용하려고 하는데, 직원이 이용 절차를 알려주고 있다. 정답은 보기 Ⓑ.

2. 체육관 직원은 학생에게 어떤 정보를 알려달라고 하는가?
　　Ⓐ 병력과 운동 기록
　　Ⓑ 키, 몸무게, 건강 정보
　　Ⓒ 긴급 시에 대비한 연락처
　　Ⓓ 체육관 운동복을 빌리는데 필요한 옷 치수

해설 직원은 학생의 가장 기본적인 인적사항으로 비상 연락처를 요구하고 있다. 따라서 정답은 보기 Ⓒ.

대화의 일부를 다시 들으시오. 그리고 나서 질문에 답하시오.
여 : 그렇게 해주시면 정말 좋겠어요. 제가 양식을 다 작성하고 나서 함께 둘러볼 수 있을까요?
남 : 저요? 전 데스크를 지켜야 해요, 대신 여기서 일하는 학생 트레이너를 불러드리죠. 지금 4명이 있는데,
　　한 명을 오라고 할게요.

3. 남자가 이것을 말할 때 암시하는 것은 무엇인가: 🎧
　　남 : 저요? 전 데스크를 지켜야 해요, 대신 여기서 일하는 학생 트레이너를 불러드리죠. 지금 4명이 있는
　　　　데, 한 명을 오라고 할게요.

　　Ⓐ 트레이너가 학생보다 더 낫다.
　　Ⓑ 남자는 학생에게 체육관을 보여줄 수 없다.
　　Ⓒ 남자는 서류 업무를 처리해야 한다.
　　Ⓓ 남자는 운동에 대해 잘 모른다.

해설 여자가 체육관 시설을 소개해달라는 말에 남자는 자신은 데스크를 지켜야 한다고 말하며 대신 트레이너
　　를 불러 주겠다고 한다. 이 말은 자신은 투어를 못 시켜준다는 뜻이다. 정답은 보기 Ⓑ.

4. 대화에서, 남자는 학생에게 몇 가지를 일러주고 있다. 아래 표의 각 보기가 남자가 언급한 사항에 속하는
　　지 표시하시오. 각 보기에 맞는 칸에 클릭하시오.

	Mentioned	Not Mentioned
Ⓐ 트레이너와 시간을 정하기		
Ⓑ 수영부와 함께 운동하기		
Ⓒ 적당한 옷과 신발을 준비하기		
Ⓓ 운동 기구를 잘 관리하기		

해설 여자가 어떻게 운동해야 하는지 걱정하자 남자가 트레이너와 이야기를 해보고 운동 시간을 정하라고 제
　　안했다. 그리고 대화 마지막 부분에서 적당한 운동복을 준비하라고 하였다. 따라서 정답은 보기 Ⓐ와
　　Ⓒ. 보기 Ⓑ의 수영부(swim team)는 수영장 이용 시간과 관련하여 언급된 내용으로 만든 오답이며, 보
　　기 Ⓓ 역시 대화에 언급된 운동 기구(exercise equipment)를 이용하여 만든 오답이다.

5. 이 대화에 이어 바로 일어날 일은 무엇인가?
　　Ⓐ 학생은 운동복을 살 것이다.
　　Ⓑ 학생은 수영장에서 수영을 할 것이다.
　　Ⓒ 학생은 남자와 약속을 정할 것이다.
　　Ⓓ 학생은 체육관을 둘러볼 것이다.

 대화에 뒤이어 일어날 일은 토플 리스닝 섹션에서 자주 등장하는 문제 중 하나이다. 대화의 마지막 부분을 주의 깊게 들으면 쉽게 풀 수 있는 문제이다. 대화의 중간 부분에서 직원이 학생에게 체육관을 트레이너와 함께 둘러볼 것을 제안했고, 대화의 마지막에서 트레이너가 오고 있다고 했다. 따라서 학생은 이제 트레이너와 함께 체육관 시설을 둘러볼 것임을 유추할 수 있다. 정답은 보기 ⑩.

[Questions 1–5] Listen to part of a conversation at a gym.

M : How can I help you? You look a little bit lost.

W : Yes, thanks. I want to register to use the gym, but I've never used one before, and I'm not sure how to get started.

M : Oh, no problem. I can help.

W : Um, do I need to fill out any forms?

M : Yes, you do, but it's very simple. We just need to keep some very basic information on file.

W : What kind of information?

M : Just your emergency contacts, in case you get hurt while you're working out.

W : Oh, I see.

M : You're new here, so if you want, we can show you around the gym. You can see what facilities we have. Obviously this is a new gym, so everything's in good shape: the pool, all the exercise equipment……．

W : That's really great. Will you give me the tour after I fill out the form?

M : Me? Uh, I need to stay here at the desk, but I'll get one of the student trainers for you. There are four here right now, so I'll have one come down.

W : Great. And... uh, what about working out? I don't know much about lifting weights and using the machines. I don't want to hurt myself by exercising the wrong way.

M : Don't worry. You should talk about that with the trainer. You can schedule sessions with them. We have about 12 who work at different times.

W : That'll do. I have one more question to ask you... uh, are there certain times of day when the pool is not available?

M : Wait a second... right, here's a copy of the schedule. The swim team actually uses a different pool most of the time, so don't worry about that.

W : Is there anything else I should do?

M : Well, you ought to make sure you have proper clothes for the gym: shoes with good support, comfortable shorts that aren't too loose or too tight, a good swimsuit and goggles if you'll be using the pool, that kind of thing. It's a good investment.

W : That's terrific. Thanks for your help!

M : My pleasure – and here's the trainer.

Now get ready to answer the questions. You may use your notes to help you answer.

Listen again to part of the conversation. Then answer the question.
W : That's really great. Will you give me the tour after I fill out the form?
M : Me? Uh, I need to stay here at the desk, but I'll get one of the student trainers for you. There are four here right now, so I'll have one come down.

남 : 무엇을 도와줄까요? 좀 헤매고 있는 것 같은데요.
여 : 네, 감사합니다. 체육관 이용 등록을 하고 싶은데, 전에 한 번도 와본 적이 없어서 무엇부터 해야 하는 건지 잘 모르겠어요.
남 : 걱정 말아요. 내가 도와줄게요.
여 : 양식 같은 걸 작성해야 하나요?
남 : 그래요, 하지만 아주 간단해요. 아주 기본적인 사항만 파일에 입력해 놓으면 되죠.
여 : 어떤 사항이죠?
남 : 운동하다가 다칠 경우를 대비해서 비상 연락처가 필요해요.
여 : 아, 알겠습니다.
남 : 새로 왔으니 학생이 원한다면 함께 다니며 체육관 시설을 소개해줄 수 있어요. 어떤 시설을 갖추고 있는지 알 수 있을 거예요. 새로 지은 체육관이라 모두 상태가 아주 좋아요. 수영장이라던가, 각종 운동기구 같은 것들 말이죠……
여 : 그렇게 해주시면 정말 좋겠어요. 제가 양식을 다 작성하고 나서 함께 둘러볼 수 있을까요?
남 : 저요? 전 데스크를 지켜야 해요, 대신 여기서 일하는 학생 트레이너를 불러드리죠. 지금 4명이 있는데, 한 명을 오라고 할게요.
여 : 좋아요. 그런데요... 운동은 어떡하죠? 전 역기 들기나 기계 사용에 대해서 아는 것이 거의 없어요. 운동을 잘못 하다가 다치고 싶지는 않아요.
남 : 걱정 말아요. 트레이너와 그 부분에 대해 이야기 해보도록 해요. 트레이너와 함께 하는 운동 시간을 잡을 수 있어요. 12명의 트레이너가 교대로 근무하고 있어요.
여 : 그러면 되겠네요. 질문이 하나 더 있는데요... 수영장을 이용하지 못하는 시간대가 따로 있나요?
남 : 잠깐만요... 아, 여기 스케줄 표를 참조하도록 해요. 수영부는 주로 다른 수영장을 이용하고 있으니까, 그 부분은 걱정 안 해도 될 겁니다.
여 : 제가 해야 하는 게 뭐 또 있나요?
남 : 운동을 할 때는 적당한 복장을 갖추는 것이 좋아요. 몸에 무리가 가지 않는 신발을 신도록 하고, 너무 헐렁하거나 꽉 끼지 않는 편안한 바지를 입고, 수영을 할 때는 적당한 수영복과 물안경을 준비하도록 해요. 나중에 보면 다 좋은 투자죠.
여 : 정말 친절하게 잘 알려주시네요. 도와주셔서 감사합니다!
남 : 별거 아닌걸요, 아 저기 트레이너가 오네요.

어휘 | lost 길 잃은 | gym 체육관 | emergency contact 비상 연락처 | in good shape 좋은 상태의 | equipment 장비 | lift weight 역기를 들다 | proper 적당한 | comfortable 편안한 | goggle 물안경 | investment 투자 | terrific 굉장한 |

[문제 6-11] 세계사 강의의 일부를 들으시오.

6. 교수는 주로 무엇에 관해 이야기 하고 있는가?
    Ⓐ 가황 처리법의 발명
    Ⓑ 중앙아메리카인들의 고무 사용
    Ⓒ 고무의 역사와 발달
    Ⓓ 고무 산업

해설 이 강의는 유럽인들이 고무를 발견하기 이전부터 중앙아메리카와 남아메리카에서 고무가 사용된 역사와
    그 이후의 고무의 발달에 관해 이야기 하고 있다. 따라서 정답은 보기 Ⓒ.

7. 파라고무 나무는 어떤 나라가 원산지인가?
    Ⓐ 인도네시아
    Ⓑ 브라질
    Ⓒ 포르투갈
    Ⓓ 나이지리아

해설 강의의 앞부분에서 파라고무 나무는 브라질이 원산지라고 하였다. 스크립트의 ‘it is native to Brazil’
    이란 부분을 질문지에서 ‘is indigenous to what country’로 paraphrase(바꾸어 쓰기)하여 물어보고
    있다. 정답은 보기 Ⓑ.

8. 강의에서, 교수는 중앙아메리카인과 남아메리카인의 초기 고무 사용에 대해 이야기 하고 있다. 아래 표
    의 각 보기가 이 쓰임새 중 하나인지 표시하시오. 각 보기에 맞는 칸에 클릭하시오.

	Yes	No
Ⓐ 풍선		
Ⓑ 방수 천		
Ⓒ 신발		
Ⓓ 타이어		
Ⓔ 공		

해설 중앙아메리카와 남아메리카에서는 기원전 1600년경부터 고무공을 이용한 스포츠를 즐겼고, 마야인들은
    고무 밑창을 댄 신발을 신었으며, 각종 도구의 손잡이에 고무를 이용했고, 방수 옷을 만들기도 하였다.
    따라서 정답은 보기 Ⓑ, Ⓒ, Ⓔ. 보기 Ⓐ의 풍선은 언급되지 않았고, 보기 Ⓓ의 타이어는 경화 방법이 발
    명되고 나서 만들어졌다.

강의의 일부를 다시 들으시오. 그러고 나서 질문에 답하시오.
*마야인들은 각종 도구의 손잡이에도 고무를 덧대었고 방수 옷을 만들기도 했죠. 다시 말하지만, 이런 것들은
그 당시 유럽인들의 생활 모습과는 완전히 다른 것으로, 유럽인들은 상상도 못하던 것이었어요. 방수 천 샘플
이 포르투갈에 가져가졌을 때, 마녀의 농간이라는 비난과 고발이 난무했죠!*

9. 교수가 이것을 말할 때 암시하는 것은 무엇인가?
    방수 천 샘플이 포르투갈에 가져가졌을 때, 마녀의 농간이라는 비난과 고발이 난무했죠!

Ⓐ 대부분의 유럽 기술은 중앙아메리카인의 발명에 기초하고 있다.
Ⓑ 유럽인들은 훌륭한 기술 개척자였으며, 다른 문명의 새로운 기술에 개방적이었다.
Ⓒ 유럽인들은 흔히 새로운 발명이 초자연력으로 인해 생겨나는 것이라고 생각했다.
Ⓓ 유럽인들은 다른 문명이 가지고 있던 기술을 훔쳐 그 기술을 자신들의 공로로 돌렸다.

해설 마야인들이 일상생활에 고무를 사용하던 당시 유럽인들은 이런 생활과는 거리가 멀었다고 하였다. 포르투갈인들이 새로운 물건을 처음 보고 마녀의 농간이라고 비난했다는 것은 이들이 다른 문명의 새로운 기술에 개방적이지 않았으며 악마와 마녀의 농간 등 초자연력이 존재한다고 믿었다는 것을 암시한다. 따라서 정답은 보기 Ⓒ.

10. 강의 내용에 따라, 고무에 관해 추론할 수 있는 것은 무엇인가?
Ⓐ 고무라는 이름은 고무의 특성 가운데 하나를 본떠 붙여졌다.
Ⓑ 생고무가 합성 고무보다 품질이 우수하다.
Ⓒ 고무 사용이 줄어들고 있다.
Ⓓ 고무는 유럽인들이 최초로 발견했다.

해설 강의 주제인 고무에 관해 추론할 수 있는 것을 묻는 문제이므로, 지문 내용을 전반적으로 이해하고 있어야 한다. 보기 Ⓐ를 확인하려면 고무의 이름이 언급된 부분을 스크립트에서 찾아보자. 스크립트의 3단락 첫 부분을 보면, 고무라는 명칭은 Joseph Priestley라는 사람이 연필 자국을 문질러 지우는 고무의 성질에 착안해 붙인 것이라 하였다. 이를 통해 고무라는 이름이 고무의 특성 가운데 하나를 본떠 붙여진 것이라고 추론할 수 있다. 따라서 정답은 보기 Ⓐ. 보기 Ⓑ의 합성 고무는 언급된 바가 없고, 보기 Ⓒ 역시 언급된 적이 없고, 보기 Ⓓ는 강의 내용과 일치하지 않는다.

11. 고무를 화학물과 섞고 가열하여 강화하는 처리법의 이름은 무엇인가?
Ⓐ 가황 처리법
Ⓑ 껍질 뚫기
Ⓒ 채집하기
Ⓓ 응고 작용

해설 강의의 마지막 부분에서 가황 처리법이 소개되면서 고무가 상업적으로 널리 쓰이게 되었다고 하였다. 고무를 화학물과 섞고 이 혼합물을 가열하여 강화하는 처리법이 바로 가황 처리법이다. 정답은 보기 Ⓐ.

🎧 [Questions 6-11] Listen to part of a lecture in a world history class.

P(M) : Everyone's ready? All right, as I told you last class, today we're going to take a look at one of the modern essentials, rubber. In scientific terms, it is an elastic hydrocarbon polymer that we derive from the sap of certain plant species. The primary source of rubber sap is from the Para rubber tree, which is in the Euphorbia genus. From the Latin name, you can probably guess that it is native to Brazil. Well, a wound in the bark of the rubber tree produces more sap... and that's how people discovered that they could cultivate rubber and harvest sap and put it to practical use.

Do you think rubber is a recent invention? Well, some of you might be surprised to hear this, but, uh, the ancient civilizations of Central and South America played sports using rubber balls as long ago as 1600 B.C., according to radiocarbon dating. In fact, the Spanish Conquistadores were shocked at the way the balls would bounce – because they had never seen anything like them in Europe – that they thought demons must be involved. And the Maya were arguably the inventors of rubber-soled shoes: they'd dip their feet into liquid rubber and let it dry. They put rubber to other intelligent uses, such as grips for tool handles and uh, making waterproof cloth. Again, these were developments far beyond what the Europeans were doing at the time. When samples of this waterproof cloth were brought back to Portugal, there were accusations of witchcraft!

Actually, the name rubber came along much later, in 1770, when a man named Joseph Priestley noticed that rubber could be used as an eraser. It was good at rubbing out pencil marks. The name stuck. Rubber production spread quickly around the world, after its discovery by Europeans. One large batch of seeds went from Brazil to England in 1876. From there, the British Empire dispatched rubber seeds throughout its tropical colonies, to the places that are now Sri Lanka, Indonesia, Singapore, Malaysia, India, and Nigeria, among others.

Now, when it comes to the rubber harvesting techniques, well, they are fairly standard: the plantation worker pierces the tree bark with a sharp, hollow stick, and allows latex to drip into a container overnight. The sap from many trees is mixed with a coagulant, usually formic acid, which causes the rubber molecules to clump together. These clumps of rubber are flattened into sheets and sent off to factories to be processed. Rubber really became useful commercially when vulcanization was invented by Charles Goodyear in 1839. This was a process that involved mixing rubber with chemicals like sulfur and heating and strengthening it. Vulcanization made rubber suitable for use in tires and other products that required more durability.

Now get ready to answer the questions. You may use your notes to help you answer.

Listen again to part of the lecture. Then answer the question.
They put rubber to other intelligent uses, such as grips for tool handles and uh, making waterproof cloth. Again, these were developments far beyond what the Europeans were doing at the time. When samples of this waterproof cloth were brought back to Portugal, there were accusations of witchcraft!

9. What does the professor imply when he says this: 🎧
When samples of this waterproof cloth were brought back to Portugal, there were accusations of witchcraft!

P : 모두들 준비됐죠? 좋아요, 지난 시간에 말한 대로, 오늘은 현대 사회의 필수품 가운데 하나인 고무에 대해 살펴보겠어요. 과학 용어로 고무는 특정 식물 종의 수액에서 얻어지는 탄성이 있는 탄화수소 중합체이죠. 고무 수액은 주로 등대풀 속에 속하는 파라고무 나무에서 나죠. 라틴어 명칭으로 볼 때, 이 나무는 브라질이 원산이란 걸 알 수 있을 거예요. 고무 나무 껍질을 벗기면 더 많은 수액이 나오죠... 이를 보고 사람들이 고무나무를 심어서 수액을 채취하여 실용화하게 되었어요.
여러분은 고무가 최근에 발명된 것이라고 생각하나요? 이 이야기를 듣고 놀라는 사람들도 있을 텐데요, 방사성 탄소에 의한 연대 측정 결과를 보면 기원전 1600년경에 중앙아메리카와 남아메리카에서 발생한 고대 문명인들이 고무공을 이용하여 스포츠를 즐겼다고 해요. 사실, 스페인 정복자들은 유럽에서는 고무공 같은 것을 본 적이 없었기 때문에 공이 튀는 모습을 보고 너무 놀라 악마가 꾸민 짓이라고 생각하기도 했어요. 또 마야인들은 논란의 여지는 있지만 최초로 고무 밑창을 덧댄 신발을 만들어 신었는데, 신을 신은 발을 고무 액체에 담근 후에 말렸어요. 마야인들은 각종 도구의 손잡이에도 고무를 덧대었고 방수 옷을 만들기도 했죠. 다시 말하지만, 이런 것들은 그 당시 유럽인들의 생활 모습과는 완전히 다른 것으로, 유럽인들은 상상도 못하던 것이었어요. 방수 천 샘플이 포르투갈에 가져가졌을 때, 마녀의 농간이라는 비난과 고발이 난무했죠!

음, 고무(rubber)라는 이름은 훨씬 나중인 1770년에 붙여졌는데, Joseph Priestley(조셉 프리슬리)라는 남자가 고무를 지우개로 사용할 수 있다는 걸 알게 되었죠. 고무는 연필 자국을 문질러 지우는데(rubbing out) 탁월했어요. 그래서 그 이름이 붙여지게 된 거죠. 유럽인들이 고무를 발견한 후에는 전 세계로 고무 생산이 빠르게 퍼져나갔어요. 1876년에 브라질에서 많은 양의 고무나무 종자가 영국으로 들여져 왔죠. 영국인들은 영국으로 들여온 이 종자를 영국의 열대 식민지 전역으로 보급했는데, 지금의 스리랑카와 인도네시아, 싱가포르, 말레이시아, 인도, 나이지리아 같은 곳들이죠.

자, 고무 채취 과정에 대해 이야기 해보자면, 음, 채취 과정은 꽤 표준적이죠. 고무 농장 인부가 끝이 날카롭고 속이 비어있는 막대로 나무껍질에 구멍을 내어 고무 유액이 흘러나오게 하고, 이 유액이 밤새도록 용기에 떨어져 내리도록 해요. 나무에서 얻어진 수액은 대개는 포름산인 응고제를 넣고 섞는데, 이렇게 하면 고무 분자가 응고하게 되는 것이죠. 이 응고한 고무 덩어리가 납작하게 압축되어 가공 처리를 위해 공장으로 보내집니다. 고무는 Charles Goodyear(찰스 굿이어)가 1839년에 가황 처리법을 고안해냄으로써 상업적으로 널리 쓰이게 되었어요. 가황 처리법은 고무를 황과 같은 화학물과 결합시킨 후, 이 혼합물을 가열하여 강하게 만드는 가공법이에요. 이 가황 처리법을 이용하여 고무는 타이어와 기타 내구성이 필요한 제품에 적합하게 쓰이게 되었죠.

어휘 | essential 필수적인 것 | term 용어 | elastic 탄성이 있는 | hydrocarbon 탄화수소 | polymer 중합체 | derive 얻다, 유래하다 | sap 수액 | primary 주요한 | source 원천 | genus 속 | native to ~가 원산인 | wound 상처 | bark 나무껍질 | cultivate 심다, 경작하다 | put A to use A를 사용하다, 이용하다 | recent 최근의 | invention 발명 | civilization 문명 | radiocarbon dating 방사성 탄소에 의한 연대 측정 | Conquistador 신대륙 정복자(16세기에 멕시코와 페루를 정복한 스페인 사람) | bounce 튀다 | demon 악마 | arguably 논란의 여지가 있는 | sole 밑창 | dip 담그다 | liquid 액체 | grip 손잡이 | waterproof 방수의 | beyond ~의 범위를 넘어서 | accusation 비난, 고발 | witchcraft 마법, 마력 | eraser 지우개 | rub out 문질러 지우다 | batch 한 묶음, 일단 | seed 씨앗, 종자 | dispatch 발송하다, 급파하다 | fairly 꽤, 상당히 | plantation 농원, 플랜테이션 | pierce 뚫다, 찌르다 | hollow 속이 텅 빈 | latex 유액 | drip 방울이 떨어지다 | coagulant 응고제 | formic acid 포름산 | clump 응고하다, 덩어리 | flatten 압축하다, 평평하게 하다 | process 가공하다 | commercially 상업적으로 | vulcanization 가황 처리, 경화 처리 | chemical 화학물 | sulfur 유황 | suitable 적합한 | durability 내구성 |

Review

1. 1. 그만두다 2. 승인 3. 유창함 4. 개요 5. 수수께끼 같은 6. 임금 7. 통계 8. 발급하다 9. 일손이 부족한 10. 제출하다 11. experiment 12. rusty 13. reference 14. atmosphere 15. diameter 16. expand 17. erupt 18. rare 19. periodically 20. inevitable

2. 1. as a matter of fact 실은 2. benefit from ~에서 이득을 얻다 3. come by 들르다 4. run out of ~을 다 써 버리다 5. out of print 절판된 6. result from ~에서 생겨나다 7. beyond expression 형용할 수 없는 8. so to speak 이를테면 9. come to an end 끝나다 10. work out 운동하다

3. 1. proper 2. accusations 3. accompanied 4. intervention 5. compare 6. subtitled
해석 | 1. 운동을 할 때는 적당한 복장을 갖추는 것이 좋아요.
2. 방수 천 샘플이 포르투갈에 가져가졌을 때, 마녀의 농간이라는 비난과 고발이 난무했죠!
3. 안타깝게도 이런 호황기 뒤에는 재화의 가격이 인상하는 인플레이션이 뒤따르게 되요.
4. 일부에서는 정부가 경제 활동에 적극 개입해야 한다고 말하고, 또 다른 측에서는 정부의 개입이 상황을 더 악화시킬 뿐이라고 말하죠.
5. 제가 하고 싶은 건 미국 중소 도시의 임금을 살펴보고 부동산 가격과 비교해보는 거예요.
6. 나쁘지는 않네요, 그런데 문제는 강의 시간에 보게 되는 영화에는 자막이 들어있지 않아요.

Chapter 3 Inference

Office Hours

1. Ⓑ 2. Ⓐ 3. Ⓒ

1. 대화가 끝나고 나서 학생은 무엇을 할 것 같은가?
Ⓐ 결정하기 전에 교수에게 다시 한 번 조언을 더 구할 것이다.
Ⓑ 경비를 충당할 방법을 찾아볼 것이다.
Ⓒ 인턴 근무를 한 학기 미룰 것이다.
Ⓓ 아르바이트를 더 할 것이다.

Dictation | ① in a predicament ② it doesn't pay much ③ my tuition and all my expenses
④ find a way to do it ⑤ some kind of raise ⑥ I'll look into it

남 : 제가 좀 곤란한 상황에 처했는데, 조언 좀 해주시겠어요?
여 : 그래, 무슨 일이니?
남 : 제가 Washington D.C.에 있는 국립 미술관의 인턴 근무를 제의 받았는데요, 보수가 적어요. 정말 좋은 기회이긴 하지만, 생활비와 학비, 기타 경비 등을 어떻게 충당할지 모르겠어요.
여 : 어머, 그래도 정말 굉장한 곳이잖니. 네가 그 곳에서 인턴으로 근무하기를 고대했었잖아.
남 : 네, 그랬죠. 그런데 지금은 어떡해야 할지 잘 모르겠어요. 나중에 제 경력에 큰 도움이 되겠지만, 재정 문제가 정말 걱정되거든요.
여 : 내 생각엔 그 일을 할 수 있는 방법을 찾아봐야 할 것 같구나. 가족에게 도움을 받거나, 학자금 대출과에 알아보거나, 국립 미술관 인사부에도 알아보거나. 네 상황을 설명하고, 음, 보수를 좀 올려줄 수 있는지 알아볼 수도 있잖니?
남 : 보수를 올려주는 그런 일은 일어날 것 같지 않아요.
여 : 해 보기 전까지는 모를 일이란다.
남 : 교수님 말씀이 맞아요, 한 번 알아볼게요. 감사합니다!

2. 다음 중 학생에 관해 추론할 수 있는 것은?
   Ⓐ 오늘 수업 시간에 결석할 것이다.
   Ⓑ 발목이 제대로 낫지 않아서 수술을 해야 한다.
   Ⓒ 제출 기한이 지났기 때문에 리포트를 다시 써야 한다.
   Ⓓ 진료 예약 시간을 바꿀 것이다.

Dictation | ① can I interrupt you ② to turn in my paper ③ make it to class ④ the weather's getting cold ⑤ it healed right way ⑥ have to live with

여 : Banks 교수님, 잠시 뵐 수 있을까요?
남 : 그래, 어서 들어오렴. 무슨 일이니?
여 : 리포트를 제출하려고 왔습니다. 오늘 수업 시간까지 제출하라고 하셨어요.
남 : 그래. 그럼 그 때 제출하지 그러니?
여 : 그게 말이죠, 오늘 오후에 병원에 가야 해서 수업에 못 갈 것 같아요.
남 : 아픈 건 아니지? 다 괜찮니?
여 : 괜찮아요. 지난 학기에 발목을 다쳤는데 날이 추워지니까 좀 아파서요. 엑스레이를 찍어보고 다 나았는지 확인하려고 해요.
남 : 그렇구나. 큰 일이 아니었으면 좋겠구나.
여 : 앞으로 계속 겪어야 할 일들 가운데 하나겠죠.
남 : 그래. 행운을 빌게.

3. 대화를 통해 학생에 관해 추론할 수 있는 것은 무엇인가?
   Ⓐ 특별 점수를 받는 것에는 관심이 없다.
   Ⓑ 리포트를 잘 썼다고 생각했다.
   Ⓒ 사람들 앞에서 발표를 많이 해본 적이 없다.
   Ⓓ 자신에게 무대 공포증이 있다고 생각해본 적이 없다.

Dictation | ① keep it short ② give a presentation in class ③ I'm really flattered ④ be a great illustration ⑤ give it a try

여 : 수업이 끝나고 남아줘서 고맙구나. 짧게 얘기하도록 할게.
남 : 왠지 안 좋은 일인 것 같네요.
여 : 겁난다고? 그런 게 아니라, 무대 공포증에 관해서 쓴 네 리포트가 정말 잘 쓰여져서, 다음 수업 시간에 네가 발표를 했으면 해.
남 : 아... 감사합니다! 과찬이세요, 그런데... 발표요? 제가 잘할 수 있을지 모르겠어요.
여 : 너도 무대 공포증 같은 것이 있니?
남 : 네! 그래서 제가 그 주제로 리포트를 쓴 거예요.

어휘 | scary 무서운 | anxiety 걱정, 불안 | flatter 우쭐하게 하다 | illustration 실례, 예증 | credit 점수 |

Service Encounters

1. Ⓑ　**2.** Ⓒ　**3.** Ⓐ

1. 대화를 통해 학생에 관해 결론 내릴 수 있는 것은 무엇인가?
　Ⓐ 유럽을 제외한 다른 지역을 알아볼 것이다.
　Ⓑ 학생은 알바니아에서 진행되는 프로그램을 선택할 것이다.
　Ⓒ 다양한 분야에서 활동할 수 있는 몰도바로 갈 것이다.
　Ⓓ 이 부서에서 더 많은 정보를 요청할 것이다.

Dictation | ① more about the volunteer programs　② something helpful over the summer
　　　　　　③ at an English literacy program　④ open to more subjects　⑤ double-majoring in

어휘 | volunteer 자원봉사 | helpful 도움이 되는 | literacy 읽고 쓸 줄 앎 | subject 과목, 분야 |
　　double-major 복수전공하다 | brochure 소책자 |

2. 대화를 통해 학생에 관해 추론할 수 있는 것은 무엇인가?
  Ⓐ BIO221 수강을 포기할 것이다.
  Ⓑ 남자에게 대기자 명단에 올려달라고 요청할 것이다.
  Ⓒ Yuen 교수의 수업에 수강신청 할 것이다.
  Ⓓ 생물학 수업은 아무것도 듣지 않을 것이다.

Dictation ┃ ① figure out how to get into ② there's a waiting list ③ there's one slot left ④ fit
              into your schedule

여 : Winerock 교수님의 보존 생물학 수업을 듣고 싶은데, 컴퓨터를 확인해보니 이미 인원이 찼다고 나
      와요.
남 : 강의 번호가 뭐죠?
여 : BIO338이에요.
남 : 맞아요, 그 수업은 이미 인원이 찬데다 이미 5명의 학생이 대기자 명단에 올라 있어요.
여 : 그럼 안 되는데. 방법이 없을까요?
남 : BIO221이란 환경 과학 수업에서 비슷한 내용을 다뤄요. 어디 보자... Yuen 교수님이 가르치는 수업
      이네요.
여 : 그 분을 알아요. 제 친구가 전에 그 분 강의를 들었는데, 그 분의 강의가 좋다는 얘기를 들어본 적이
      있어요. 그걸 들을 수 있을 것 같아요. 자리가 있나요?
남 : 네, 한 자리가 남아있네요. 학생의 스케줄에도 맞을 거예요.

어휘 ┃ figure out 이해하다, 알아내다 ┃ conservation 보존 ┃ ahead of ~에 앞서 ┃ opening 빈자리 ┃
          slot 자리, 지위 ┃ fit into ~에 들어맞다 ┃

3. 대화를 통해 데이터베이스 기록에 관해 결론 내릴 수 있는 것은 무엇인가?
  Ⓐ 뭔가 착오가 있는 것 같다.
  Ⓑ 가을 방학 이후에 데이터베이스가 업데이트 되었다.
  Ⓒ 다른 기숙사에 해당하는 기록이다.
  Ⓓ 기록이 확실히 맞다.

Dictation ┃ ① vacating my dorm room ② the procedure for that ③ there aren't any fines or
              late fees ④ hang on ⑤ at fall break ⑥ go upstairs and you inspect ⑦ take it
              easy

여 : 이번 학기 기숙사 방을 비울 예정인데요. 어떤 절차를 거쳐야 하나요?
남 : 학생이 방을 비우고 나면 내가 가서 방을 점검하고 카드 키를 수거기만 하면 됩니다. 그리고 컴퓨터
      조회를 해서 벌금이나 연체료 같은 게 없는지 확인해야 하죠... 음, 말이 나온 김에, 지금 하도록 할
      까요? 컴퓨터가 켜져 있으니까요. 학생 이름이 뭐죠?
여 : Blair Waldorf입니다.
남 : 잠깐만요…….
여 : 다 괜찮은가요?
남 : 음, 기록을 보니까 미수금이 있는 것 같군요. 의자가 없어졌다고 나오네요.

어휘 | vacate 비우다, 퇴거하다 | procedure 절차 | inspect 검사하다, 점검하다 | empty 빈 | collect 수거하다, 모으다 | fine 벌금 | late fee 연체료 | outstanding 미결제의 | missing 분실한 | upstairs 위층 |

Lectures

1. 1) Ⓐ 2) Ⓒ **2.** 1) Ⓒ 2) Ⓓ **3.** 1) Ⓒ 2) Ⓒ 3) Ⓑ

1. 조류학 수업

1. 다음 중 어느 것이 바우어(둥지)에 관해 사실일 것 같은가?
   Ⓐ 새들의 개인적인 취향 때문에 각각의 바우어는 모양이 다르다.
   Ⓑ 바우어를 꾸미는 물건의 배열은 임의적이다.
   Ⓒ 장식용 물건 대부분은 먹을 수 있는 것이다.
   Ⓓ 거의 모든 바우어가 복잡한 구조를 가지고 있다.

2. 강의 내용에 따라, 수컷 바우어새에 관해 추론할 수 있는 것은 무엇인가?
   Ⓐ 짝짓기 의식 동안 조용하다.
   Ⓑ 깃털 색깔이 화려하다.
   Ⓒ 시각 기억력이 좋다.
   Ⓓ 모든 수컷이 암컷에 의해 선택된다.

Dictation | ① worthy of some note ② indigenous to the tropical parts ③ their mating ritual ④ its own distinguished characteristics ⑤ elaborate and sophisticated ⑥ sneak in and move something ⑦ looks around each bower ⑧ part of courtship rituals

어휘 | be worthy of note 주목할 만하다 | courtship 구애(행동) | ritual 의식 | weird 이상한 | indigenous to ~가 원산인 | peculiar 특이한 | decorate 장식하다 | nest 둥지 | distinguished 두드러진 | fairly 꽤 | plain 단순한, 간소한 | earth 흙 | twig 나뭇가지 | elaborate 정교한 | sophisticated 정교한, 복잡한 | stack 쌓다 | arrangement 배열 | object 물건 | berry 딸기류의 열매 | shell 조개껍질 | feather 깃털 | sneak in 몰래 들어오다, 서성대다 |

2. 세계사 수업

1. 나폴레옹과 현대 이탈리아의 관계에 대해 교수가 암시하는 것은 무엇인가?
   Ⓐ 나폴레옹은 이탈리아의 군제를 현대화했다.
   Ⓑ 나폴레옹은 피할 수도 있었던 유혈사태를 일으켰다.
   Ⓒ 나폴레옹은 이탈리아가 통일되게 하였다.
   Ⓓ 나폴레옹은 교황보다 훨씬 덜 중요한 인물이었다.

2. 교수가 나폴레옹에 관해 암시하지 않는 것은?
   Ⓐ 나폴레옹은 정보 수집이 전쟁 승리의 핵심이라고 생각했다.
   Ⓑ 나폴레옹은 기습공격을 하는 것으로 유명했다.
   Ⓒ 나폴레옹은 포병과 보병 둘 모두의 중요성을 알고 있었다.
   Ⓓ 나폴레옹은 대 영국, 러시아, 오스트리아 전쟁을 승리로 이끌었다.

Dictation | ① the great military leaders of history ② compare with his military accomplishments ③ which was sold to France ④ It should be no surprise ⑤ merged a number of them ⑥ an extensive knowledge of military strategy ⑦ put more emphasis on ⑧ concealing his troops and striking ⑨ manage to capture ⑩ in a coup ⑪ decades of wars against

어휘 | compare with ~에 필적하다 | accomplishment 업적 | surpass ~를 능가하다 | in that regard 그 점에 있어서는 | general 장군 | genius 특출한 재능 | elevate 높이다, 의기양양하게 하다 | prominence 탁월, 걸출함 | invasion 침략 | unify 통일하다, 단일화하다 | independent 독립된 | merge 합병하다, 병합하다 | predecessor 전임자, 조상 | battle 전투 | artillery 포병 | infantry 보병 | conceal 숨기다, 감추다 | embark on ~에 착수하다 | coup 쿠데타 | contract 줄어들다, 수축하다 |

3. 연극 수업

1. 교수는 주로 무엇에 관해 이야기 하고 있는가?
  Ⓐ Sidney Howard의 너무 이른 죽음(요절)
  Ⓑ Sidney Howard가 주로 다루었던 주제
  Ⓒ 극작가로서의 Sidney Howard의 삶
  Ⓓ Sidney Howard의 많은 재능

강의의 일부를 다시 들으시오. 그러고 나서 질문에 답하시오.

2. 교수가 이것을 말할 때 암시하는 것은 무엇인가:
  여러분이 위대한 미국 극작가를 떠올릴 때, Sidney Howard가 가장 먼저 떠오르지는 않죠?

  Ⓐ 학생들은 Sidney Howard에 관해 더 잘 알고 있었어야 했다.
  Ⓑ Sidney Howard는 생전에 작품을 많이 쓰지 않았다.
  Ⓒ 많은 학생들이 Sidney Howard와 그의 작품을 잘 모르고 있다.
  Ⓓ Sidney Howard는 호평을 받지 못했다.

3. Sidney Howard에 관해 추론할 수 있는 것은 무엇인가?
  Ⓐ 영화 시나리오 작가로 더 잘 알려져 있었다.
  Ⓑ 프랑스어에 능통했다.
  Ⓒ 생전에 퓰리처 상과 아카데미 상을 받았다.
  Ⓓ 코미디물에 관심이 많았다.

Listen again to part of the lecture. Then answer the question.

What does the professor imply when he says this: 🎧
When you think about the great American playwrights, Sidney Howard probably isn't the first name that enters your mind, is it?

P : 여러분이 위대한 미국 극작가를 떠올릴 때, Sidney Howard(시드니 하워드)가 가장 먼저 떠오르지는 않죠? 오늘은 이 작가에 관해 이야기 해볼까 해요, 왜냐하면 Sidney Howard라는 이름이 사람들이 흔히 알고 있는 이름은 아니지만, 그렇게 되어야 하기 때문이죠. 1891년에 태어나 1939년에 생을 마감한 Howard는 퓰리처 상과 아카데미 상을 모두 수상한 최초의 작가였어요. 여러 언어를 유창하게 구사할 줄 알았고, 후에는 번역가가 되었죠. 특히 그는 프랑스 극작가인 Charles Vildrac과 Rene Fauchois를 좋아했고, 그들의 작품을 영어로 번안해서 인기를 얻었어요. 그 즈음에는 이미 본인의 작품으로 비평가들의 호평을 받고 있었어요. 1924년에 발표된 '그들은 무엇을 원하는지 알고 있었다(They Knew What They Wanted)'와 같은 희곡은 사람들의 관심을 불러일으켰죠. Howard는 온정적이고 동정적인 작풍으로 사회 문제를 다루었어요. 작품 속 등장인물에 도덕적 판단을 주입시키는 대신, 더 큰 관점을 가지고 등장인물을 그냥 결점이 있는 인간으로 보았어요, 우리 모습이 그런 것처럼요. 20년대 후반부터 30년대 본인의 작품으로 큰 인기와 성공을 누렸고, 브로드웨이와 런던에서 상연된 작품은 매진되기도 했고요. Howard는 1939년에 사고로 비극적인 죽음을 맞이하죠. 바로 그 해에 '바람과 함께 사라지다(Gone with the Wind)'를 시나리오로 각색하여 사후에 아카데미 상을 받았어요. 뛰어난 재능을 가진 많은 훌륭한 작가들과 예술가들이 요절을 했는데, Sidney Howard 역시 이런 경우죠. Howard의 요절로 미국의 극문학계는 큰 손실을 입었다고 할 수 있어요.

어휘 | playwright 극작가 | household name 흔히 쓰는 말, 일반화된 용어 | translator 번역가 | adaptation 번안, 각색 | warm-hearted 인정이 있는, 온정의 | sympathetic 동정적인 | flawed 결점이 있는 | sold-out 매진된 | tragically 비극적으로 | posthumously 사후에 |

Practice

[1-5] 1. Ⓑ   2. Ⓐ   3. Ⓒ   4. Ⓓ   5. Mentioned – Ⓐ, Ⓓ, Ⓔ Not Mentioned – Ⓑ, Ⓒ
[6-11] 6. Ⓓ   7. Ⓓ   8. Yes – Ⓑ, Ⓓ, Ⓔ No – Ⓐ, Ⓒ   9. Ⓒ   10. Ⓐ   11. Ⓒ

[문제 1-5] 학생과 캠퍼스 경비 직원 사이의 대화의 일부를 들으시오.

1. 남자는 무슨 문제를 가지고 있는가?
Ⓐ 강의실에서 귀중품을 잃어버렸다.
Ⓑ 기숙사에서 자신과 룸메이트의 물건을 도난당했다.
Ⓒ 룸메이트가 자신의 소지품을 훔쳤다.
Ⓓ 기숙사에서 물건을 훔쳐서 체포되었다.

해설 남자가 찾아온 이유는 기숙사 방에 누군가 침입해서 물건을 훔쳐 갔기 때문에 도난 신고를 하러 온 것이다. 따라서 정답은 보기 ⑧.

대화의 일부를 다시 들으시오. 그리고 나서 질문에 답하시오.
여 : 그렇다니 다행이군요. 왜 여기로 전화를 하지 않았어요?
남 : 어, 전화번호를 몰랐어요. 알았다면 휴대폰으로 전화를 했을 거예요. 뭐, 어쨌든 가까우니까요. 이렇게 직접 오면, 전화상으로 기다릴 필요는 없잖아요.

2. 남자가 이것을 말할 때 암시하고 있는 것은 무엇인가: 🎧
    남 : 뭐, 어쨌든 가까우니까요. 이렇게 직접 오면, 전화상으로 기다릴 필요는 없잖아요.

   Ⓐ 직접 찾아와 신고하는 것이 전화하는 것보다 더 빠르다.
   Ⓑ 직원이 기숙사에 들렀어야 한다.
   Ⓒ 전화번호를 기억하고 있을 필요가 없다.
   Ⓓ 휴대폰을 별로 사용하지 않는다.

해설 왜 전화로 신고하지 않았느냐는 직원의 질문에 학생은 전화번호를 몰라서 못했다고 말하면서도, 가깝기 때문에 직접 찾아오면 전화상으로 오래 기다리지는 않아도 된다고 말하였다. 이 말은 직접 찾아와 신고하는 것이 전화상으로 신고하는 것보다 더 접수가 빠르다는 것을 암시하고 있다. 따라서 정답은 보기 Ⓐ.

3. 다음 중 도난당한 물품이 아닌 것은?
    Ⓐ 컴퓨터
    Ⓑ 음악 플레이어
    Ⓒ 휴대 전화
    Ⓓ 책

해설 학생이 도난 물품으로 언급한 것은 컴퓨터와 MP3 플레이어, CD, DVD, 교재이다. 보기 Ⓒ의 휴대 전화 (cell phones)는 도난 물품으로 언급된 것이 아니라, 전화번호를 몰라서 전화로 신고를 하지 못했다는 것을 설명하기 위해 언급되었다. 따라서 정답은 보기 Ⓒ.

대화의 일부를 다시 들으시오. 그리고 나서 질문에 답하시오.
남 : 어떻게 이런 일이 있는지 모르겠어요. 우리한테 이런 일이 일어나다니 믿을 수가 없어요!
여 : 학생의 심정은 잘 알아요. 정말 일어나서는 안 되는 일이죠. 캠퍼스를 안전하게 지키기 위해 최선을 다하고 있지만, 가끔씩 나쁜 사람들이 이런 행동을 저지르죠, 우리가 아무리 노력을 해도 말이에요.

4. 여자가 이것을 말할 때 도난 사고에 관해 어떻게 생각하고 있는 것 같은가: 🎧
    여 : 학생의 심정은 잘 알아요. 정말 일어나서는 안 되는 일이죠. 캠퍼스를 안전하게 지키기 위해 최선을 다하고 있지만, 가끔씩 나쁜 사람들이 이런 행동을 저지르죠, 우리가 아무리 노력을 해도 말이에요.

   Ⓐ 여자는 학교 측에서 학생들을 보호하기 위해 모든 것을 했다고 생각한다.
   Ⓑ 여자는 학생들을 돕는데 관심이 없다.
   Ⓒ 여자는 학생들에게도 어느 정도 책임이 있다고 생각한다.
   Ⓓ 여자는 유감으로 생각하며, 어느 정도 책임감을 느끼고 있다.

해설 학생이 왜 이런 일이 일어났는지 도무지 모르겠다고 하자, 여자는 학생의 심정을 이해한다고 말하면서, 최선을 다함에도 불구하고 안 좋은 일들이 가끔씩 일어난다고 이야기 하고 있다. 따라서 여자는 도난 사고가 발생한 것을 유감으로 생각하며, 책임감을 느끼고 있음을 알 수 있다. 정답은 보기 ⓓ.

5. 대화에서, 캠퍼스 경비 직원은 학생에게 앞으로 무슨 일이 일어날지 말하고 있다. 아래 표의 각 보기가 여자가 언급한 사항에 속하는지 표시하시오. 각 보기에 맞는 칸에 클릭하시오.

	Mentioned	Not Mentioned
ⓐ 시 경찰이 학생과 그의 룸메이트와 이야기를 나눌 것이다		
ⓑ 캠퍼스 경비 직원이 학생의 교수에게 전화를 할 것이다		
ⓒ 학생과 그의 룸메이트는 가족과 함께 지내야 한다		
ⓓ 가족들이 보험 배상을 청구해야 한다		
ⓔ 잠금 장치가 교체될 것이다		

해설 직원이 학생에게 앞으로 일어날 일과 해야 할 일로 언급한 것은 경비 직원이 기숙사에 함께 가보는 것과, 시 경찰이 기숙사를 방문하는 것, 도난당한 물품 목록을 작성하는 것, 가족에게 연락해서 보험 처리를 하는 것, 잠금 장치를 교체하는 것, 교수에게 제출할 확인서를 써 주는 것이다. 이에 해당하지 않는 것은 보기 ⓑ와 ⓒ이다. 정답은 보기 ⓐ, ⓓ, ⓔ.

🎧 [Questions 1–5] Listen to part of a conversation between a student and a campus security officer.

W : Can I help you? You look pretty upset.

M : Yes, I just came straight here from my dorm. Somebody broke into my room and stole a lot of stuff. My roommate's there right now.

W : Oh, nobody's got hurt?

M : Fortunately, no.

W : That's good to hear. Why didn't you call us?

M : Um, I didn't know the number. Otherwise I'd have called from my cell phone. Anyway, it's close by. This way, I wouldn't have to wait on hold.

W : OK, no problem. Can you tell me what was taken?

M : As far as I know, both of our computers were taken. My roommate has a new desktop system and I have a – had a – laptop that was a couple of years old. Um, what else... his MP3 player, all our CDs and DVDs, some textbooks. I'm not sure.

W : I'm so sorry to hear that. Look, I'll tell you what we need to do. First, I'll get a security officer to go back to the dorm with you. I'll call the metropolitan police now, too, and ask that an officer meet you at the room as well. You and your roommate will need to make a list of everything that's missing.

M : This is so awful. I can't believe this happened to us!

W : I know. It's really terrible. We try really hard to provide a secure campus but sometimes bad people do things like this, despite our best efforts.

M : Of course you do. I know that. Um, is there anything else we should do?

W : Yes. You might as well contact your families. You ought to be covered by their insurance policies, and your parents will need to file claims so you can get your stuff replaced.

M : I'll do that. And will someone change the locks on our doors?

W : Yes, that will be done tonight. You'll have new keys before you go to sleep. And we'll give you notes for your professors, in case you've lost any assignments when your PCs were stolen.

M : OK, thanks for your help. I guess I'd better get back to my room.

W : Good luck, and I'm sorry!

Now get ready to answer the questions. You may use your notes to help you answer.

Listen again to part of the conversation. Then answer the question.

W : That's good to hear. Why didn't you call us?

M : Um, I didn't know the number. Otherwise I'd have called from my cell phone. Anyway, it's close by. This way, I wouldn't have to wait on hold.

2. What does the man imply when he says this: 🎧

   M : Anyway, it's close by. This way, I wouldn't have to wait on hold.

Listen again to part of the conversation. Then answer the question.

M : This is so awful. I can't believe this happened to us!

W : I know. It's really terrible. We try really hard to provide a secure campus but sometimes bad people do things like this, despite our best efforts.

4. How does the woman seem to feel about the situation when she says this: 🎧

   W : I know. It's really terrible. We try really hard to provide a secure campus but sometimes bad people do things like this, despite our best efforts.

여 : 무엇을 도와줄까요? 뭔가 안 좋은 일이 있는 것 같군요.

남 : 네, 지금 기숙사에서 곧장 오는 길이에요. 우리 방에 누군가 침입해서 물건들을 훔쳐갔어요. 지금 제 룸메이트가 거기 있어요.

여 : 저런, 다친 사람은 아무도 없나요?

남 : 다행히도 아무도 안 다쳤어요.

여 : 그렇다니 다행이군요. 왜 여기로 전화를 하지 않았어요?

남 : 어, 전화번호를 몰랐어요. 알았다면 휴대폰으로 전화를 했을 거예요. 뭐, 어쨌든 가까우니까요. 이렇게 직접 오면, 전화상으로 기다릴 필요는 없잖아요.

여 : 알겠어요. 도난당한 물품이 무엇이죠?

남 : 지금까지 알고 있는 건, 저랑 제 룸메이트의 컴퓨터가 모두 없어졌어요. 룸메이트는 새 데스크톱 컴퓨터를 가지고 있고, 저는 한 2년 정도 된 노트북을 가지고 있어요, 아니 가지고 있었죠. 그리고 또... 룸메이트의 MP3 플레이어랑 CD, DVD, 그리고 교재들도요. 아직 잘 모르겠어요.

여 : 소지품을 많이 잃어버렸다니 유감이네요. 앞으로 무엇을 해야 하는지 알려주도록 할게요. 먼저, 우리 경비직원이 학생과 함께 기숙사로 가보도록 하죠. 시 경찰국에도 지금 전화를 해서 경찰이 학생의 방을 방문하도록 할게요. 학생과 룸메이트는 없어진 모든 물건의 목록을 작성해야 합니다.

어휘 | straight 곧바로 | break into ~에 침입하다 | steal 훔치다 | stuff 물건 | fortunately 다행히 | close by 바로 곁에 | on hold 통화하기를 기다리고 있는, 보류 상태의 | metropolitan police 시 경찰서 | awful 심한 피해가 있는 | terrible 가혹한, 무시무시한 | secure 안전한 | despite ~에도 불구하고 | effort 노력 | insurance policy 보험, 보험 증권 | file claim 배상을 청구하다 |

[문제 6–11] 교육학 강의의 일부를 들으시오.

6. 교수는 주로 무엇에 관해 이야기 하고 있는가?
    Ⓐ 마리아 몬테소리의 삶
    Ⓑ 이탈리아의 다양한 교육 방식
    Ⓒ 유년기 교육
    Ⓓ 몬테소리식 교육법

해설 이 강의는 이탈리아의 여성 교육가인 Montessori(몬테소리)가 주창한 아동의 자주성 신장을 중시한 교육법, 즉 몬테소리 교육법에 관해 설명하고 있다. 따라서 정답은 보기 Ⓓ.

강의의 일부를 다시 들으시오. 그러고 나서 질문에 답하시오.

7. 교수가 이것을 말할 때 의미하는 것은 무엇인가: 🎧
몬테소리 교육법이 소개된 지 이제 100년이 조금 넘었는데요, 이 교육방법은 전 세계의 교육계에 많은 영향을 끼쳤어요.

    Ⓐ 몬테소리 교육법은 오래되고 낡은 교육 철학이다.
    Ⓑ 몬테소리 교육법은 흥미롭지만 유용하지 않다.
    Ⓒ 몬테소리 교육법은 많은 비판가들이 경시하는 교육법이다.
    Ⓓ 몬테소리 교육법은 상당한 영향력을 가지고 있다.

해설 개발된 지 100년이 조금 넘은 몬테소리 교육법이 전 세계 교육계에 큰 영향을 끼쳤다고 하였다. 스크립트의 'it has made important inroads into ~'라는 표현의 문맥상 의미를 파악하면 쉽게 풀 수 있는 문제이다. 정답은 보기 ⓓ.

8. 강의에서, 교수는 몬테소리 교육법의 근본 원리들을 언급하고 있다. 아래 표의 각 보기가 이 원리에 속하는지 표시하시오. 각 보기에 맞는 칸에 클릭하시오.

	Yes	No
ⓐ 모든 수업이 이탈리아어로 이루어진다.		
ⓑ 교사는 아이들을 관찰하고 피드백을 준다.		
ⓒ 학생들의 놀이 시간이 일반 학생들의 놀이 시간보다 더 길다.		
ⓓ 학생들 스스로 학습을 주도한다.		
ⓔ 학습 활동에 오감이 모두 동원된다.		

해설 몬테소리 교육법의 핵심 원리가 언급된 스크립트의 2단락 내용을 들으면서 잘 정리해 두었으면 한층 쉽게 풀 수 있는 문제이다. 몬테소리 교육법의 핵심은 아이들 스스로가 학습을 주도하는 자주성, 아이들의 행동을 관찰하고 방향 제시를 하는 교사의 역할, 오감을 동원한 감각교육이다. 정답은 보기 ⓑ, ⓓ, ⓔ.

강의의 일부를 다시 들으시오. 그러고 나서 질문에 답하시오.

점수를 매겨 성적표를 나눠주는 대신, 몬테소리 프로그램은 관찰과 평가를 더 중시하죠... 학생들의 강점과 약점이 무엇인지, 그런 것들을 관찰하죠. 이게 재미있는 부분인데, 몬테소리 교육법 중 이와 같은 관찰과 평가 부분이 부모들이 아이들의 A 학점, B 학점에 신경을 쓰는 미국 학교에서는 호응을 못 받았어요. 일부 몬테소리 학교에서는 부모들을 만족시키기 위해 점수를 매긴 성적표를 나눠주기 시작했죠.

9. 교수가 이것을 말할 때 암시하는 것은 무엇인가: 🎧
일부 몬테소리 학교에서는 부모들을 만족시키기 위해 점수를 매긴 성적표를 나눠주기 시작했죠.

ⓐ 몬테소리 교육법은 지능이 더 높은 학생들에게도 잘 통한다.
ⓑ 몬테소리 교육자들은 교육 원칙을 고수하는 편이다.
ⓒ 몬테소리 교육법은 특정 교육 환경에 맞게 변모했다.
ⓓ 더 많은 미국 학교에서 몬테소리 프로그램을 채택하고 있다.

해설 학생들의 학습 성취도를 점수로 평가하지 않는 몬테소리 교육법이 미국 학교에서 호응을 받지 못하자, 일부 몬테소리 학교에서 성적을 매겨 성적표를 나눠주기 시작했다고 하였다. 이는 특정 교육 환경에 적합하게 교육방식을 일부 변경했다는 것을 나타낸다. 따라서 정답은 보기 ⓒ. 이미 몬테소리 프로그램을 시행하는 일부 학교에서 교육방식을 약간 변경한 것이기 때문에, 보기 ⓓ에서처럼 더 많은 미국 학교에서 몬테소리 교육법을 채택하고 있다고는 말할 수 없다.

10. 다음 중 어느 것이 마리아 몬테소리에 관해 맞지 않는가?
ⓐ 아동 교육과 성인 교육 접근법은 비슷하다고 생각했다.
ⓑ 20세기 초에 자신만의 독특한 교육법을 고안해냈다.
ⓒ 어린 아이들 교육에 관심이 있었다.
ⓓ 이탈리아인이다.

해설 스크립트의 3단락을 보면 마리아 몬테소리의 교육 철학이 드러나 있다. 몬테소리는 아동과 성인의 학습법이 근본적으로 다르다고 생각했다. 따라서 아동 교육과 성인 교육 접근법은 당연히 차이가 날 수 밖에 없다. 정답은 보기 Ⓐ.

11. 다음 중 어느 것이 몬테소리 교육법에 관해 사실 같은가?
Ⓐ 몬테소리 교육협회는 이탈리아 로마에 기반을 두고 있다.
Ⓑ 각 나라마다 몬테소리 교육 표준이 다르다.
Ⓒ 누구나 몬테소리라는 명칭과 교육방법을 이용할 수 있다.
Ⓓ 몬테소리 교사를 인증하는 국제단체가 있다.

해설 스크립트의 마지막 부분을 들어보면 몬테소리라는 이름은 등록된 상표도 아니고 몬테소리 교육법을 규제하거나 증진하는 독립협회도 없다고 하였다. 따라서 누구나 이 이름과 교육법을 사용할 수 있을 것이다. 현재 미국에 수천 개의 몬테소리 학교가 있다는 것 역시 이러한 사실을 뒷받침한다. 정답은 보기 Ⓒ.

[Questions 6–11] Listen to part of a lecture in an education class.

P(W): Does anyone think you are in a Montessori classroom today? Yes, no? All right, those of you who said you are not in a Montessori classroom were correct. The Montessori Method has been around for a little over 100 years now, and it has made important inroads into educational systems worldwide. Toward the end, I'd like to talk a little more about where we're finding the new Montessori programs, but for now, let's start with some background information.

The Italian educator Maria Montessori developed the method in the early 1900s. It started out as a method of teaching very young children, in kindergarten and elementary schools. Originally she was working with mentally retarded children, as well. Her interest was in educating the children with the most challenges and obstacles. So this method focuses on what aspects? The method emphasizes self-directed learning. In other words, students are allowed to select what they want to study. That doesn't mean they never have to learn how to solve math problems, or they graduate from high school without knowing anything about grammar. But the lessons are given to them in a self-paced, self-motivated way, I mean, in an ideal environment. Then do they not need teachers at all? Well, the teacher's role is to function more like a guide, or a director. Rather than giving out letter grades, Montessori programs tend to rely more on observation and evaluation... like, what are the student's strengths and weaknesses. That's an interesting part, you know, that part of the method hasn't been popular in American schools, where parents tend to be concerned about As and Bs. Some Montessori schools have begun assigning letter grades to keep the parents happy. Another unique and groundbreaking principle of the Montessori Method was its incorporation of elements of all the five senses. You've heard about the theory of multiple intelligences, right? And you're probably aware that people have their own unique learning styles – kinesthetic, auditory, visual, and so on? Well, the learning activities in Montessori schools enable kids to touch and manipulate objects or teaching aids while also absorbing educational content unconsciously.

In Montessori's original conception of the method, she felt it was important to look at education as a series of steps, or building blocks, which the children could assemble on their own. All you had to do was provide the correct guidance, and explanations when they were needed, and children would do the rest of the work themselves. Montessori felt that the learning styles of children and adult were fundamentally different. Other educators had sometimes tended to treat children as small adults, and Montessori disagreed rather strongly with that view.

Today, the name Montessori is not trademarked, and there is no single organization to regulate or promote the method. There are several thousand Montessori schools in the U.S. today, and there are even Montessori high schools. Montessori's method is yielding good results and is becoming popular in inner-city schools, as well. Many schools claim to use the method, but one school might be quite different from the next.

Now get ready to answer the questions. You may use your notes to help you answer.

Listen again to part of the lecture. Then answer the question.

7. What does the professor mean when she says this: 🎧
The Montessori Method has been around for a little over 100 years now, and it has made important inroads into educational systems worldwide.

Listen again to part of the lecture. Then answer the question.
Rather than giving out letter grades, Montessori programs tend to rely more on observation and evaluation... like, what are the student's strengths and weaknesses. That's an interesting part, you know, that part of the method hasn't been popular in American schools, where parents tend to be concerned about As and Bs. Some Montessori schools have begun assigning letter grades to keep the parents happy.

9. What does the professor imply when she says this: 🎧
Some Montessori schools have begun assigning letter grades to keep the parents happy.

P : 여러분 중에 지금 몬테소리 수업에 참여하고 있다고 생각하는 사람 있어요? 맞아요, 아니에요? 자, 그렇지 않다고 대답한 학생들이 맞았어요. 몬테소리 교육법이 소개된 지 이제 100년이 조금 넘었는데요, 이 교육방법은 전 세계의 교육계에 많은 영향을 끼쳤어요. 강의 마지막 부분에 새로운 몬테소리 교육 프로그램을 시행하고 있는 곳에 대해 알아볼 건데, 지금은 배경 지식을 알아보는 것으로 수업을 시작합시다.

이탈리아 교육가인 Maria Montessori(마리아 몬테소리)가 1900년대 초반에 몬테소리 교육법을 개발했어요. 유치원과 초등학교에서 아주 어린 아이들을 가르치는 교육법으로 시작했죠. 처음에는 지적 발육이 늦은 아이들을 대상으로 했죠. 몬테소리는 어려움과 장애가 있는 아이들을 교육하는데 관심이 있었어요. 그럼 몬테소리 교육법은 어떤 면에 중점을 두는 걸까요? 바로 아이들 스스로가 자발적으로 학습을 하는 자유성을 강조해요. 즉, 학생들이 공부하고 싶은 것을 직접 선택할 수 있는 거죠. 그렇다고 해서 아이들이 수학 문제를 푸는 법을 배우지 않는다거나 문법을 전혀 모른 채로 고등학교를 졸업한다는 건 아니에요. 다만 자기 진도에 맞춰 스스로 동기 부여를 하며 학습이 이루어진다는 것이죠, 이상적인 환경에서 말이에요. 그럼 아이들에게 선생님은 전혀 없어도 되는 걸까요? 교사는 안내자나 길잡이 같은 역할을 가집니다. 점수를 매겨 성적표를 나눠주는 대신, 몬테소리 프로그램은 관찰과 평가를 더 중시하죠... 학생들의 강점과 약점이 무엇인지, 그런 것들을 관찰하죠. 이게 재미있는 부분인

데, 몬테소리 교육법 중 이와 같은 관찰과 평가 부분이 부모들이 아이들의 A 학점, B 학점에 신경을
쓰는 미국 학교에서는 호응을 못 받았어요. 일부 몬테소리 학교에서는 부모들을 만족시키기 위해 점
수를 매긴 성적표를 나눠주기 시작했죠. 몬테소리 교육법만의 독특하고 획기적인 또 다른 핵심 원리
는 모든 감각 기관, 즉 오감을 동원한 학습이죠. 다중 지능 이론에 대해 들어본 적이 있죠? 그리고 사
람들에게는 자기만의 고유한 학습법, 가령 운동 감각이나, 청각, 시각과 같은 학습법이 있다는 것을
알고 있죠? 몬테소리 학교의 학습 활동은 아이들이 물건이나 교구를 만지고 조작하면서 동시에 교육
내용을 무의식적으로 흡수하게 해주죠.
몬테소리가 이 학습법을 처음 고안해 낼 때, 그녀는 교육을 단계별 학습, 또는 아이들이 스스로 조립
할 수 있는 블록 쌓기와 같은 것으로 인식하는 것이 중요하다고 생각했어요. 우리가 할 일은 올바른
방향과 필요한 경우에는 설명을 제공하는 것이고, 그 나머지는 아이들이 알아서 하는 것이죠. 몬테소
리는 아이들과 어른의 학습법이 근본적으로 차이가 있다가 생각했어요. 어떤 교육자들은 아이들을 작
은 어른으로 대하기도 했지만, 몬테소리는 다소 강력하게 그런 의견에 반대했죠.
오늘날, 몬테소리란 명칭은 등록된 상표가 아닐뿐더러 몬테소리 교육법을 규제하고 증진하는 단일 기
구가 있는 것도 아니에요. 미국에는 수천 개의 몬테소리 학교가 있고, 몬테소리 고등학교도 있어요.
몬테소리 교육법은 좋은 결과를 내고 있고 대도시 중심부의 저소득층이 다니는 학교에서 호응이 높
아지고 있죠. 많은 학교에서 몬테소리 교육법을 활용한다고 자랑하지만, 학교마다의 특성은 아주 다
르기도 해요.

어휘 | make inroads into ~에 진출하다, 잠식하다 | kindergarten 유치원 | mentally retarded children 지적
발육이 늦은 아이, 정신 지체아 | obstacle 장애 | aspect 면, 국면 | emphasize 강조하다 |
self-directed 자발적인 | grammar 문법 | self-paced 자기 진도에 맞춰 학습할 수 있는 |
self-motivated 스스로 동기 부여를 하는 | give out 나눠주다, 배포하다 | observation 관찰 |
evaluation 평가 | strength 강점 | weakness 약점 | groundbreaking 획기적인 |
incorporation 혼합, 결합 | multiple intelligences 다중 지능 | kinesthetic 운동 감각의 |
auditory 청각의 | visual 시각의 | manipulate 조작 | teaching aid 교구 | absorb 흡수하다 |
unconsciously 무의식적으로 | conception 고안, 착안 | assemble 조립하다 | fundamentally 근본적으로 |
disagree 일치하지 않다, 의견이 다르다 | view 관점 | trademark ~의 상표를 등록하다 | regulate 규제하다 |
promote 증진하다 | yield 산출하다 | inner-city 대도시 중심부의 저소득층 거주 지역 |

Review

1. 1. 이름이 난, 세상에 알려진 2. 기회 3. 낮다 4. 걱정 5. 방해하다 6. 자원봉사 7. 읽고 쓸 줄 앎
8. 보존 9. 절차 10. 벌금 11. inspect 12. overflow 13. ritual 14. decorate
15. arrangement 16. accomplishment 17. invasion 18. predecessor 19. sympathetic
20. playwright

2. 1. in a predicament 곤경에 처한 2. look into 조사하다 3. turn in 제출하다 4. give it a try 시도해
보다 5. make an appointment 약속을 정하다 6. figure out 이해하다, 알아내다 7. ahead of ~에
앞서 8. take a rest 휴식을 취하다 9. turn down 소리를 줄이다 10. worthy of note 주목할만한

3. 1. assignments 2. obstacles 3. groundbreaking 4. flawed 5. emphasis 6. attract

해석 | 1. 그리고 컴퓨터가 도난당했을 때 중요한 숙제를 잃어버렸을 경우를 대비해서 교수님에게 제출할 확인서도 써주도록 할게요.
2. 그녀는 어려움과 장애가 있는 아이들을 교육하는데 관심이 있었어요.
3. 몬테소리 교육법만의 독특하고 획기적인 또 다른 핵심 원리는 모든 감각 기관, 즉 오감을 동원한 학습이죠.
4. 작품 속 등장인물에 도덕적 판단을 주입시키는 대신, 더 큰 관점을 가지고 등장인물을 그냥 결점이 있는 인간으로 보았어요, 우리 모습이 그런 것처럼요.
5. 그리고 다른 군 지도자들과 비교하여 정보 수집에 열을 올렸죠.
6. 수컷 바우어새는 암컷을 유인하기 위해 화려하게 장식된 둥지인 바우어(bower)를 지어요.

Chapter 4 Connecting Information

Office Hours

1. Yes – Ⓑ, Ⓒ, Ⓔ No – Ⓐ, Ⓓ **2.** Music – Ⓐ, Ⓓ Chemistry – Ⓑ, Ⓒ
3. Suggested – Ⓑ, Ⓒ Not Suggested – Ⓐ, Ⓓ

1. 대화에서, 교수는 학생에게 장학금 수여자 선정 상황에 관해 알려주며 몇 가지 서류를 제출하라고 말하고 있다. 아래 표의 각 보기가 제출 서류에 해당하는지 표시하시오. 각 보기에 맞는 칸에 클릭하시오.

	Yes	No
Ⓐ 관련 학문 이슈에 관한 에세이		
Ⓑ 학업 계획서		
Ⓒ 학과장님께 쓰는 편지		
Ⓓ 봉사 활동 증명서		
Ⓔ 성적 증명서		

Dictation | ① the scholarship nomination ② whatever it takes ③ you're the best candidate ④ a statement of purpose ⑤ explain your academic goals ⑥ who you are as a person ⑦ the best of luck

여 : 들러줘서 고맙구나. 네가 장학금 수상자 후보라는 것을 알려주고 싶었단다... 네가 상위 2명에 들었어!
남 : 정말이세요?
여 : 그래, 그런데 추가로 제출해야 할 서류들이 몇 가지 있단다.
남 : 그런가요? 뭐든지 할게요!
여 : 음, 왜 네가 최상의 후보자라고 생각하는지를 설명하는 편지를 인문학부 학과장님께 써야 해.
남 : 네.
여 : 학업 계획서도 써야 한단다.
남 : 그게 뭔가요? 무슨 내용을 써야 하는 건가요?
여 : 학업 계획서라고 들어본 적 없니? 학업 계획서에는 너의 학업 목표를 명확하게 드러내야 해, 가령 네가 선택한 분야에 대한 적성이나 능력, 의지 등과 같은 것 말이야. 학과장님께 쓰는 편지는 네가

어휘 | nomination 지명, 추천 | finalist 결승 진출자 | candidate 후보자 | statement of purpose 학업 계획서 |
qualification 적성, 자격, 능력 | commitment 헌신, 의지 | confusing 헷갈리는 | hand in 제출하다 |
transcript 성적 증명서 |

2. 대화에서, 학생은 음악과 화학 중 어떤 것을 전공으로 선택해야 하는지 여러 이유를 제시하고 있다. 아래 표에 각 과목을 전공해야 하는 이유를 표시하시오. 각 보기에 맞는 칸에 클릭하시오.

	Music	Chemistry
Ⓐ 학생이 이것을 하는 걸 정말 좋아한다.		
Ⓑ 학생은 안정적인 보수를 벌 수 있다.		
Ⓒ 학생의 아버지가 같은 분야에 종사하신다.		
Ⓓ 학생이 재능을 보인다.		

Dictation | ① choose my major ② must be very talented ③ would be an easier choice
④ follow in his footsteps ⑤ the income would be more reliable

어휘 | chemistry 화학 | talented 재능 있는 | chemist 화학자 | follow in a person's footsteps ~의 뒤를 잇다 |
income 수입 | reliable 믿을 수 있는, 확실한 |

3. 화자들은 무용단을 수업에 초청하는 것에 관해 논의하고 있다. 아래 표의 각 보기가 교수가 제안한 대안에 속하는지 표시하시오. 각 보기에 맞는 칸에 클릭하시오.

	Suggested	Not Suggested
Ⓐ 공연 장소 변경		
Ⓑ 가나 무용수들의 공연 시간을 변경		
Ⓒ 다른 팀에게 공연을 요청		
Ⓓ 예정되어 있던 무용 공연을 취소		

Ⅾictation | ① replies to my e-mails right away ② plenty of time left ③ that might interrupt the class ④ At all events ⑤ have a backup plan in place

여 : 가나 전통 무용단의 방문 계획은 어떻게 되어 가고 있니? 연락은 하고 있니? 공연을 할 수 있대?
남 : 실은, 교수님께 그 말씀을 드리려 했어요. 무용단 단장님이 정말 좋으신 분이고 제가 보낸 이메일에 바로 답장을 보내주시는데요, 그 분께서 지금 공연 일정이 너무 빡빡하다고 말씀하셨어요. 시간이 별로 없는 것 같아요.
여 : 문제가 생길 수도 있겠구나. 아직 학기 중에 남은 시간이 많으니까, 일정을 재조정 하는 것이 어떻겠니?
남 : 그렇게 해도 괜찮나요? 수업 흐름에 방해가 될까 봐요... 그럼, 일정을 확인해보도록 할게요.
여 : 그리고 다른 무용단도 알아보는 것이 좋을 거야. 지금 미국 순회공연을 하고 있는 아프리카 무용단이 적어도 한 팀 더 있다고 알고 있어, 유럽 무용단도 두 팀 정도 되고 말이야. 한 팀 이상도 초청할 수 있겠네! 어쨌든 항상 예비 계획은 준비해두고 있어야 해.
남 : 명심하도록 하겠습니다. 감사합니다!

어휘 | traditional 전통적인 **|** dance troupe 무용단 **|** director 단장 **|** interrupt 방해하다 **|** backup 예비, 보충 **|** at all events 여하튼 간에 **|** in place 적절한, 제자리에 **|**

1. Yes – Ⓒ, Ⓓ No – Ⓐ, Ⓑ, Ⓔ **2.** Mentioned – Ⓐ, Ⓑ, Ⓔ Not Mentioned – Ⓒ, Ⓓ
3. Mentioned – Ⓐ, Ⓒ, Ⓓ Not Mentioned – Ⓑ, Ⓔ

1. 대화에서, 여자는 새로 개방되는 주차장을 무료로 이용할 수 있는 사람들을 언급하고 있다. 아래 표의 각 보기가 주차장을 사용할 수 있는 사람들인지 표시하시오. 각 보기에 맞는 칸에 클릭하시오.

	Yes	No
Ⓐ 1학년과 2학년생		
Ⓑ 모든 풀타임 등록 학생		
Ⓒ 교직원		
Ⓓ 3학년과 4학년 풀타임 등록 학생		
Ⓔ 일반 대중		

남 : 주차 문제에 관해 질문이 있습니다.

여 : 주차 위반 벌금을 내러 오셨나요?

남 : 아뇨, 새로 개방되는 주차장 이용에 대해 알고 싶어요. 그곳 시설을 이용하려면 주차 이용료가 얼마나 되죠?

여 : 음, 경우에 따라 다릅니다. 4개 층은 교직원만 이용할 수 있어요. 교직원이신가요?

남 : 아뇨. 전 학생이에요. 학생들은 사용할 수 없는 건가요?

여 : 사용할 수는 있지만, 몇 가지 조건이 있어요. 3학년과 4학년, 대학원생 중 풀타임으로 등록한 학생들만 허가증이 발급될 예정이에요.

남 : 네, 알겠습니다. 그런데 일반인들에게 유료로 개방되는 구역도 있다고 알고 있었는데요?

여 : 맞아요, 하지만 아직 요금이 정해지지 않았어요. 지금 알려드릴 수 있는 건 일반 학생들이 이용하기에는 부담스러울 정도로 비쌀 거라는 겁니다.

남 : 학교에 자주 차를 몰고 오지는 못하겠네요.

어휘 | permit 허가, 허가증 | circumstance 상황, 환경 | issue 발급하다 | rate 요금 | discourage 말리다, 단념시키다 |

2. 대화에서, 우체국 직원은 학생이 보낸 항공 우편이 배달되지 않은 채 반송된 이유를 설명하고 있다. 아래 표의 각 보기가 그러한 이유로 언급되었는지 표시하시오. 각 보기에 맞는 칸에 클릭하시오.

	Mentioned	Not Mentioned
Ⓐ 우체국 직원들이 학생의 필체를 못 알아봤을 수도 있다.		
Ⓑ 새로 온 직원이 봉투를 부주의하게 붙였을 수도 있다.		
Ⓒ 우표를 충분히 붙이지 않았을 수도 있다.		
Ⓓ 학생이 우편물을 보내려고 했던 국가에서는 허가 없이 우편물을 배달할 수 없다.		
Ⓔ 포장재에 안전상의 문제가 있었을 수도 있다.		

Dictation | ① about 3 weeks ago　② should've brought it　③ for security reasons　④ that doesn't seem likely　⑤ rule out the possibility

남 : 저기, 제가 한 3주 전에 친구에게 항공 우편으로 보낸 편지가 오늘 반송되었는데요, 이유를 모르겠어요. 좀 도와주시겠어요?

여 : 그래요, 제가 한 번 보죠.

남 : 실은 기숙사에 두고 왔어요. 가져왔어야 하는 건데.

여 : 괜찮아요. 그럼 흔히 반송되는 경우를 알려줄게요.

남 : 감사합니다. 어떤 경우들이죠?

여 : 안전상의 이유 때문에 우편물이 거부되는 경우가 있어요. 미국의 우편 보안은 상당히 엄격히 지켜지고 있어요. 우편물 겉봉에 하얀 가루 같은 것을 흘렸다면, 그것 때문에 반송되었을 수도 있어요.

남 : 그런 것 같지는 않아요.

여 : 우편물 취급하는 사람이 주소를 제대로 못 읽었을 가능성도 있어요. 주소를 손으로 썼나요?

어휘 | airmail 항공 우편 | take a look 보다 | cause 이유, 원인 | reject 거부하다 | security 보안, 안보 |
strict 엄격한 | spill 흘리다 | powder 가루 | handler ~를 취급하는 사람 | handwritten 손으로 쓴 |
rule out 배제하다 | seal 밀봉하다, 봉인하다 | sloppy 너절한, 조잡한 |

3. 대화에서, 학자금 대출과 직원은 학자금 융자 신청을 철회하는 절차를 설명하고 있다. 각 보기가 남자가
언급한 이 절차에 해당하는지 아래 표에 표시하시오. 각 보기에 맞는 칸에 클릭하시오.

	Mentioned	Not Mentioned
Ⓐ 상환 연기 신청서를 작성하기		
Ⓑ 학과장님에게 감사 편지 쓰기		
Ⓒ 현재 학자금 융자 신청 내용을 취소하는 양식 작성하기		
Ⓓ 장학금 통지서 사본 가져오기		
Ⓔ 앞으로 모든 과목에서 A 학점 받기		

Dictation | ① it's pretty simple　② won't need loans you've applied for　③ anything else　④
last but not least　⑤ have a saucy tongue

어휘 | indicate 나타내다 | deferment 연기 | saucy 건방진 |

1. 파충류학 수업

1. 오늘 강의에서, 교수는 무슨 주제에 관해 이야기 하고 있는가?

    Ⓐ 뱀의 구멍 기관

    Ⓑ 뱀의 서식지

    Ⓒ 많은 종의 뱀

    Ⓓ 생물 적응

2. 강의에서, 교수는 뱀의 구멍 기관의 여러 기능을 이야기 하고 있다. 아래 표의 각 보기가 이 기능들 중 하나인지 표시하시오. 각 보기에 맞는 칸에 클릭하시오.

	Yes	No
Ⓐ 온도 조절		
Ⓑ 적외선 방출		
Ⓒ 포식자를 발견하여 피하기		
Ⓓ 먹이 찾기		
Ⓔ 다른 뱀과 의사소통		

Ⅾictation | ① fascinating biological adaptations   ② not their habitat   ③ on either side of their head   ④ Most of all   ⑤ wearing night-vision goggles   ⑥ it works the same way   ⑦ aren't clear on whether   ⑧ with terrific accuracy   ⑨ find shelter from the sun

P : 자, 이제 특정 뱀 종의 구멍 기관에 관해 잠깐 알아볼까요? 이 기관은 홈이 있는 각종 독사에게서 찾아볼 수 있고, 일부 비단뱀과 보아뱀도 이 기관을 가지고 있죠. 이 구멍 기관은 굉장한 생물 적응 형태임이 틀림없어요. 내가 파충류 공부를 시작하기 전에 이 홈이 있는 독사들(pit viper)이 사실은 구덩이(pit)에 살고 있지 않다는 것을 알고 놀란 적이 있어요. 그래요, 여러분이 잘 짐작하듯 'pit viper'란 이름은 뱀의 서식지가 아닌 뱀의 감각 기관과 관련이 있어요. 이 기관은 보통 뱀의 눈과 코 사이 양쪽에 있어요. 그럼 이 구멍 기관은 무슨 역할을 할까요? 무엇보다도, 구멍 기관은 뱀이 열이라고도 알려져 있는 적외선을 탐지하게 해주죠. 액션 영화를 보면 등장인물들이 야간 투시경을 착용하고 있는 걸 볼 수 있는데, 이 안경은 주변에 있는 생명체의 열 분포도를 보여주어 착용자가 어두운 곳에서 잘 볼 수 있도록 해주죠. 뱀의 경우에도 같은 방식으로 작용해요. 온혈 동물은 열을 방출하는데, 뱀은 구멍 기관 안팎의 온도를 비교하여 이 열을 감지하죠. 과학자들은 구멍 기관이 발달한 이유가 포식자를 탐지하기 위한 것인지, 먹잇감을 탐지하기 위한 것인지는 정확히 몰라요. 하지만 구멍 기관이 발달하게 된 환경적 이유가 많이 있었을 거예요. 그 원인이 무엇이든 구멍 기관은 뱀이 한 치의 착오도 없이 정확하게 먹이를 공격하게 해주죠. 설치류나 새와 같은 먹이가 열을 내면, 구멍 기관이 이를 탐지하는 거예요. 구멍 기관은 체온 조절 기능도 가지고 있어요. 뱀이 더 따뜻한 곳이나 더 서늘한 곳을 찾아내게 해줘요, 가령 햇볕을 피할 곳을 찾고 있다면 말이에요. 실험 결과를 보아도 이를 알 수 있죠.

2. 생태학 수업

1. 숲이 왜 사라지고 있는가? 2개의 답을 클릭하시오.

Ⓐ 상업적 용도로 나무를 베어버림

Ⓑ 가축 방목

Ⓒ 해수면 상승

Ⓓ 주택가 확장

2. 강의에서, 교수는 삼림 벌채로 인해 생겨나는 결과에 관해 이야기 하고 있다. 아래 표의 각 보기가 이 결과들 중 하나인지 표시하시오. 각 보기에 맞는 칸에 클릭하시오.

	Yes	No
Ⓐ 토양 침식		
Ⓑ 생물의 다양성의 감소		
Ⓒ 자외선 양의 감소		
Ⓓ 홍수		
Ⓔ 지구 온난화		

Dictation | ① in the midst of a major ecological crisis ② take the appropriate action ③ through deliberate human activity ④ for urban use ⑤ such disposable products as ⑥ end up as wasteland ⑦ species are dying off ⑧ less wood available for fuel ⑨ there's no chance of cultivation ⑩ outweighs all the consequences ⑪ be dealt with immediately

P : 우리 모두 지구가 심각한 생태학적 위기를 겪고 있다는 것을 알고 있어요. 따라서 그에 대한 적절한 조처를 취할 수 있도록 문제를 올바로 이해하는 일은 매우 중요하죠. 그런 의미에서 오늘은 삼림 벌채 문제에 관해 이야기하고 싶군요. 삼림 벌채란 인간의 계획적인 활동을 통해, 또는 환경 퇴화의 결과로 인해 숲의 용도가 바뀌는 걸 말해요. 농경 활동이나 목축을 목적으로 숲이 개간되기도 하죠. 대형 패스트푸드 체인점들은 햄버거를 만들기 위해 소고기를 구매할 방법을 찾고 있으니까요. 도시 개발에 이용되기도 하고요. 종이나 젓가락 같은 일회용품을 만드는데 쓰기 위한 벌채도 큰 문제죠. 결국 안타깝게도 숲이 황무지로 변해버리게 되요.
자, 이 무자비하고 파괴적인 활동의 결과는 천차만별이에요. 물론 환경 자체가 훼손되죠. 숲이 이전과 같은 수의 생물 종을 유지할 수 없기 때문에 생물의 다양성이 줄어들어요. 실제로 급속한 속도로 생물 종이 사라지고 있기 때문에 우리가 살고 있는 현재를 대멸종의 시대라고도 하죠. 그런데 이 삼림 벌채의 결과가 여기서 멈추지 않아요. 땔감으로 사용할 목재도 줄어들죠. 토양 침식 역시 큰 문제입니다. 모든 나무가 베어지기 때문에 토양이 제자리에 고정되어 있지 않고, 따라서 필수 토양분이 없어지죠. 결국 작물을 재배할 기회가 사라지니 동물과 인간이 소비할 식량도 줄어들게 되는 것이죠. 삼림 벌채의 결과로 언급해야 할 것이 하나 더 남아 있는데, 조금 전에 이야기 했던 모든 결과들을

어휘 | ecological crisis 생태학적 위기 | take action 조처를 취하다 | deforestation 삼림 벌채, 산림 개간 | conversion 전환, 변환 | deliberate 계획적인, 고의의 | consequence 결과 | degradation 퇴화 | clear 개간하다 | livestock 가축 | beef 소고기 | logging 벌목 | disposable product 1회용품(사용 후 바로 버릴 수 있는 물품) | wasteland 황무지, 폐허 | devastating 황폐화시키는 | biodiversity 생물의 다양성 | extinction 멸종 fuel 연료, 땔감 | soil erosion 토양 침식 | nutrient 영양분 | outweigh ~를 능가하다 | convert A into B A를 B로 바꾸다 | It goes without saying that ~는 말할 나위도 없다 |

3. 경영학 수업

1. 다음 중 어느 것이 비용이 가장 많이 드는가?
   Ⓐ 라디오 광고
   Ⓑ TV 광고
   Ⓒ 지하철 포스터
   Ⓓ 신문 광고

2. 교수는 두 가지 형태의 광고를 설명하고 있다. 아래의 각 보기가 어떤 형태의 특징인지 아래 표에 표시하시오. 각 보기에 맞는 칸에 클릭하시오.

	Print Ads	TV/Film Ads
Ⓐ 등장인물들이 광고 되는 물건을 사용한다		
Ⓑ 팸플릿이 포함된다		
Ⓒ 가장 비용이 많이 든다		
Ⓓ 걸으면서 사람들이 집어 간다		

Dictation | ① hundreds of advertisements ② a form of communication ③ deliver a one-way message ④ chosen by the sponsor, not the consumer ⑤ fall into the category ⑥ In contrast ⑦ the most effective ⑧ cost millions of dollars ⑨ paid for by the companies that make and sell

는 상업 광고는 가장 효과적인, 따라서 가장 중요한 광고로 인식되지요. 따라서 가장 비싸기도 하고 요. 많은 관중이 지켜보는 미식축구 경기에 나오는 광고 1개에 수백만 달러가 드니까요. TV 프로그램 이나 영화 속에서 등장인물들이 특정 물건을 사용하거나 언급하는 간접 광고(PP)도 있어요. 등장하는 물건을 만들고 파는 회사가 비용을 지불하죠. 간접 광고는 할리우드 영화나 유명한 미국 TV 프로그램에서 흔히 찾아볼 수 있는 광고 형태입니다.

어휘 one-way 한쪽의, 일방적인 distribute 배포하다 fall into ~에 속하다 audience 관중

Practice

[1-5] 1. Ⓓ 2. Ⓒ 3. Ⓑ 4. Mentioned – Ⓑ, Ⓒ, Ⓔ Not Mentioned – Ⓐ, Ⓓ 5. Ⓓ
[6-11] 6. Ⓑ 7. Ⓐ 8. Ⓓ 9. Ⓓ 10. Mentioned – Ⓒ, Ⓓ, Ⓔ Not Mentioned – Ⓐ, Ⓑ 11. Ⓒ

[문제 1–5] 학생과 교수 사이의 대화의 일부를 들으시오.

1. 화자들은 주로 무엇에 관해 이야기 하고 있는가?
  Ⓐ 학생의 교생 실습이 원만하지가 않다.
  Ⓑ 교수는 학생이 교생 실습을 나가길 원한다.
  Ⓒ 학생은 어린 아이들과 잘 지내지 못하고 있다.
  Ⓓ 교수가 학생이 리포트를 수정하는데 조언을 해주고 있다.

해설 교수와 학생은 학생의 교생 실습과 실습 보고서에 관해 대화를 나누고 있다. 학생은 이미 보고서 초안을 제출한 상태이고, 교수가 이 초안 수정 방향에 대해 조언을 해주고 있다. 따라서 정답은 보기 Ⓓ.

2. 학생에 관해 추론할 수 있는 것은 무엇인가?
  Ⓐ 세부 전공 분야를 학급 관리로 바꿀지도 모른다.
  Ⓑ Joanna Smith와는 안면이 없다.
  Ⓒ 초등학교에서 교생 실습을 했다.
  Ⓓ 리포트에 어떤 내용을 써야 하는지 잘 모른다.

해설 어린 아이들(little kids)과 유년기 학습 방식(early childhood learning styles)에 관해 언급한 부분을 통해 학생이 초등학교로 교생 실습을 갔었음을 유추할 수 있다. 따라서 정답은 보기 Ⓒ. 보기 Ⓐ는 대화를 통해 전혀 추론할 수 없는 내용이고, 보기 Ⓑ는 전에 Joanna Smith를 만난 적이 있다고 했으므로 오답이며, 보기 Ⓓ는 교수가 학생에게 초안을 잘 썼다고 하였으므로 오답이다.

3. 교수에 따르면 학생은 어떤 교육 분야에서 어려움을 느끼고 있는가?
  Ⓐ 유년기 교육
  Ⓑ 특수 교육
  Ⓒ 아동 심리학
  Ⓓ 학급 관리

해설 교수는 학생이 특수 아동을 가르치는데 약간의 문제가 있는 것 같다고 하였다. 이에 학생은 자신의 세

부 전공 분야가 아니라서 그렇다며, 그래도 잘 한 것 같다고 말하고 있다. 정답은 보기 ⓑ. Special-needs와 special education 모두 특수 교육 분야를 가리킨다.

4. 대화에서, 교수는 학생의 리포트를 보강할 수 있는 몇 가지 방법을 언급하고 있다. 아래 표의 각 보기가 이러한 방법 가운데 하나인지 표시하시오. 각 보기에 맞는 칸에 클릭하시오.

	Mentioned	Not Mentioned
ⓐ 학습 장애와 정서 장애에 대한 조사하기		
ⓑ 특수 교육을 전공하고 있는 동료 학생에게 조언을 얻기		
ⓒ 이론에 관한 내용을 줄이고 실제 경험을 더 많이 소개하기		
ⓓ 특별한 보살핌을 필요로 하는 아이들과 더 많은 시간을 보내기		
ⓔ 특정 분야로 범위를 좁혀 그 분야를 중점적으로 쓰기		

해설 교수가 학생에게 리포트 수정 방향에 관해 조언을 준 부분은 크게 3가지이다. 첫째로 너무 방대한 내용을 모두 담으려 하지 말고 특정 분야를 정해 구체적으로 기술하기, 둘째로 특수 아동 교육에 관하여 동료 학생에게 조언을 받기, 마지막으로 이론적인 내용보다는 실습을 하면서 겪은 체험을 바탕으로 리포트를 작성하기 등이다. 따라서 정답은 보기 ⓑ, ⓒ, ⓔ. 보기 ⓐ와 ⓓ는 지문에 언급되었던 표현을 이용해 만들어진 오답들로 혼동하지 않도록 주의해야 한다.

대화의 일부를 다시 들으시오. 그러고 나서 질문에 답하시오.
남 : 그리고 특수 교육을 필요로 하는 아이들과 잘 지내지 못한 것 같더구나. 학습 장애와 정서 장애는 다루기가 쉽지 않단다. 다들 알고 있는 일이지...
여 : 네, 그렇지만 제 전문 분야가 아니었어요. 그래도 잘 하고 있다고 생각했었는데요.

5. 학생이 이것을 말할 때 암시하는 것은 무엇인가: 🎧
여 : 네, 그렇지만 제 전문 분야가 아니었어요. 그래도 잘 하고 있다고 생각했었는데요.

ⓐ 자신이 가르치는 모든 아이들을 똑같이 사랑한다.
ⓑ 특수 아동에 관해서는 아는 것이 없어서 당혹해 하고 있다.
ⓒ 특수 교육 분야를 더 연구하고 싶지 않다.
ⓓ 특수 아동들을 가르치는데 별 문제가 없다고 생각했다.

해설 교수가 학생의 특수 아동 교육 실습에 약간의 문제가 있었다고 하자, 학생은 자신의 세부 전공 분야는 아니지만 잘 해왔다고 생각했다고 말하고 있다. 따라서 정답은 보기 ⓓ.

🎧 [Questions 1–5] Listen to part of a conversation between a student and a professor.

M : Well, I've been hearing good things about your practicum. You seem to have a natural talent for working with little kids!

W : Thanks, that's really nice to hear. I really love little children. So, um, how'd you feel about the rough draft of my report?

M : It's all right, but it needs some edits. You're on the right track, so don't worry. You only need to polish it up a little.

W : Oh? What do you recommend?

M : Before anything else, I think you've tried to include too much. It's too broad, and that makes it seem vague. You need to focus only on a couple of specific areas, like what you've learned about classroom management so far, or what you've witnessed firsthand about early childhood learning styles. Simply put, don't try to include everything under the sun.

W : OK, I guess I know what you mean. I can see how that would be a problem.

M : You also seemed to have had a little trouble with the special-needs kids. Learning disabilities and emotional disorders are tough to work with. Everyone understands that...

W : Yes, but it wasn't really my specialization. I thought I was doing all right, though.

M : You were. Like I said, don't worry. What I want you to do is talk to Joanna Smith, who's also doing her practicum there. She is in special education, and she's very knowledgeable. She'll be happy to give you some practical suggestions for dealing with this group of kids. I think it'll help you take things less personally when you get frustrated. Incorporate that into your paper, too.

W : Ooh, that's a really great idea. I think I've met her before. I appreciate that.

M : Finally, when you're editing, be sure to put the focus on your own experiences, and not so much on the theories. The faculty wants to see that you're applying what you've learned, instead of just repeating something you've memorized.

W : Those are great ideas. Thanks for taking the time to explain them to me!

M : Sure, you're welcome. Keep up the good work!

Now get ready to answer the questions. You may use your notes to help you answer.

Listen again to part of the conversation. Then answer the question.

M : You also seemed to have had a little trouble with the special-needs kids. Learning disabilities and emotional disorders are tough to work with. Everyone understands that...

W : Yes, but it wasn't really my specialization. I thought I was doing all right, though.

5. What does the student imply when she says this: 🎧

W : Yes, but it wasn't really my specialization. I thought I was doing all right, though.

남 : 네가 교생 실습을 아주 잘 해냈다는 이야기를 들었단다. 어린 아이들을 돌보며 가르치는 일에 소질이 있는 것 같구나.

여 : 감사합니다, 그렇게 말씀해 주시니 기분이 좋네요. 전 어린 아이들을 정말 좋아해요. 그럼, 제 실습 보고서 초안에 대해서는 어떻게 생각하세요?

남 : 괜찮았는데, 약간의 수정을 해야 할 것 같구나. 보고서 방향은 잘 잡았으니, 걱정하지는 말고. 약간 다듬기만 하면 될 거야.

여 : 그런가요? 어떤 점을 바꿔야 하죠?

남 : 먼저, 너무 많은 내용을 다루려고 한 것 같더구나. 내용이 너무 광범위해서, 논점이 모호해졌어. 몇 가지 구체적인 포인트를 정하도록 하렴. 가령, 학급 관리에 대해 지금까지 알게 된 것이라던가, 유년기 아이들의 학습 방식에 대해 네가 직접 느낀 점 같은 것들 말이야. 간단히 말하면, 모든 내용을 다 쓰려고 하지 않도록 하렴.

여 : 네, 무슨 말씀이신지 알 것 같아요. 왜 그런 점이 문제가 되는지 이해할 수 있을 것 같아요.

어휘 | practicum 교사 실습 과목 | rough draft 초안 | on the right track (생각 등이) 타당한, 사고 방식이 바른 |
polish up 끝마무리 하다, 다듬다 | before anything else 먼저 | vague 모호한, 애매한 | firsthand 직접 |
simply put 간단히 말하면 | under the sun 이 세상의, 지상의 | learning disability 학습 장애 |
emotional disorder 정서 장애 | tough 힘든 | specialization 전문 분야 | knowledgeable 아는 것이
많은 | incorporate 구체화하다 | theory 이론 | keep up 유지하다 |

[문제 6-11] 생리학 강의의 일부를 들으시오.

6. 교수가 오늘 다루고 있는 강의 주제는 무엇인가?
　Ⓐ 전염병 확산
　Ⓑ 척추동물의 면역 체계
　Ⓒ 화학적 면역 방어 체계
　Ⓓ 피부와 피부의 질병 예방

해설 전반적으로 인간과 동물의 면역 시스템에 관해 이야기 하고 있는데, 교수가 스크립트의 3단락에서 특히
　　　오늘은 척추동물의 면역 시스템에 관해 중점적으로 이야기 하겠다고 말하였다. 따라서 정답은 보기 Ⓑ.
　　　보기 Ⓒ의 화학적 면역 방어 체계는 다음 시간에 공부할 내용이다.

강의의 일부를 다시 들으시오. 그러고 나서 질문에 답하시오.
*면역 기능을 돕는 특수 장기와 세포도 있어요. 가령, 여러분의 간을 생각해봐요. 간이 생체 여과기 기능을 한
다는 것을 깨닫기 전까지는 사람들이 간에 대해 별로 생각해보지 않아요.*

7. 교수는 왜 이것을 말하는가: 🎧
　가령, 여러분의 간을 생각해봐요.

　Ⓐ 면역 체계에 있어 특수 기관의 역할에 대한 학생들의 이해를 돕기 위해
　Ⓑ 인간 장기의 예를 들어주기 위해

ⓒ 신체 기능에 있어 간의 중요성을 강조하기 위해
ⓓ 사람들이 간의 기능을 잘 모른다는 것을 지적하기 위해

해설 교수가 면역 기능을 돕는 특수 기관과 조직이 있다고 말한 후에, '예를 들어 간을 생각해보라'고 말하였다. 이는 간이 어떤 기능을 하는지를 보여줌으로써 면역 체계에 있어 특수 기관의 역할을 학생들이 이해하도록 하기 위한 것이다. 정답은 보기 Ⓐ. 보기 ⓒ와 같이 단순히 간의 중요성을 강조하려고 한 말은 아니다.

8. 강의에 따르면, 왜 사람들은 피부에 난 벤 상처나 찔린 상처를 조심스럽게 치료해야 하는가?
ⓐ 피부가 저절로 낫는데 시간이 너무 오래 걸린다.
ⓑ 상처에서 피가 너무 많이 날 것이다.
ⓒ 피부에 흉터가 남을 것이다.
ⓓ 피부는 1차 감염 경로이다.

해설 피부는 신체의 감염을 막는 1차 방어선이기 때문에 벤 상처와 찔려서 난 상처를 아주 조심스럽게 치료하는 것이 중요하다고 하였다. 교수가 한 말 중, 'It's the first line of defense against infection' 이 보기 ⓓ에서는 'the skin is the first route of infection' 으로 바뀌어 표현되었다. 정답은 보기 ⓓ.

9. 디프테리아, 천연두, 파상풍에 대한 면역 반응은 어떤 신체 작용을 통해 이루어지는가?
ⓐ 정화
ⓑ 돌연변이
ⓒ 효소
ⓓ 면역기억반응

해설 이 세 질병은 면역기억반응과 백신 작용을 설명하면서 언급되었다. 정답은 보기 ⓓ.

10. 강의에서, 교수는 면역 시스템의 여러 기능을 언급하고 있다. 아래의 각 보기가 이런 기능으로 언급되었는지 아래 표에 표시하시오. 각 보기에 맞는 칸에 클릭하시오.

	Mentioned	Not Mentioned
ⓐ DNA가 이로운 쪽으로 돌연변이 하게 함		
ⓑ 병에 걸리지 않도록 새로운 특별한 세포를 만들어 냄		
ⓒ 어떤 세포와 조직이 이롭고 어떤 것들이 그렇지 않은지를 인지함		
ⓓ 몸에서 세균과 병균을 제거함		
ⓔ 몸속에 들어왔던 이물질을 기억해내어 공격함		

해설 우리 몸의 면역 시스템은 병원균과 같은 이물질을 감지하여 공격하고, 한 번 노출되었던 바이러스나 박테리아를 기억하여 또 다시 침입하면 공격하고, 병원체를 깨끗이 씻어내는 기능을 한다. 정답은 보기 ⓒ, ⓓ, ⓔ.

11. 면역 시스템이 병원균을 없애는 방법이 아닌 것은?
ⓐ 재채기
ⓑ 기침
ⓒ 침 뱉기
ⓓ 코 풀기

[Questions 6–11] Listen to part of a lecture in a physiology class.

P(M) : Humans and animals have immune systems... which is lucky for us. They protect us from disease and they fight off infections. Even bacteria have enzymes that protect them against harmful viruses. The immune system is one of the most amazing evolutionary developments, and that's saying a lot.

So, how the immune system works in a specific way... the first task for any immune system is identification. You know, it needs to know the difference between healthy cells and tissues, and invaders. The immune system can identify a number of possible threats: viruses, tumors, harmful bacteria, fungi, and parasites. Uh, this is always a complicated process, because the body faces a wide variety of pathogens that can cause disease. Plus, as you know, bacteria and viruses are always mutating. Just when you've developed some immunity against one form of the common cold, another strain comes along.

The immune system of vertebrates, and we'll focus on that today, is a network of several levels of the anatomy. Let's see... at the molecular level, there are certain proteins that are involved with identifying pathogens and attacking them, or neutralizing them. This also happens on the cellular level: T-cells and phagocytes, for example. There are also specialized organs and tissues that assist in providing immunity. Think of your liver, for example. It's not an organ people often think about much until they realize that it acts as the body's filter. Another example of immunity at the tissue-and-organ level is, quite simply, the skin. It's the first line of defense against infection, which is why it's so important to treat cuts and punctures carefully. Once something breaches the barrier, then other defenses are activated.

Another process that happens within us is called immunological memory. This is how vaccination works: the body is exposed to a weakened or killed version of a harmful virus or bacteria, and it organizes an immune response. Later, if it is exposed to the same threat again, the defenses are already there. They remember it immediately and make a quick, effective attack. This is a concept people have understood – somewhat imperfectly – for centuries. Two thousand years ago, plague survivors in Athens cared for the sick, and they realized they were safe from a second infection. This was the basis for our understanding of immunization. People developed a better understanding of disease, especially diphtheria, smallpox, and tetanus.

The body also has ways of cleansing itself of pathogens. Things that we might find annoying are actually important processes for keeping ourselves healthy. Think about the last time you had a cold and you had to blow your nose a hundred times. Well, mucus like nasal mucus traps invading bacteria, and flushes them out. Coughing, sneezing, crying, and relieving yourself in the bathroom also serve this purpose.

The immune system is wonderfully complex, as I've said, and unfortunately that's all we have time for today. Tomorrow, we'll talk in more detail about chemical immune

defenses.
Now get ready to answer the questions. You may use your notes to help you answer.

Listen again to part of the lecture. Then answer the question.
*There are also specialized organs and tissues that assist in providing immunity. Think of
your liver, for example. It's not an organ people often think about much until they realize that
it acts as the body's filter.*

7. Why does the professor say this: 🎧
Think of your liver, for example.

P : 인간과 동물은 면역계를 가지고 있어요... 우리로서는 다행스런 일이죠. 면역계는 질병으로부터 우리
를 보호해주고, 감염을 퇴치해주죠. 박테리아도 효소를 가지고 있는데, 이 효소가 해로운 바이러스로
부터 박테리아를 보호해줘요. 면역계는 역사상 가장 놀라운 진화 형태 중 하나에요, 굉장한 일이죠.
면역계가 구체적으로 어떻게 작용하냐 하면.... 면역 시스템이 첫 번째로 하는 일은 몸 안의 물질을
감지하는 거예요. 건강한 세포 및 조직과 침입자를 구별해내야 하는 거죠. 면역 시스템은 수많은 잠
재적 위험 요소를 구별해낼 수 있어요. 바이러스와 종양, 유해한 박테리아, 각종 균들, 기생충 같은
것이죠. 이 모든 과정은 언제나 복잡한데, 몸이 질병을 일으키는 수많은 병원균에 대항해야 하기 때
문이에요. 게다가, 다들 아는 것처럼, 박테리아와 바이러스는 항상 돌연변이를 일으켜요. 일반적인 감
기 바이러스에 면역성을 발달시키는 그 순간 변종 바이러스가 나타나는 것이죠.
척추동물의 면역 시스템, 아, 오늘은 이 부분을 중점적으로 다룰 건데요, 이 척추동물의 면역 시스템
은 세포, 조직 등 몸의 각 레벨이 서로 제휴 관계를 유지하며 기능을 해요. 어디 보자... 분자 레벨에
서는 병원체를 감지하고 공격 또는 무력화시키는 특정 단백질이 있어요. 이러한 기능은 세포 레벨에
서도 일어나는데, 예를 들면 T 세포와 식세포가 있죠. 면역 기능을 돕는 특수 장기와 세포도 있어요.
가령, 여러분의 간을 생각해봐요. 간이 생체 여과기 기능을 한다는 것을 깨닫기 전까지는 사람들이
간에 대해 별로 생각해보지 않아요. 조직 및 장기 레벨에서 일어나는 면역 기능의 또 다른 예로는 피
부가 있어요. 피부는 신체의 감염을 막는 1차 방어선으로, 바로 그런 점 때문에 벤 상처와 찔려서 난
상처를 아주 조심스럽게 치료하는 것이 중요한 거에요. 이물질이 이 장벽을 돌파하여 체내에 침투하
면 다른 방어 시스템이 활성화되지요.
체내에서 일어나는 또 다른 방어 기능 중에 면역기억반응이라는 것이 있어요. 이게 바로 백신의 비밀
이죠. 신체가 약화된, 또는 죽은 비이러스나 박테리아에 노출되면 몸이 면역반응을 유도하죠. 나중에
우리 몸이 똑같은 위험에 노출되면, 방어 시스템은 이미 준비되어 있어요. 위험 물질을 즉시 기억해
내어 빠르고 효과적인 공격을 감행하는 거죠. 사람들은 불완전하기는 하지만 이러한 생각을 수세기
전부터 해왔어요. 2천년 전에 아테네를 휩쓸었던 역병에서 살아난 사람들이 환자들을 돌보았는데, 그
들은 자신들이 2차 감염의 위험으로부터 안전하다는 것을 알게 되었어요. 바로 이 발견이 우리가 면
역 체계를 이해하는 기초가 되었죠. 디프테리아, 천연두, 파상풍과 같은 질병에 대해서도 더 잘 이해
하게 되었어요.
우리 몸은 병원체 정화 기능도 가지고 있어요. 성가시다고 생각되는 것들도 실은 건강을 유지하는데
있어 중요한 과정이에요. 여러분이 마지막으로 감기에 걸려 코를 수백 번은 풀어야 했던 때를 생각해
봐요. 콧물 같은 점액은 침투하는 박테리아를 가두어서 씻겨 내버려요. 기침이나 재채기, 눈물을 흘리
는 것이나, 화장실에서 용변을 보는 것들도 모두 이러한 목적을 가지고 있어요.
아까 말했듯이 면역 시스템은 매우 복잡한 체계를 갖고 있는데, 아쉽지만 오늘 수업은 여기서 마쳐야
겠네요. 내일은 화학적 면역 방어 시스템에 대해 자세히 알아보겠어요.

Review

1. 1. 지명, 추천 2. 후보자 3. 헌신, 의지 4. 수입 5. 방해하다 6. 예비, 보충 7. 회복하다
8. 몹시 바쁜 9. 요금 10. 단념시키다 11. strict 12. seal 13. spill 14. deferment
15. refund 16. author 17. habitat 18. detect 19. prey 20. consequence

2. 1. hand in 제출하다 2. follow in a person's footsteps ~의 뒤를 잇다 3. rule out 배제하다 4. fill
out 작성하다 5. bring back 반환하다 6. give off 방출하다, 내뿜다 7. take action 조처를 취하다
8. It goes without saying that ~는 말할 나위도 없다 9. fall into ~에 속하다 10. give out 나눠주다

3. 1. harmful 2. audience 3. referred 4. accuracy 5. collapsed 6. qualifications
해석 | 1. 박테리아도 효소를 가지고 있는데, 이 효소가 해로운 바이러스로부터 박테리아를 보호해줘요.
2. 많은 관중이 지켜보는 미식축구 경기에 나오는 광고 1개에 수백만 달러가 드니까요.
3. 실제로 급속한 속도로 생물 종이 사라지고 있기 때문에 우리가 살고 있는 현재를 대멸종의 시대
라고도 하죠.
4. 그 원인이 무엇이든 구멍 기관은 뱀이 한 치의 착오도 없이 정확하게 먹이를 공격하게 해주죠.
5. 네가 알고 있을 수도 있을 텐데, 캠퍼스 프랑스어 클럽이 전에 있었단다. 대학 측의 재정이 부족
하게 되어서 작년에 문을 닫았지.
6. 학업 계획서에는 너의 학업 목표를 명확하게 드러내야 해, 가령 네가 선택한 분야에 대한 적성
이나 능력, 의지 등과 같은 것 말이야.

Chapter 5 Stance/Function

Office Hours

1. Ⓑ 2. Ⓐ 3. Ⓑ

대화의 일부를 다시 들으시오. 그러고 나서 질문에 답하시오.
남 : Frist 교수님, 아동 심리학 305 수업 리포트에 관해 여쭤보고 싶은 것이 있습니다.
여 : 내가 한 번 맞춰보도록 할게. 제출했던 리포트를 아직 못 돌려받아서 온 것 아니니?

1. 교수가 이것을 말할 때 암시하는 것은 무엇인가: 🎧

> *여 : 내가 한 번 맞춰보도록 할게. 제출했던 리포트를 아직 못 돌려받아서 온 것 아니니?*

Ⓐ 교수는 학생이 지각하는 것을 꾸짖고 싶어 한다.
Ⓑ 교수는 학생이 자신을 찾아올 거라고 예상하고 있었다.
Ⓒ 교수는 학생의 리포트에 큰 문제가 있다고 생각한다.
Ⓓ 교수는 학생이 무슨 이야기를 하는 건지 전혀 모르고 있다.

Dictation | ① Let me guess ② did an outstanding job ③ if I could use it as a model
④ remove your name

남 : Frist 교수님, 아동 심리학 305 수업 리포트에 관해 여쭤보고 싶은 것이 있습니다.
여 : 내가 한 번 맞춰보도록 할게. 제출했던 리포트를 아직 못 돌려받아서 온 것 아니니?
남 : 네, 그래서 온 거에요! 모두들 오늘 리포트를 돌려받는데, 저는 못 받아서…….
여 : 실은 네 리포트에 관해 너와 이야기를 하고 싶었단다. 놀이 치료에 관한 리포트를 정말 잘 썼더구나,
　　매우 훌륭했어. 네 리포트를 모델 에세이로 사용하면 어떨지 생각하고 있었단다.
남 : 모델 에세이요?
여 : 그래, 추후 강의용으로 말이야. 물론 네 이름은 지울 거야. 학생들이 A+, A, B+ 리포트가 어떤 것인
　　지 알 수 있도록 샘플 리포트를 모아둔단다. 그렇게 해도 괜찮겠니?
남 : 그럼요! 과찬의 말씀이십니다!

어휘 | outstanding 뛰어난 | remove 지우다, 제거하다 |

대화의 일부를 다시 들으시오. 그러고 나서 질문에 답하시오.
남 : 그래서 너희 그룹에 문제가 생겼겠구나.
*여 : 정말 그렇다니까요. 그것 말고도 John이 아직 자기가 맡은 부분을 끝내지 않았다는 것을 알게 되었어요.
　　일이 많아서 아직 못했다고 하는데, 정말이지 John이 하는 변명들은 지긋지긋해요. 저희들도 모두 아르
　　바이트를 하거든요.*

2. 학생이 이것을 말할 때 의미하는 것은 무엇인가: 🎧

> *여 : 정말 그렇다니까요.*

Ⓐ 학생의 그룹은 John의 불성실한 행동 때문에 곤란에 처해 있다.
Ⓑ 학생은 교수에게 왜 John이 자신의 그룹에 속해 있는지 알려 달라고 요청한다.
Ⓒ 학생은 교수가 John을 만나 직접 이야기하기를 원한다.
Ⓓ 학생의 그룹은 새로운 멤버를 들여야 한다.

Dictation | ① in a bad mood today ② Tell me about it ③ he hasn't done his part of the
research ④ a little sick and tired of his excuses ⑤ get the project done

남 : 어서 오렴, Penelope. 여기 앉도록 해.
여 : 시간을 내주셔서 감사합니다, Wahlberg 교수님.

어휘 | be in a bad mood 기분이 안 좋다 | sick and tired of ~이 지긋지긋한 | excuse 변명 | reasonable 합당한 |

대화의 일부를 다시 들으시오. 그러고 나서 질문에 답하시오.
여 : 시나리오를 쓰는 비법 좀 가르쳐주실 수 있나 해서요. 전에 써 본적이 없거든요.
남 : 그게 내 수업과 어떻게 관련이 있는지 잘 모르겠군요.

3. 교수는 왜 이것을 말하는가: 🎧
   남 : 그게 내 수업과 어떻게 관련이 있는지 잘 모르겠군요.

   Ⓐ 학생이 원하는 것이 무엇인지 모르겠다는 것을 나타내려고
   Ⓑ 학생이 뭔가를 잘못 알고 있다고 암시하려고
   Ⓒ 너무 바빠서 학생의 질문에 답할 수 없다는 것을 암시하려고
   Ⓓ 학생 스스로가 방법을 찾아야 한다는 것을 나타내려고

Dictation | ① questions about the course ② how that's related to my class ③ you're getting it
         mixed up ④ how books are adapted for film ⑤ shoot a film

Listen again to part of the conversation. Then answer the question.
W : Um, I'm wondering if you could suggest tips for writing screenplays. I've never done that
   before.
M : I'm not sure how that's related to my class.

Why does the professor say this: 🎧
M : I'm not sure how that's related to my class.

여 : 학기도 이제 막 시작해서 지금 바쁘신 건 아는데요, 교수님의 영화 수업에 관해 질문 좀 드려도 될까요?
남 : 그래요, 강의에 관해 질문이 있나요?
여 : 시나리오를 쓰는 비법 좀 가르쳐주실 수 있나 해서요. 전에 써 본적이 없거든요.
남 : 그게 내 수업과 어떻게 관련이 있는지 잘 모르겠군요.
여 : 교수님의 강의에서 만들 영화 시나리오를 학생들이 쓰는 게 아닌가요?
남 : 아니에요, 내가 보기엔 학생이 상급 과정과 혼동을 한 것 같군요. 내가 가르치는 200 레벨 수업은

주로 책 이야기가 영화로 각색되는 과정을 다뤄요. 이 수업에서는 책을 많이 읽고, 기말 프로젝트로는 소설 책 한 권을 모두 읽고, 그 소설의 각색 버전을 읽어야 하죠.

여 : 어머, 제가 정말 크게 착각했나 봐요.

남 : 영화를 찍고 싶다면, 400 레벨 강의들을 알아보도록 해요.

어휘 | tip 비결, 비법 | screenplay 영화각본, 시나리오 | adapt 각색하다 | novel 소설 |

Service Encounters

1. Ⓐ   2. Ⓒ   3. Ⓒ

대화의 일부를 다시 들으시오. 그러고 나서 질문에 답하시오.

남 : 좋아요. 여기 있는 양식을 작성하기만 하면 되고, 필름을 담을 통이 여기 있어요.

여 : 저... 이렇게 하는데 보증제도 같은 것이 있나요?

1. 학생은 왜 이것을 말하는가?

여 : 저... 이렇게 하는데 보증제도 같은 것이 있나요?

Ⓐ 필름이 손상될까 걱정하고 있다.

Ⓑ 필름에 뭔가 문제가 생기면 전액 환불을 원한다.

Ⓒ 사진이 프로젝트 마감일 전까지 완성된다는 것을 확인하고 싶어한다.

Ⓓ 이것이 진짜 무료 서비스라고 생각하지 않는다.

Dictation | ① for free   ② come to the right place   ③ any kind of guarantee   ④ let the more experienced students develop   ⑤ taking your chances

Listen again to part of the conversation. Then answer the question.

M : All right. You just need to fill out this little form, and here's a bag for your film.

W : So... is there any kind of guarantee with this?

Why does the student say this:

W : So... is there any kind of guarantee with this?

여 : 안녕하세요, 여기서 무료로 사진을 현상해준다고 하던데, 맞나요?

남 : 맞아요, 학생들이 사진을 현상해도 별 상관없다면 제대로 찾아왔군요.

여 : 돈도 별로 없고, 수업 프로젝트 마감일도 코앞이라서요...

남 : 선택의 여지가 별로 없군요, 그렇죠?

여 : 그렇죠! 정말 그래요.

남 : 좋아요. 여기 있는 양식을 작성하기만 하면 되고, 필름을 담을 통이 여기 있어요.

여 : 저... 이렇게 하는데 보증제도 같은 것이 있나요?

어휘 | develop 현상하다 | guarantee 보증 | take chances 운에 맡기고 해보다, 위험을 무릅쓰다 |

대화의 일부를 다시 들으시오. 그러고 나서 질문에 답하시오.
여 : 그러죠. 학생증을 보여주겠어요?
남 : 여기 있습니다.
여 : 네... 음, 참 이상한 일이네요.

2. 여자가 이것을 말할 때 암시하는 것은 무엇인가: 🎧
    여 : 네... 음, 참 이상한 일이네요.

    Ⓐ 여자는 학생증 사진이 학생의 얼굴과 닮지 않았다고 생각한다.
    Ⓑ 여자는 뭔가 재미있는 일이 학생에게 일어났다는 것을 알게 되었다.
    Ⓒ 여자는 컴퓨터 기록에 문제가 있다는 것을 발견했다.
    Ⓓ 여자는 학생의 문제에 관해 별 관심을 기울이지 않는다.

Dictation | ① when I checked my account online ② several students weren't paid ③ must be
a computer error ④ until the end of the day

여 : 기록에는 학생 계좌가 전혀 존재하지 않는다고 나오네요. 그럴 리가 없는데 말이에요. 컴퓨터 오류 때문인 것 같군요.

남 : 정말이지, 전 똑같은 은행 계좌를 갖고 있어요!

여 : 네, 학생 말을 믿어요. 그 점에 대해서는 걱정 말아요. 내 생각엔 우리 쪽에 더 큰 문제가 있는 것 같 군요. 제 상사와 이야기를 나누어봐야겠어요.

남 : 제가 언제 급료를 받을 수 있을지 알 수 있으세요?

여 : 오늘 오후까지 시간을 주면 무슨 일이 잘못되었는지 확인하도록 할게요.

남 : 네, 그렇게 하세요, 그러는 게 괜찮을 것 같아요.

어휘 | account 계좌 | deposit 예금하다 |

대화의 일부를 다시 들으시오. 그러고 나서 질문에 답하시오.

여 : 있긴 있어요. 7층까지 올라가서 분수대에서 왼쪽으로 돌면, 도서관에서 서고로 사용하는 공간을 찾을 수 있을 거예요.

남 : 거기에 올라가도 되나요? 지도를 가지고요?

3. 학생이 이것을 말할 때 의미하는 것은 무엇인가: 🎧

남 : 거기에 올라가도 되나요? 지도를 가지고요?

Ⓐ 서고를 사용하려면 예약이 필수라고 생각했다.
Ⓑ 서고에 큰 테이블이 없다고 생각했다.
Ⓒ 서고를 사용하면 안 된다고 생각했다.
Ⓓ 서고에 지도가 있다고 생각했다.

Dictation | ① for geography class   ② spread out large maps   ③ go all the way up   ④ taking books out of the library   ⑤ a lot of junk   ⑥ don't mind moving a few stacks of books

Listen again to part of the conversation. Then answer the question.

W : Actually, there is. If you go all the way up to the 7th floor and turn left at the water fountain, and you'll see an area the library uses for storage.

M : Is it OK to go up there? I mean taking the maps?

What does the student mean when he says this: 🎧

M : Is it OK to go up there? I mean taking the maps?

남 : 지금 지리학과 학생들이랑 함께 있는데요, 좀 더 큰 테이블이 놓여있는 공간이 있는지 알고 싶습니다.

여 : 무슨 일 때문이죠?

남 : 지리학 수업 때문이에요. 큰 지도들을 펼쳐 놓고 비교해 봐야 하거든요.

여 : 알겠어요. 안됐지만 오늘 개인학습공간은 모두 예약이 되어있네요.

남 : 저런, 큰 테이블이 있는 또 다른 공간이 있나요?

여 : 있긴 있어요. 7층까지 올라가서 분수대에서 왼쪽으로 돌면, 도서관에서 서고로 사용하는 공간을 찾을 수 있을 거예요.

어휘 | geography 지리학 | spread out 펼치다 | map 지도 | book 예약하다 | water foundation 분수대 |
without permission 무단으로, 허가 없이 | junk 잡동사니 | stack 더미, 쌓아 올림 (stacks of 많은) |

Lectures

1. 1) Ⓐ 2) Ⓓ **2.** 1) Ⓒ 2) Ⓑ **3.** 1) Ⓑ 2) Ⓑ 3) Ⓒ

1. 해양학 수업

강의의 일부를 다시 들으시오. 그리고 나서 질문에 답하시오.

P : 좋아요. 음, 이러한 연구 결과가 암시하는 바는 물론 기념비적인 것이었죠. 그의 연구는 동물의 의사소통과 인간의 의사소통 사이의 유사성을 보여주었어요. 모두 알고 있듯, 동물은 인간이 언어를 통해 의사소통을 하는 것과 같은 방식으로 의사소통을 하지는 않지만, 의사소통을 하기 위해 특정한 행동 패턴이 나타나는 것은 확실해요.

1. 교수가 이것을 말할 때 암시하는 것은 무엇인가:

   P : 그의 연구는 동물의 의사소통과 인간의 의사소통 사이의 유사성을 보여주었어요.

   Ⓐ 커뮤니케이션이 항상 구어를 통해 이루어지는 것은 아니다.
   Ⓑ 동물의 특정 행동 패턴이 인간의 행동 패턴과 유사하다.
   Ⓒ 동물의 의사소통은 해석하기가 어렵지 않다.
   Ⓓ 의사소통은 동물 행동의 한 형태이다.

강의의 일부를 다시 들으시오. 그리고 나서 질문에 답하시오.

P : 잘 알려져 있지는 않지만, 그의 이전 발견들만큼 흥미로운 발견이 바로 물고기에게 청력이 있다는 것이죠. 물고기의 측선이 감각기관 기능을 한다고 알려져 있어요. 이 측선에서 진동과 움직임을 감지하죠. 하지만, 물고기에게는 인간의 귀에서 발견되는 것과 유사한 내이에 있는 뼈인 이석을 갖춘 귀가 있어요.

2. 교수가 이것을 말할 때 암시하는 것은 무엇인가:

   P : 잘 알려져 있지는 않지만, 그의 이전 발견들만큼 흥미로운 발견이 바로 물고기에게 청력이 있다는 것이죠.

   Ⓐ 대부분의 사람들은 물고기가 색깔을 구분하는 능력만 가지고 있다고 생각했었다.
   Ⓑ 물고기에게 측선이 있다는 사실을 모르는 사람이 많았다.
   Ⓒ 물고기에게 예민한 청각이 있다는 사실은 널리 알려져 있었다.
   Ⓓ 대부분의 사람들은 물고기에게 청력이 없다고 믿었다.

Listen again to part of the lecture. Then answer the question.
P : Good. Well, the implications of this, of course, were monumental. His work showed the parallels between animal communication and human communication. As you know, animals do not communicate the way humans do, via language, but certain behavior patterns definitely occur for the purpose of communication.

1. What does the professor imply when he says this: 🎧
P : His work showed the parallels between animal communication and human communication.

Listen again to part of the lecture. Then answer the question.
P : Perhaps not as well known, but equally interesting, was his discovery that fish can hear. It is known that the lateral line of fishes functions as a sensory organ: it detects vibration and motion. However, fishes do have an ear – complete with an otolith, an internal ear bone similar to what can be found in the human ear.

2. What does the professor imply when he says this: 🎧
P : Perhaps not as well known, but equally interesting, was his discovery that fish can hear.

P : 중요한 동물학자들에 관한 토론을 이어가도록 Karl von Frisch(카를 폰 프리슈)에 관해 이야기 하도록 하겠어요. 그는 많은 혁신적이고 선구적인 발견을 한 장본인이죠. 그가 발견한 것들에 대해 누구 이야기해보고 싶은 사람 있어요?
S : 사실, 그는 1973년에 노벨상을 수상했어요. 초기의 연구에서는 물고기와 꿀벌이 색깔을 구별하는 능력을 가지고 있고, 꿀벌이 비슷한 많은 꽃향기를 구분할 수 있다는 것을 증명했죠. 또한 최초로 꿀벌의 8자 춤에 나타나는 의사소통 패턴을 해석해내기도 했고요.
P : 좋아요. 음, 이러한 연구 결과가 암시하는 바는 물론 기념비적인 것이었죠. 그의 연구는 동물의 의사소통과 인간의 의사소통 사이의 유사성을 보여주었어요. 모두 알고 있듯, 동물은 인간이 언어를 통해 의사소통을 하는 것과 같은 방식으로 의사소통을 하지는 않지만, 의사소통을 하기 위해 특정한 행동 패턴이 나타나는 것은 확실해요.
S : 하지만 제가 알기로는 이러한 연구 결과를 발표할 당시 회의적인 시각이 많았다고 하던데요?
P : 맞아요, 대부분의 위대한 발견이 그러했던 것처럼요. 사실, 그의 발견이 과학적 사실로 확립된 것은 비교적 최근의 일이죠. 잘 알려져 있지는 않지만, 그의 이전 발견들만큼 흥미로운 발견이 바로 물고기에게 청력이 있다는 것이죠. 물고기의 측선이 감각기관 기능을 한다고 알려져 있어요. 이 측선에서 진동과 움직임을 감지하죠. 하지만, 물고기에게는 인간의 귀에서 발견되는 것과 유사한 내이에 있는 뼈인 이석을 갖춘 귀가 있어요.

어휘 | zoologist 동물학자 | pioneer 선구적인 | be capable of ~할 수 있다 | distinguish 구별하다 | scent 향기 | interpret 해석하다 | waggle dance 꿀벌의 8자 춤 | implication 암시, 의미 | monumental 기념비적인 | parallel 유사성 | via ~를 통해 | skepticism 회의론 | relatively 비교적 | lateral line 측선 | sensory organ 감각기관 | vibration 진동 | otolith 이석 | internal ear 내이 |

2. 언어학 수업

강의의 일부를 다시 들으시오. 그러고 나서 질문에 답하시오.
언어의 여러 측면 가운데 아직 우리가 다루지 않은 것이 있는데, 바로 제스처와 기타 시각적 신호에요...
이는 언어 학습에 있어 빠지지 않는 필수적인 구성 요소로, 아무리 강조해도 지나치지 않죠.

1. 교수는 왜 이것을 말하는가? 🎧
   아무리 강조해도 지나치지 않죠.

   Ⓐ 제스처와 기타 시각적 신호를 이해하는 것은 스트레스 쌓이는 일이라는 것을 암시하기 위해
   Ⓑ 제스처에 관해 이야기 할 시간이 별로 없다는 것을 나타내기 위해
   Ⓒ 제스처와 시각적 신호가 언어 습득에 있어 중요한 역할을 한다는 것을 강조하기 위해
   Ⓓ 왜 시각적 신호가 필수적인 요소인지 이해 못하겠다는 것을 표현하기 위해

강의의 일부를 다시 들으시오. 그러고 나서 질문에 답하시오.
그럼 유아의 제스처 발달 양식에 관해 알아보는 것이 좋을 것 같군요, 음, 이 과정을 이해하면 어떻게 제스처가 언어라는 전체적인 그림의 한 부분을 이루는지를 이해할 수 있을 거예요. 모두 알다시피 언어 습득은 선천적인 면과 후천적인 면을 모두 가지고 있기 때문에... 이 부분을 다시 되풀이 할 필요는 없겠죠?

2. 교수가 이것을 말할 때 암시하는 것은 무엇인가: 🎧
   이 부분을 다시 되풀이 할 필요는 없겠죠?

   Ⓐ 학생들은 그 부분에 관한 내용을 교재에서 찾아 읽을 수 있다.
   Ⓑ 학생들은 전시간에 그 부분을 배웠다.
   Ⓒ 학생들은 이 내용에 대해 알 필요가 없다.
   Ⓓ 학생들은 이 내용을 복습했었어야 한다.

Dictation | ① for second language learners ② we haven't yet touched on ③ but another thing to speak it ④ how it fits into the big picture of language ⑤ babies don't utter their first words ⑥ convey their thoughts, desires, and needs ⑦ a variety of emotions

Listen again to part of the lecture. Then answer the question.
Well, there is one aspect of language that we haven't yet touched on and that is gestures and other visual cues... these are, ah, these are essential – now, I can't stress this enough – to learning a language.

1. Why does the professor say this: 🎧
   now, I can't stress this enough

Listen again to part of the lecture. Then answer the question.
So, um, basically I want to look at the development of gesture from infancy, uh, I think this will give you a good understanding of how it fits into the big picture of language. Because, as you know, language acquisition is both innate and learned... I don't have to go over this again, do I?

2. What does the professor imply when she says this: 🎧
I don't have to go over this again, do I?

P : 자, 모두들 자리에 앉아요... 그럼, 지난 시간에 다루었던 내용으로 돌아가봅시다. 다들 알겠지만, 그 동안 언어 패턴에 관해 많은 이야기를 나누어보았는데요, 제 2 외국어 학습자들에게는 특히 중요한 부분이죠. 언어의 여러 측면 가운데 아직 우리가 다루지 않은 것이 있는데, 바로 제스처와 기타 시각적 신호에요... 이는 언어 학습에 있어 빠지지 않는 필수적인 구성 요소로, 아무리 강조해도 지나치지 않죠. 음, 외국어를 배워본 적이 있는 사람이라면, 글로 써져 있는 것을 읽는 것과 그것을 말로 하는 것은 별개의 문제라는 것을 알고 있을 거에요. 그리고 사람들이 무엇을 말하는지, 그 의미가 무엇인지를 이해하는 것은 또 다른 문제죠.
그럼 유아의 제스처 발달 양식에 관해 알아보는 것이 좋을 것 같군요, 음, 이 과정을 이해하면 어떻게 제스처가 언어라는 전체적인 그림의 한 부분을 이루는지를 이해할 수 있을 거에요. 모두 알다시피 언어 습득은 선천적인 면과 후천적인 면을 모두 가지고 있기 때문에... 이 부분을 다시 되풀이 할 필요는 없겠죠? 특히, 언어 습득은 생후 18개월 동안에 빠르게 진행돼요. 보통 아기가 12개월까지는 말을 못하는 것이 사실이기 하지만, 아기들에게는 자기의 생각과 욕구, 필요한 것을 표현할 수 있는 방법들이 있어요... 예를 들면, 신생아는 팔과 다리를 이리저리 움직여서 다양한 감정을 표출하죠... 뭔가 불편하면 발가락을 꼼지락꼼지락 움직이기도 할테고, 무슨 말인지 알겠죠.

어휘 | cue 신호 | one thing... another (thing) ~와 ~는 별개이다 | infancy 유아 | acquisition 습득 | innate 타고난, 선천적인 | learned 학습에 의한, 후천적인 | go over 복습하다, 되풀이하다 | utter 말하다, 중얼거리다 | convey 표출하다 | needs 욕구, 필요한 것 | newborn 신생아 | uncomfortable 불편한 |

3. 범죄 심리학 수업
  1. 강의의 주제는 무엇인가?
    Ⓐ 거짓말 탐지기의 역사
    Ⓑ 폴리그래프의 이용과 한계
    Ⓒ 고대 중국인의 거짓말 탐지 기법
    Ⓓ 거짓말 탐지기의 정확성

  2. 다음 중 어느 것이 폴리그래프로 측정되지 않는가?
    Ⓐ 맥박
    Ⓑ 타액 분비
    Ⓒ 혈압
    Ⓓ 호흡

강의의 일부를 다시 들으시오. 그러고 나서 질문에 답하시오.
P : 지금 그 점에 관해 이야기 하려던 참이었어요. 사실, 폴리그래프가 전혀 신뢰할만지 못하다는 증거가 있어요. 1997년에 행해진 한 연구 결과를 보면 이 기계의 정확성은 61%에 불과하죠. 다른 이들도 폴리그래프가 테스트 방법이 아니라고 말하는데, 이 기계가 표준화되어서는 안 된다는 뜻이죠. 그리고 스파이들이 폴리그래프를 '이겨서' 자신들의 정체를 끝까지 숨겼던 이야기들도 유명해요. 폴리그래프가 조만간 과거의 유물이 될지도 모르죠.

  3. 교수가 이것을 말할 때 암시하는 것은 무엇인가: 🎧

P : 그리고 스파이들이 폴리그래프를 '이겨서' 자신들의 정체를 끝까지 숨겼던 이야기들도 유명해요.

   Ⓐ 폴리그래프 사용이 확대되어야 한다.
   Ⓑ 폴리그래프를 표준화하는 것은 잘된 일이다.
   Ⓒ 폴리그래프는 신뢰할만한 도구가 아니다.
   Ⓓ 폴리그래프를 작동하는 사람이 서툴다.

Dictation | ① who is investigated using a lie detector ② to a suspect's body ③ what happens next ④ this instrument measures ⑤ outside of a person's conscious control ⑥ attempt to determine guilt or innocence ⑦ the technicians administering the test ⑧ it cannot be standardized ⑨ keep their identities hidden

Listen again to part of the lecture. Then answer the question.

P : *I was about to talk about that right now. In fact, there is evidence that it is not reliable at all. One study from 1997 showed that its accuracy was only 61%. Other critics say that the polygraph is not a form of testing, which means that it cannot be standardized. There are also famous examples of spies managing to 'beat' the polygraph and keep their identities hidden. It's possible that the polygraph may soon be a thing of the past.*

3. What does the professor imply when he says this: 🎧
   P : *There are also famous examples of spies managing to 'beat' the polygraph and keep their identities hidden.*

P : 여러분 모두 거짓말 탐지기를 이용해 조사 받는 사람이 등장하는 영화들을 본 적이 있죠? 누가 그것에 관해 이야기 해볼래요?
S : 제가 전에 읽은 소설에서는 경찰이 용의자의 몸에 전극을 연결한 후, 기계 전원을 켠 후, 질문을 하기 시작했어요.
P : 그렇죠, 그 다음에 무슨 일이 일어날지 정확히 알고 있을 거예요. 그 사람이 거짓말을 하고 있다면, 들통이 나겠죠. 거짓말 탐지기는 흔히 사람들이 속일 수 없는 무적의 기계처럼 보이지만, 실상은 그것보다는 좀 더 복잡하지요. 어떤 종류의 거짓말 탐지기가 실제로 가장 많이 쓰이는지 알고 있나요?
S : 폴리그래프(거짓말 탐지기의 일종)요?
P : 맞아요. 누군가 조사를 받는 동안, 이 기계는 심장 박동과 혈압, 맥박, 호흡과 같은 생리적 반응을 측정해요. 이러한 현상들은 모두 교감 신경계의 통제를 받는데, 사람의 의식 제어력을 벗어난 곳이죠. 스트레스와 불안이 이러한 신체 변화를 유발해요. 이런 사실은 고대 중국 시대부터 알려졌는데, 그 당시에 사람들은 누군가가 유죄인지 무죄인지를 알아내기 위해 그 사람에게 입에 쌀을 물고 있게 했어요. 사람이 불안함을 느끼면 타액 분비가 멈춘다고 믿어졌기 때문에, 심문을 끝낼 즈음에 쌀이 건조한 채로 남아있으면, 그 사람은 거짓말을 하고 있는 것이라고 여겨졌죠. 그와 비슷한 생각이 오늘날의 거짓말 탐지에 기초가 되었어요. 예비 인터뷰를 통해 심문 받는 사람의 일반적인 상태가 기록되고 나면, 진짜 질문이 이어지게 되는데, 테스트를 실시하는 전문가가 어떤 변화를 찾고 있는지 알고 있기 때문이에요.
S : 그럼, 이 폴리그래프가 항상 정확한가요?
P : 지금 그 점에 관해 이야기 하려던 참이었어요. 사실, 폴리그래프가 전혀 신뢰할만하지 못하다는 증거가 있어요. 1997년에 행해진 한 연구 결과를 보면 이 기계의 정확성은 61%에 불과하죠. 다른 이들도 폴리그래프가 테스트 방법이 아니라고 말하는데, 이 기계가 표준화되어서는 안 된다는 뜻이죠. 그리고 스파이들이 폴리그래프를 '이겨서' 자신들의 정체를 끝까지 숨겼던 이야기들도 유명해요. 폴리그래프가 조만간 과거의 유물이 될지도 모르죠.

어휘 | lie detector 거짓말 탐지기 | electrode 전극 | suspect 용의자 | invincible 무적의 | complicated 복잡한 |
instrument 기계 | physiological 생리적인 | heartbeat 심박동 | blood pressure 혈압 | pulse 맥박 |
respiration 호흡 | sympathetic nervous system 교감 신경계 | conscious 의식 | anxiety 근심, 불안 |
guilt 유죄 | innocence 무죄 | salivation 타액 분비 | underpin 버팀목을 대다, 지지하다 |
preliminary 예비의 | administer 실행하다 | evidence 증거 | reliable 신뢰할만한 |
standardize 표준화하다 | identity 정체 | hidden 감추어진 |

Practice

[1-5] **1.** Ⓑ   **2.** Ⓑ   **3.** Ⓒ   **4.** Suggested – Ⓑ, Ⓒ, Ⓓ Not Suggested – Ⓐ, Ⓔ   **5.** Ⓓ
[6-11] **6.** Ⓒ   **7.** Ⓑ   **8.** Ⓑ   **9.** Romanticism – Ⓐ, Ⓑ, Ⓔ Neoclassicism – Ⓒ, Ⓓ   **10.** Ⓓ   **11.** Ⓒ

[문제 1-5] 학생과 교수 사이의 대화의 일부를 들으시오.

1. 학생이 교수와 대화를 나누는 이유는 무엇인가?
 Ⓐ 학생은 대학원 입학 지원서를 작성하는데 어려움을 느끼고 있다.
 Ⓑ 학생은 어느 학교 대학원에 가야 할지 결정을 못 내리고 있다.
 Ⓒ 학생은 학교에 남아 공부를 계속할지 취직을 할지 결정을 내리려고 한다.
 Ⓓ 학생은 교수에게 취직하는데 도움을 요청하고 있다.

해설 학생은 학부 졸업 후 바로 대학원에 가고 싶어 한다. 아직 어떤 학교를 선택해야 할지 결정을 못 내리고
 있어서 교수에게 조언을 구하고 있다. 정답은 보기 Ⓑ.

대화의 일부를 다시 들으시오. 그러고 나서 질문에 답하시오.
여 : 우리 학교 프로그램도 생각 중이라고 했으니까, 네가 내 선입견을 배제하고 듣는다면 내 생각을 말해줄게.
남 : 그렇게 해주세요.

2. 교수가 이것을 말할 때 암시하는 것은 무엇인가: 🎧
 여 : 우리 학교 프로그램도 생각 중이라고 했으니까, 네가 내 선입견을 배제하고 듣는다면 내 생각을 말해줄게.

 Ⓐ 교수는 학생의 상황에 대해 마음의 결정을 내리려 하고 있다.
 Ⓑ 교수가 이 학교에서 일하기 때문에 교수의 견해는 중립적이지 않다.
 Ⓒ 교수는 학생이 올바른 결정을 내리지 않았다고 생각한다.
 Ⓓ 교수는 어떤 프로그램이 학생에게 가장 적합한지 확신을 못하고 있다.

해설 교수는 지금 다니고 있는 학교의 대학원 프로그램의 장점을 이야기 하려 하고 있다. 교수 역시 이 학교
 직원이라 한 쪽으로 치우칠 수도 있기 때문에, 자신이 하는 말에 들어있는 선입견을 배제하고 들으라는
 의미이다. 따라서 정답은 보기 Ⓑ.

3. 학생에 관해 추론할 수 있는 것은 무엇인가?
 Ⓐ 학생은 봄방학 때 직장 경력을 쌓을 것이다.
 Ⓑ 학생은 학비를 댈 여력이 없다.
 Ⓒ 학생은 미생물학을 전공하고 있다.
 Ⓓ 학생의 성적은 평균 이하이다.

4. 대화에서, 교수는 학생에게 지금 다니는 학교에 남아 공부를 하면 좋을 몇 가지 이유를 제시하고 있다. 아래 표의 각 보기가 교수가 제시한 이유에 속하는지 표시하시오. 각 보기에 맞는 칸에 클릭하시오.

	Suggested	Not Suggested
Ⓐ 부모님과 가까이 살게 될 것이다.		
Ⓑ 주(state) 거주자이기 때문에 학비가 더 저렴하다.		
ⓒ 명성이 높은 학문 프로그램을 보유하고 있다.		
Ⓓ 교수들과 친분이 있다.		
Ⓔ 같은 곳에 계속 사는 것이 지역사회에서 취직하는데 더 낫다.		

5. 다음 중 어느 것이 학생에 관해 맞는가?
    Ⓐ 올해 졸업을 한다.
    Ⓑ 부모님께서 학생이 다른 주로 가는 것을 원하신다.
    ⓒ 외국에서 공부하는데 관심이 없다.
    Ⓓ 메릴랜드 주와 뉴욕 주에 친구가 있다.

[Questions 1–5] Listen to part of a conversation between a student and a professor.

M : Professor Merkel, do you have time to talk to me about something?

W : Can we make it quick? I have a faculty meeting.

M : It won't take long. I'm a senior this year, and I'll graduate in spring. I want to go to graduate school right after my graduation, but I'm having a really tough time deciding where to go.

W : Have you submitted your applications yet? Or have you already heard from some of the programs you were interested in?

M : I haven't, but I thought I'd apply for seven schools.

W : Why seven?

M : Because it's a lucky number? No, to be honest, I can only afford to apply for seven. You know, the application fees are so expensive, I mean, for students like me.

W : You can say that again. Does your 7 include our program here?

M : Actually, yes, and in addition to the program here, I'm thinking about several others in the country and maybe a couple out of the country.

W : You're a good student, so I'm sure you'll be accepted in several places.

M : I really hope so.

W : Well, you said you've considered our program, so if you can ignore my bias for a minute,

I'll give you my opinion.

M : Please do.

W : Our microbiology program is a nationally ranked one. We're not in the top 10, but we have a good reputation from professors as well as students. Also, you know the professors here, and you have a good relationship with them.

M : That counts for a lot.

W : Right. Don't underestimate good relationships. You can save your trouble getting accustomed to the new environment, like professors, dorms, libraries... I mean everything at the new school. And there's one other thing you might want to consider: in-state tuition. If you stay here, you're still a resident, so it's a lot cheaper.

M : That's a big advantage for sure, but I might get funding for other programs, right? I mean my grades are good, and I have some good professional experience, also.

W : That's true. Besides, it's valuable to live in different parts of the country or overseas. Do you have family and friends in these other locations you have in mind?

M : Yes, in Maryland and New York.

W : I see. Well, maybe you'd better narrow down your options to those two, plus this one.

M : That's an idea.

Now get ready to answer the questions. You may use your notes to help you answer.

2. Listen again to part of the conversation. Then answer the question.

W : Well, you said you've considered our program, so if you can ignore my bias for a minute, I'll give you my opinion.

M : Please do.

What does the professor imply when she says this: 🎧

W : Well, you said you've considered our program, so if you can ignore my bias for a minute, I'll give you my opinion.

남 : Merkel 교수님, 잠깐 시간 좀 있으세요?

여 : 이야기를 빨리 끝낼 수 있을까? 교수회의가 있어서 말이야.

남 : 오래 걸리지는 않을 거예요. 제가 올해 4학년인데요, 내년 봄에 졸업을 해요. 졸업하자마자 대학원에 진학하고 싶은데, 어느 학교로 가야 할지 결정을 못 내리고 있어요.

여 : 입학신청서는 제출했니? 아니면 관심 있는 학교에서 벌써 연락을 받았니?

남 : 아직이요, 그런데 7개 학교에 지원할까 해요.

여 : 왜 7개 학교니?

남 : 행운의 숫자니까요? 실은 그런 게 아니라, 지금 사정상 7개 학교 밖에 지원을 못해요. 저 같은 학생에게는 신청비도 만만치 않으니까요.

여 : 그렇긴 하지. 그 7개 학교 중에 우리 학교 프로그램도 들어가니?

남 : 네, 그리고 우리 학교 프로그램 말고도 국내 학교 몇 곳과 외국 학교 두 곳 정도를 생각하고 있어요.

여 : 넌 공부도 잘하고 착실한 학생이니까 여러 학교에 합격할 거야.

남 : 정말 그랬으면 좋겠어요.

여 : 우리 학교 프로그램도 생각 중이라고 했으니까, 네가 내 선입견을 배제하고 듣는다면 내 생각을 말해줄게.

남 : 그렇게 해주세요.

여 : 우리 학교 미생물학 프로그램은 전국적으로 명성이 높지. 아직 상위 10위권에 들지는 못했지만, 학생들과 교수들 모두로부터 평판이 좋단다. 그리고 넌 우리 학교 교수님들도 잘 알고 있고, 관계도 좋잖니.

어휘 | ignore 무시하다 | bias 선입견, 편견 | reputation 평판 | underestimate 과소평가하다 |
get accustomed to ~에 익숙해지다 | in-state tuition 주립 대학의 주(state) 거주 학생에게 적용
되는 학비(out-of-state tuition에 비해 혜택이 있음) |

[문제 6-11] 영문학 강의의 일부를 들으시오.

6. 교수는 주로 무엇에 관해 강의하고 있는가?
  Ⓐ 영문학 유산
  Ⓑ 신고전주의 시와 낭만주의 시의 비교
  Ⓒ William Wordsworth의 글
  Ⓓ 유명한 낭만주의 시인들의 작품

해설 낭만주의 문예 사조를 대변하는 대표 시인인 윌리엄 워즈워드의 작품과 시풍 등에 관해 강의하고 있다.
  정답은 보기 Ⓒ.

강의의 일부를 다시 들으시오. 그리고 나서 질문에 답하시오.
*자, William Wordsworth(윌리엄 워즈워드)는 영국 낭만주의(romantic) 시인을 대표하는 문학가로, 그렇다
고 해서 젊은 연인들 사이에 일어나는 로맨스(romance)를 말하는 건 아니에요. 자, 낭만주의는 19세기 후반
과 20세기 초반에 영국 문학을 주름잡았던 문예 사조입니다.*

7. 교수는 왜 이 말을 하는가:
  그렇다고 해서 젊은 연인들 사이에 일어나는 로맨스(romance)를 말하는 건 아니에요.

  Ⓐ 젊은 커플들에 대해 농담을 하려고
  Ⓑ 용어에 대해 흔히 생겨나는 오해를 명확히 밝혀두려고
  Ⓒ 많은 사람들이 사랑의 정표로 시를 쓴다는 것을 제시하려고
  Ⓓ 낭만주의가 로맨스와 간접적으로 연관이 있다는 것을 설명하려고

해설 낭만주의 문예 사조를 뜻하는 romantic과 연인들 사이의 애정 관계를 나타내는 romance는 서로 다른
  용어임을 설명하기 위해 언급한 말이다. 따라서 정답은 보기 Ⓑ.

8. 왜 비평가들은 Wordsworth의 작품을 싫어했는가?
  Ⓐ 그의 작품에는 시골 지역의 풍경과 너무 완벽하다고 생각되는 사람들이 묘사되어 있었다.

ⓑ 그의 작품은 부유한 사람들이 가난한 사람들보다 더 흥미진진하다는 생각에 위배되었다.
ⓒ 그의 작품은 Samuel Coleridge라는 하층민의 작품과 함께 출판되었다.
ⓓ 그의 작품에는 엘리트 계층이 알아볼 수 있는 영어 말씨가 쓰이지 않았다.

해설 워즈워드는 일상적인 언어를 사용하여 평범한 삶의 모습을 자신의 작품에 묘사했다. 주로 상류층의 삶을 다루는 신고전주의 사상에 빠져 있던 당시의 비평가들은 그의 이러한 시풍을 좋아하지 않았다. 정답은 보기 ⓑ.

9. 강의에서, 교수는 신고전주의 문학과 낭만주의 문학을 비교하고 있다. 아래 표의 각 보기가 어느 범주에 속하는지 표시하시오. 각 보기에 맞는 칸에 클릭하시오.

	Romanticism	Neoclassicism
ⓐ 평범한 사람들의 언어를 사용		
ⓑ 자연과 인간 사이의 관계를 찬양		
ⓒ 개인의 감정 표현을 억제		
ⓓ 복잡한 어휘		
ⓔ 가난한 노동 계층에 대한 관심		

해설 낭만주의 문학 작품은 평범한 사람들이 일상 생활에서 사용하는 언어로 쓰여져 있고, 자연과 인간의 관계를 찬양하는 내용이 담겨져 있으며, 가난한 계층에 대한 관심을 드러낸다. 따라서 낭만주의 문학의 특징은 보기 ⓐ, ⓑ, ⓔ. 보기 ⓒ와 ⓓ는 신고전주의 문학의 특징이다.

강의의 일부를 다시 들으시오. 그리고 나서 질문에 답하시오.
많은 문학팬들은 Wordsworth의 시가 말년 경에는 단조롭고 지루하며 독창성이 결여되어 있다고 말해요. 특히 젊었을 때 쓰여진 서정적인 문체와 비교하면요. 공정하게 말하자면, 그는 실제로 1814년과 1822년경에 그의 초창기 영광을 그대로 재현한 훌륭한 시편들을 창작했어요.

10. 교수는 왜 이 말을 하는가? 🎧
공정하게 말하자면, 그는 실제로 1814년과 1822년 경에 그의 초창기 영광을 그대로 재현한 훌륭한 시편들을 창작했어요.

ⓐ 교수는 학생들이 Wordsworth의 시를 불공평하게 판단하지 않기를 원한다.
ⓑ 교수는 Wordsworth가 후기에 오직 두 편의 작품만을 출간했다는 것을 설명해주기를 원한다.
ⓒ 교수는 Wordsworth의 후기 작품을 비판한 것을 사과하기를 원한다.
ⓓ 교수는 Wordsworth의 후기 작품의 진가를 알아주기를 원한다.

해설 초기 시절과 비교하여 말년의 시풍이 단조로워지기는 했지만, 꼭 그렇다고 할 수는 없는 훌륭한 작품들도 있었다는 것을 강조하고 싶어한다. 정답은 보기 ⓓ.

11. 교수에 따르면, 왜 Wordsworth의 시가 중요한가?
ⓐ 그의 시는 미국에서 활동하는 모든 낭만주의 작가를 대변한다.
ⓑ 그의 시는 이전 세대의 시와 현대시를 이어주는 연결 고리이다.
ⓒ 그의 시의 평이한 문체는 격조가 높고 위엄이 있다.
ⓓ 그의 시는 전통적인 시와 비교하여 완벽하다.

해설 워즈워드의 시가 사람들의 마음을 매료시키는 것은 힘과 우아함이 공존하기 때문이다. 정답은 보기 ⓒ.

P(M) : So, William Wordsworth is perhaps the best example of English romantic poets, and by that, I do not mean the kind of romance that occurs between young lovers. No, romanticism was an artistic movement that dominated English literature during the late nineteenth and early twentieth century. Anyway, Wordsworth was one of the key writers in this genre and did a lot to make poetry more accessible to the general public. He used simple vocabulary and wrote in a more casual style. And, like all romantic poets, he celebrated the relationships between humanity and nature, and believed that morality was a consequence of these two.

Now, at the time that Wordsworth began his career, the major themes of literature were neoclassical in nature. So, um, for example, authors would write epic poems about idealistic heroes, or utopian worlds. Art, as well, centered on the representation of perfect features, both of the human body and of the idyllic surroundings. Wordsworth, on the other hand, incorporated novel ideas into his poems and used the opportunity to express his own desires and also his own faults. This was very different and not at all welcomed by the critics. They hated his contributions to Lyrical Ballads, a famous collection of poetry published in 1798, along with works by Samuel Coleridge.

But Wordsworth took everything in stride. He even responded to his critics in a new preface of Ballads when the second edition was published a couple of years later. In it, he stated that he considered his unconventional poetry to be a source of emotional tranquility. Or, rather, he saw his poems as emerging out of feeling, not thinking. He rejected academic approaches to writing that removed the emotive expression, and emphasized the importance of natural human emotions. Well, uh, this kind of makes sense if you just think about his subject matter. He wrote about everyday events and people using everyday language. He even went so far as to suggest that his works were just ways to experiment with common language – he meant the language of the lower class – and that he wanted to see if he could use this diction to create pure poetic art. This may sound strange to some of you, but at the time, there were... well, it was almost like there were two different dialects of English spoken. One was the high English of the upper class and was used almost exclusively in neoclassical poetry. But, the other was the speech of the working class – this was what Wordsworth, and later, all romantic poets, were interested in writing about.

Still, this new preface did nothing to quell the hostility of his critics. But, romanticism is, by definition, a really rebellious form of creating art. I mean, not only Wordsworth, who is credited as the first major star of this movement, but others who came after him. They pushed the boundaries of, uh, well, of class and economic status. Who would believe that the poor in the rural areas had as interesting of lives as the rich? Certainly not those who subscribed to neoclassical beliefs.

Well, like all teenage rebels, Wordsworth eventually toned down his anger, and this is also reflected in his writing. Many literature buffs say that his writing just became dull and uninspired toward the end of his life, especially compared to the lyrical style of writing in his youth. To be fair, he did produce some good works around 1814 and 1822 that reflected his earlier glory. But even The Excursion, a collection that continued on from his seminal publication, The Prelude, it, well, he just couldn't regain his greatness as an older man, which is unfortunate, because those early poems were just incredible.

What is worth remembering is that Wordsworth's easy flow of language in blank verse had power and grace. He felt a deep connection to nature and true humanity, not the idealized works of his predecessors, and his finest writings are now part of the romantic heritage of English literature.

Now get ready to answer the questions. You may use your notes to help you answer.

7. Listen again to part of the lecture. Then answer the question.

So, William Wordsworth is perhaps the best example of English romantic poets, and by that, I do not mean the kind of romance that occurs between young lovers. No, romanticism was an artistic movement that dominated English literature during the late nineteenth and early twentieth century.

Why does the professor say this: 🎧
and by that, I do not mean the kind of romance that occurs between young lovers.

10. Listen again to part of the lecture. Then answer the question.
Many literature buffs say that his writing just became dull and uninspired toward the end of his life, especially compared to the lyrical style of writing in his youth. To be fair, he did produce some good works around 1814 and 1822 that reflected his earlier glory.

Why does the professor say this: 🎧
To be fair, he did produce some good works around 1814 and 1822 that reflected his earlier glory.

P : 자, William Wordsworth(윌리엄 워즈워드)는 영국 낭만주의(romantic) 시인을 대표하는 문학가로, 그렇다고 해서 젊은 연인들 사이에 일어나는 로맨스(romance)를 말하는 건 아니에요. 자, 낭만주의 는 19세기 후반과 20세기 초반에 영국 문학을 주름잡았던 문예 사조입니다. 어쨌든 Wordsworth는 이러한 문학 장르에 있어 중요한 작가였으며, 일반 대중들이 시라는 장르에 더 쉽게 다가갈 수 있도록 많은 일을 했어요. 그는 쉬운 어휘를 사용했고, 격식을 차리지 않은 문체로 글을 썼어요. 또한 다른 낭 만주의 시인들과 마찬가지로, 인간과 자연의 관계를 찬양했고, 도덕이라는 것은 인간과 자연의 상호작 용을 통해 생겨나는 것이라고 믿었어요.

자, Wordsworth가 글을 쓰기 시작했을 무렵에는 신고전주의 문학 주제가 주류를 이루었어요. 따라서, 예를 들면, 작가들은 이상적인 영웅이나 유토피아 세계에 관한 서사시를 쓰곤 했죠. 예술 작품 역시 인간 신체와 전원 환경의 완벽한 모습을 그려내는데 주력했죠. 반면 Wordsworth는 그의 시에 새로운 아이디어를 불어넣었고, 스스로의 바람과 허물을 시를 통해 표현했어요. 이는 매우 다른 시도였고 비 평가들은 전혀 호의적이지 않았죠. 그들은 Wordsworth가 '서정가요집(Lyrical Ballads)'에 시를 실은 것도 싫어했는데, 이 책은 Samuel Coleridge(사무엘 코울리지)의 작품과 함께 1798년에 출간된 유명 한 시집이에요.

하지만 Wordsworth는 모든 것을 헤쳐 나갔어요. 그는 2년 후에 '서정가요집'의 2판이 간행되었을 때, 새롭게 실린 서문을 통해 비평가들에게 자신의 신념을 표현했지요. 서문에서 Wordsworth는 그 의 판에 박히지 않은 자유로운 시가 평온한 감정의 원천이라고 말했어요. 그보다 자신의 시는 생각을 통해서가 아닌, 마음에서 느껴지는 것을 통해 쓰여지는 것이라고 여겼죠. 그는 감정적 표현을 없앤 학문적 글쓰기 접근법을 배격하고, 자연스러운 인간의 감정이 갖는 중요성을 강조했습니다. 음, Wordsworth 시의 주제를 생각해본다면 쉽게 이해가 가겠네요. 그는 일상적인 일들과 평범한 사람들 을 일상어로 표현해냈어요. 또한 그의 시가 일상어, 즉 하층 계급의 언어로 하는 실험 방식이며, 순수 시를 창작해내기 위해 이러한 시어(일상어)를 쓸 수 있을지 알기를 원했다고 말하기도 했죠. 여러분 중에는 이런 것들이 이상하게 들릴지도 모르지만, 음, 그 당시에는 2가지의 다른 영어 말씨가 있었다 고 해두죠. 하나는 상류층이 사용하던 고급 영어로, 신고전주의 시에서는 이런 영어만이 거의 쓰였어 요. 또 다른 하나는 노동 계급의 말씨였는데, 이것이 Wordsworth와 그 이후의 모든 낭만주의 시인 들이 쓰고 싶어했던 것이었죠.

하지만, 이런 새로운 서문으로도 비평가들의 적개심을 가라앉히지는 못했어요. 낭만주의란 그 문학적 정 의상으로는 정말로 기존의 것과는 반대되는 창작 예술입니다. 낭만주의 사조를 창시하고 부흥시킨 장본 인으로 평가 받는 Wordsworth 뿐만 아니라 그 뒤를 따랐던 다른 낭만주의 시인들도 마찬가지였어요. 그들은 계층과 경제적 지위의 경계를 밀어냈죠. 시골의 가난한 사람들이 부자들만큼 삶에 대해 관심을 가지고 있다는 것을 누가 믿었겠어요? 분명 신고전주의적 사상에 동조했던 사람들은 아니었겠죠. 음, 모든 10대 반항아들이 그러하듯, Wordsworth 역시 결국은 화를 누그러뜨렸고, 이러한 태도는 그의 시에도 잘 반영이 되어 있습니다. 많은 문학팬들은 Wordsworth의 시가 말년 경에는 단조롭고 지루하며 독창성이 결여되어 있다고 말해요. 특히 젊었을 때 쓰여진 서정적인 문체와 비교하면요. 공정하게 말하자면, 그는 실제로 1814년과 1822년 경에 그의 초창기 영광을 그대로 재현한 훌륭한 시편들을 창작했어요. 하지만 그의 독창적인 저서인 '서곡(The Prelude)'에서 이어진 시 모음집인 '소요(The Excursion)' 역시 나이가 들어가면서 그에게 시인으로서의 탁월함을 되찾아주지는 못했는데, 초기 시들이 정말이지 너무나도 굉장했기 때문에 안타까운 일이지요.
Wordsworth의 약강격(弱强格) 무운시(無韻詩)에서 부드럽게 읽혀져 내려가는 언어에는 힘과 우아함이 있었다는 것을 기억해야 합니다. 그는 이전 세대의 시인들에 의해 창작된 이상적인 시가 아닌, 자연과 진정한 인간성에 깊은 애착을 느꼈고, 그가 집필한 최고의 시들은 이제 영국 문학의 낭만주의 전통의 한 자리를 차지하고 있어요.

어휘 | poet 시인 | occur 발생하다 | dominate 지배하다, 우세하다 | poetry 시 | accessible 접근 용이한 | celebrate 찬양하다 | morality 도덕 | neoclassical 신고전주의의 | utopian 유토피아의 | representation 표현, 묘사 | idyllic 전원의, 목가적인 | novel 새로운 | critic 비평가 | contribution 기고 | take A in stride 쉽게 A를 뛰어 넘다, 헤쳐 나가다 | preface 서문 | unconventional 관습에 얽매이지 않은 | tranquility 평온, 고요 | emerge out of ~에서 생겨나다 | make sense 이해가 되다, 이치에 맞다 | subject matter 주제 | diction 어법 | dialect 말씨, 사투리 | upper class 상류층 | exclusively 배타적으로, 오로지 | quell 억누르다, 가라앉히다 | hostility 적개심 | by definition 정의상으로는, 당연히 | rebellious 반역하는, 반체제의 | credit ~에게 돌리다, ~ 덕분으로 돌리다 | boundary 경계 | status 지위, 상태 | the poor 가난한 사람들 | subscribe to 동의하다 | rebel 반항자 | tone down 부드럽게 하다 | anger 화 | reflect 반영하다 | buff 팬 | dull 단조롭고 지루한, 침체된 | uninspired 독창성이 없는, 상상력이 없는 | seminal 독창적인 | regain 되찾다, 회복하다 | incredible 굉장한, 훌륭한 | blank verse 약강격 무운시 | heritage 유산 |

Review

1. 1. 뛰어난, 미결제의 2. 제거하다 3. 치료 4. 보증 5. 예금하다 6. 더미, 쌓음 7. 해석하다
8. 암시, 의미 9. 진동 10. 향기 11. free 12. innate 13. acquisition 14. complicated
15. innocence 16. evidence 17. reliable 18. heritage 19. critic 20. poet

2. 1. sick and tired of ~이 지긋지긋한 2. give one's word 약속하다 3. show up 나타나다 4. take chances 운에 맡기고 해보다, 위험을 무릅쓰다 5. in charge of ~를 담당하고 있는 6. be capable of ~할 수 있다 7. go over 복습하다, 되풀이하다 8. go out of date 시대에 뒤떨어지다 9. place an order 주문하다 10. make sense 이해가 되다

3. 1. rejected 2. invincible 3. storage 4. adapted 5. skepticism 6. booked

해석 | 1. 그는 감정적 표현을 없앤 학문적 글쓰기 접근법을 배격하고, 자연스러운 인간의 감정이 갖는 중요성을 강조했습니다.
2. 거짓말 탐지기는 흔히 사람들이 속일 수 없는 무적의 기계처럼 보이지만, 실상은 그것보다는 좀 더 복잡하지요.
3. 7층까지 올라가서 분수대에서 왼쪽으로 돌면, 도서관에서 서고로 사용하는 공간을 찾을 수 있을 거예요.
4. 내가 가르치는 200 레벨 수업은 주로 책 이야기가 영화로 각색되는 과정을 다뤄요.
5. 하지만 제가 알기로는 이러한 연구 결과를 발표할 당시 회의적인 시각이 많았다고 하던데요?
6. 안됐지만 오늘 개인학습공간은 모두 예약이 되어있네요.

청소년을 위한
반석 영한대역 시리즈
(영문판, 한글판)

위대한 개츠비

지금까지 번역된 개츠비는 위대하지 않았다!
스콧 피츠제럴드 저 | 이화승 역
「위대한 개츠비」는 20세기 최고의 미국 소설이라는 작품성 덕분에 오랫동안 사랑받아온 작품이다. 기존의 어떤 번역본보다 오류가 적다는 점을 자부한다.

안네의 일기

꿈 많은 문학소녀가 남긴 생생한 감동
안네 프랑크 저 | 이화승 역
꿈 많은 유태인 소녀 안네는 열세 살 생일선물로 받은 일기장에 속마음을 털어놓는다. 독일의 유태인 탄압이 극심해지면서 안네 가족 등 8명의 2년간 '은신' 생활을 기록으로 남겼다.

어린왕자

순수성을 잃어가는 어른들을 위한 동화
앙투안 생텍쥐페리 저 | 이화승 역
이 책은 묘한 매력이 있어서 본래 '어른을 위한 동화' 지만, 어린이가 읽으면 동화가 되고 어른이 읽으면 어른과 사회에 대한 비판이 된다.

변신

현대인의 불안감을 충격적으로 묘사한 걸작!
프란츠 카프카 저 | 이화승 역
평범한 그레고르는 어느 날 벌레가 되어 버렸다. 인간의 정신을 갖고 있지만 벌레의 몸으로 살아가는데 차츰 인간의 의식마저도 희미해져 간다.

동물농장

독재체제를 통렬하게 비판하는 예언 소설
조지 오웰 저 | 조혜정 역
모든 동물은 평등하다. 하지만 어떤 동물은 다른 동물보다 더욱 평등하다! 영국 농장에서 학대받는 동물들이 농장주를 타도하는 혁명을 일으킨다.

포우 단편선

추리소설의 아버지, 포우의 단편 미학!
애드가 앨런 포우 저 | 이화승 역
초기 작품 〈검은 고양이〉는 인간의 잔혹성과 두려움에 관한 전형적 단면을 보여준다. 최초의 추리소설 〈모르그 가의 살인사건〉에서 포우는 독특한 구성과 분석, 추리를 구사하여 세계인의 경탄을 받고 있으며, 문학의 새로운 장르를 개척하여 추리소설의 아버지라고 불린다.